# NATURALIZING BULBS

# Naturalizing
# BULBS

## ROB PROCTOR

Henry Holt and Company
New York

Henry Holt and Company, Inc.
*Publishers since 1866*
115 West 18th Street
New York, New York 10011

Henry Holt® is a registered trademark of Henry Holt and Company, Inc.

Published in Canada by Fitzhenry & Whiteside Ltd.,
195 Allstate Parkway, Markham, Ontario L3R 4T8.

Library of Congress Cataloging-in-Publication Data
Proctor, Rob.
Naturalizing bulbs / Rob Proctor.—1st ed.
p.   cm.
Includes index.
1. Bulbs. I. Title.
SB425.P755  1997 97-1972
635.9′4′097—dc21

ISBN 0-8050-4631-3

Henry Holt books are available for special promotions and premiums.
For details contact: Director, Special Markets.

First Edition 1997

DESIGNED BY KATE NICHOLS

Printed in the United States of America
All first editions are printed on acid-free paper. ∞

10  9  8  7  6  5  4  3  2  1

FOR LAUREN, MY BUDDY

# ACKNOWLEDGMENTS

Gardeners are a generous lot. I'm grateful to the following people for their help and for allowing me to photograph their lovely gardens. I'm proud to call them my friends.

Panayoti Kelaidis

Christopher Woods

Diane and Tom Peace

Angela Overy

Ken Monger

Wayne Roderick

Becky and Brent Heath

Cole Burrell

Helen Dillon

Phillip Watson

Sean Hogan

Parker Sanderson

Norma and Wayne Hazen

Anne Weckbaugh

Joanna Reed

Laurie McBride

Frances Reid

Susan Eubank

Scott Ogden

Nancy Goodwin

David Turrant

Jim Reynolds

Jeff Minnich

Theresa Norford

David Pippin

Lauren Springer

David Macke

*Thanks to these beautiful gardens:*

Chanticleer—Wayne, Pennsylvania

The Huntington—San Marino, California

University of California Botanical Garden at Berkeley—Berkeley, California

Denver Botanic Gardens—Denver, Colorado

Minnesota Landscape Arboretum—Minneapolis, Minnesota

Chicago Botanic Garden—Glencoe, Illinois

San Antonio Botanical Gardens—San Antonio, Texas

Lewis Ginter Botanical Garden—Richmond, Virginia

Longwood Gardens—Kennett Square, Pennsylvania

Montrose—Hillsborough, North Carolina

Winterthur Museum and Gardens—Winterthur, Delaware

The Daffodil Mart—Gloucester, Virginia

Strybing Arboretum—San Francisco, California

University of British Columbia Botanical Gardens—Vancouver, British Columbia

Joy Creek Nursery—Scappoose, Oregon

Additional photographs courtesy of Lauren Springer, p. 14, 54, 56, 60, 67, 89, 107, 109; Christopher Woods, p. 101; C. Coleston Burrell, p. 58, 71, 83, 86, 147; Angela Overy, p. 148; Charles Mann, p. 135, 143; Tom Peace, p. 121; Panayoti Kelaidis, p. 66.

# CONTENTS

# 1

# THE NATURAL WAY

Mention the term *naturalizing,* and an image comes to mind: acres of pristine woodlands awash in golden daffodils planted by an industrious staff, all supported by a healthy bank balance. I'm out to change that.

Naturalizing is the practice of situating bulbous plants in parts of the garden where they will flourish with little care—flowering and multiplying with abandon, or simply holding their own with complementary plants. Any well-chosen, well-situated bulb that behaves as a perennial may be said to have naturalized. Sheer numbers of bulbs don't necessarily guarantee a beautiful picture and may actually be a detriment in a small garden, although extravagance certainly can pay off where appropriate.

Multiplication is not the only measure of success even if it is gratifying to the gardener's ego. Some species seed themselves with the abandon of dandelions, but others multiply slowly

*The expanding leaves of* Hosta fortunei *'Aurea' will soon cover those of English bluebells* (Hyacinthoides non-scriptus) *as they fade.*

by division or offsets. I'm just as happy that my voodoo lilies (*Sauromatum gut-tatum*) don't seed themselves in every nook and cranny. They stay put in a sheltered corner of my sunken garden—where they survive at three zones north of their assigned hardiness   and reward me with a slow but deliberate increase in leaves and vigor. No bulb is immortal (though I know some clumps that are working on it), but thoughtful placement gives a bulb the best shot for a long run in the garden.

Billions of bulbs have been stuffed in the ground across this land in the past century. It's a wonder that we're not aglow in blooming bulbs from coast to coast. Sadly, many bulbs never survive more than a season or two. It's not the bulbs' fault. The blame rests squarely on the shoulders of the gardeners, who plant inappropriate varieties for their area, situate them in unfavorable sites, and provide bad care.

Some gardeners might imagine a transformation of their property into a haze of English snowdrops and delicate cowslip primroses, followed by a sea of vibrant hybrid tulips. Unfortunately, they live in Houston.

Practicality is paramount. Before a garden fulfills a daydream, the gardener must wake up and smell the coffee. It's a big country, and it's unrealistic to transplant visions from a distant garden to a region with its own distinct climate, often radically different from the one where the vision originated. While each of us must kill an undetermined number of plants before we can call ourselves true gardeners, there must be a time when we rein in our enthusiasm and get down to earth.

Luscious photos tempt the novice gardener. Nongardening friends of mine who feel they are missing something (and they are) often pull out carefully folded magazine clippings and present them to me, saying, "This is what I want." More often than not, it's a picture from Rosemary Verey's English garden or Wave Hill in New York, where Marco Polo Stufano directs the horticultural goings-on. Who wouldn't covet such a garden? I try to explain that these are creations of uniquely talented individuals, and they are products of many years' work. The skeptical stares of my friends tell me they think I am holding back on them. Isn't there a plan or package they can buy to get this look? The magazines and catalogues are full of them.

I hate to dampen the spirits of my friends. Gardening—one of the most enduring and satisfying of life's pleasures—doesn't come in a kit. If I had to make a comparison, gardening is like playing the piano, although I have no basis for this comparison since my fingers and decidedly unmusical nature prevented it. With a little instruction, beginners learn some easy pieces. That may be all they choose to learn, or they may go on to explore every musical facet the instrument has to offer, be it classical, jazz, or rock. Only dedication brings mastery.

As far afield as this analogy runs, I'm convinced that most gardeners—once they get beyond the first exercises—intend to master their craft, just as pianists do. The road takes us in many directions, as we learn to cultivate fruits and vegetables, sow annuals and herbs, plant containers, and tend perennials. The only place where I'm truly an expert is in my own backyard. Like every other facet of gardening, bulb growing brings innumerable delights and some acute failures. My garden continues to be my most valuable teacher. It rewards me when I've done my homework and raps my knuckles when I haven't.

# Transformation

Every bulb that is buried in the ground in my garden and struggles to the surface becomes a part of a bigger picture. Its life cycle interweaves with those of every other plant in the garden and, in many ways, with my own.

I know it sounds trite, so I am almost loath to admit it: the appearance of the first wave of flowers brings me a feeling of joy. My own thoughts about the unfurling flags of *Iris reticulata* and the colonies of crocus make me understand and almost forgive the sweet poetry praising the glories of spring. This labored imagery has been handed down to us from the dawn of time, or at least from the moment the first snowdrop bloomed and a poet was nearby.

My feelings never diminish as the season progresses. Yellow trout lilies and grape hyacinths claim my attention, followed by waves of showy tulips, clumps of pungent crown imperials, heart-stopping lilies, and—just as I begin to lament the end of the season—eye-popping colchicums and crocus more lovely than those in the spring.

Bulbs have transformed my garden. They've done the same for me as a gardener. I remember the first lilies I bought many years ago. They were part of a "fantastic" offer on the back of a magazine I "could not afford to pass up" from a disreputable company that promised me hundreds of lovely flowers for an unbelievably low price. It's usually easy to spot these silly ads—promising instant hair where little or none exists, or the disappearance of wrinkles or extra pounds—so I should have known better. We all say that afterward.

My lily bulbs were about the size of a walnut. I had no idea what size they should have been, so I was not alarmed. I also harbored the unfounded suspicion that lilies were quite tender, so I planted them ten inches deep to protect them from

*Coral pink Asiatic lilies grow like gangbusters among flowering tobacco, bronze-leaf loosestrife (*Lysimachia ciliata *'Rubra'), Jupiter's beard, and pink beebalm.*

frost. I also suspected that anything that beautiful and exotic, like orchids, must need buckets of water, so I planted the bulbs in clay soil near a downspout.

I was wrong on all counts. Instead of giving up, it made me mad. I read everything I could find on lilies. Among other things, I learned I had been both gullible and ignorant. I have no idea where I came by my early assumptions about lilies, although I suspect one of my favorite movies might be a culprit. There's a scene in *The African Queen* where Katharine Hepburn and Humphrey Bogart cruise down the river framed by shots of hippos and crocodiles to convey the feeling of the exotic locale. On the bank blooms a huge clump of white lilies. Perhaps I'd seen this image enough times to assure myself that lilies—which, by the way, are not found in Africa—need a warm climate and plenty of water.

From that early disaster came my determination to know a plant's requirements before it goes in the ground. (I'm still killing plenty of plants, but they're of a higher quality and my guesses are better educated.) It also began a longstanding infatuation with lilies. The lily remains my favorite flower, but cad that I am, there are other beauties that fascinate me when no lilies grace the scene.

Growing lilies opened my eyes to an exciting new world. Although I'd been raised in a gardening family, my only exposure to the world of bulbous plants was tulips, onions, and bearded iris, for all of which I still carry a lingering fondness. I plowed through catalogues and bulb books, determined to learn the secrets of this fascinating group of plants.

*Bulb* is a general but useful catchall term for geophyte, a plant that produces a storage unit that may take the form of tuber, corm, rhizome, fleshy root stalk, or true bulb. At one time or another, I've grown almost all commercially available species and hybrids, and I've located a considerable number through sleuthing, trading, and begging. Patience is not a virtue I have ever been particularly keen about cultivating, but time, luck, and failure have led me to a good sense of what is possible in my garden.

There's no ducking homework. To grow bulbs successfully, you must select the right site for the desired effect and figure out how to accommodate the bulbs, including soil, water, and light requirements. Naturalizing is simply good gardening. If you want a lily, the options are to buy it at the flower shop or grow it. In terms of satisfaction, there's no comparison.

Each plot of soil hides its secrets. Each of us needs to discover them. Good observation is the key—watching the changing patterns of sun and shade throughout the seasons, learning the feeling and scent of the soil, and noting how plants react to conditions.

# It's a Mess

A little knowledge is indeed a dangerous thing. It seems everyone knows a bit about gardening, acquired as they grew up, absorbed from magazines or movies, and delivered across the neighbor's fence. Some of it is perfectly sound and reliable, while other "tips" are utterly useless. It used to be common practice to pull out the good old DDT at the first appearance of an aphid. We've learned to trust our gardens to work out their own ecosystems and intervene only in the most environmentally friendly way, when real trouble erupts. Why then, do we continue some of the gardening practices from the past that should have been cast out with the DDT?

I'm aghast that people who should know better hack their bearded iris into the dreaded fan shape after the flowers fade. Nature never provided this service as the iris evolved; it seems unlikely that having a plant's only source of energy reduced to four inches of leaf would be of great benefit. Iris grow so willingly, however, that they've managed to survive and even flower despite this rude treatment. The practice comes from cutting the leaves back when a clump of iris is divided. Each newly cut piece of rhizome is set in fresh soil, the theory being that the disturbed roots will become established better without a huge sail of top growth to support.

Somewhere along the line, this piece of information was lost. It reminds me of the party game where a sentence is whispered down the line, and the person at the end then repeats what he heard—usually bearing little resemblance to the original sentence. This kind of hilarity may be amusing to people, but it's hell on iris.

Somewhere along the same line, a fussy gardener—thoroughly satisfied by the barren but tidy look after they'd whacked back their iris foliage—decided that those iris looked "messy" without a yearly haircut. Iris foliage became almost universally acclaimed as messy. So did daylilies. Proponents of the "chainsaw massacre" style of pruning pop up in nearly every neighborhood. These people are deathly afraid of nature and suspicious of any flower that grows more than ankle high, and armed with steel blades and ignorance, pruning becomes a pastime that leaves no plant untouched. They seem to think a tree needs to be cut back to its main branches every once in a while just to keep it in line or that every shrub looks better as a ball.

A friend of mine who lives in Texas once came home to find that his neighbors had cut down a mature redbud in glorious bloom by their front door. When he asked what happened, they told him, "It was just too messy. The flowers kept blowing into the front hall."

I don't know when Americans became so tidy. Perhaps it was the fifties, when nearly everyone ate on a sleek chrome dinette set and began to cover their couches in plastic. A look back at the gardening magazines of the time reveals a landscape nearly as sterile as the interior. Chemical-drenched tea roses were as prized as the latest gladiolus and dinner-plate dahlias so heavily staked as to survive a Soviet air strike. Tulips and daffodils lined the walk, but it was de rigueur for the

*The gift of* Iris *'Peek-a-boo' from a special friend deserves pride-of-place in my garden with* Phlox bifida*, cushion spurge, and lily-form tulips. Rest assured that its foliage is never mutilated by a summer haircut.*

*There won't be any hand-wringing over the dying tulip foliage in this Denver garden, as vigorous peonies, poppies, phlox, and queen-of-the-meadow will soon hide the evidence.*

wealthy to have them removed the minute they finished flowering, since the leaves were so messy.

They're still messy. The "love the flowers, hate the leaves" mentality still prevails, as homeowners braid daffodil leaves into neat bundles or wrap tulip foliage with rubber bands and hairpins. Deprived of half the sunshine they need to energize for another year, the flowers decline and finally cease, while the owner wonders if maybe they bought bad bulbs or should have given them a triple dose of fertilizer and bug killer.

We've learned to deal with the leaves. We don't grow them in regimented rows so much anymore, choosing instead to plant our tulips or daffodils in "naturalistic" drifts. We take care to showcase their beauty and disguise their weakness. Set bulbs back from the front of the border, for example, and emerging perennials thoroughly obscure the withering bulb foliage as they expand up and over. On a hillside or in an orchard or meadow, grasses, daylilies, and other plants take over as the early blooming bulbs complete their season's growth.

We need to understand the life cycle of a bulb to see whether it fits our own temperament. Overly fastidious gardeners might consider therapy. It seems unhealthy to subject plants to an odd code of tidiness. It's only natural to let plants grow as nature intended, appreciating or at least tolerating them in all phases of their growth. If we can simply overcome this American obsession with neatness, we can begin to explore the opportunities that exist wherever we garden, the many areas in our gardens for planting bulbs, and the effects that can be achieved. From woodland glades to sun-drenched meadows, from city courtyard to country vista, and from streamside to arid slope, bulbs from around the world can transform our landscape.

# Natives

One of the most encouraging things about the emergence of regional gardening styles is a new appreciation for native plants, including bulbs. A general attitude of working together with nature rather than defying the elements has taken hold in many areas. It's good for the air, the water, and the birds. An important message is the responsible use of the land. Composting returns everything that came from the soil back to it. Prudent and limited use of pesticides and fertilizer protects wildlife and waterways. Water and soil conservation preserve our most precious commodities. Gardening is a wonderful way to make a positive statement: Plant a tree for oxygen and grow a hyacinth to fully enjoy the air we breathe. The optimist in me says we can save the planet.

Every once in a while, somebody gets a bee in their bonnet. In celebrating the beauty and diversity of our native plants, factions have arisen that decree that not only must we embrace our wild plants, but they're the only thing we're allowed to embrace. They hang out a sign that says "NATIVES ONLY" and mean it. In 1995 a bill in the Minnesota legislature came dangerously close to passing that would have forbidden nurseries in that state to sell any plant that was not a native. The implications are chilling.

A friend of mine in the nursery trade calls the natives-only people "flower fascists." I'm not fond of the words, but I have to agree. The environment needs protection, but this isn't it. Reasonable precautions should be taken in avoiding plants that may get out of control and threaten endangered natives. Wherever humans go, plants go with them, by design or accident. Weeds stow away in sacks of grain or catch a ride on the fur of a pet. However much we regret the unfortunate spread of pests like thistle or lythrum, we have to accept that wherever humans dwell, change is inevitable. We can't think of our own species and its often destructive effect as separate from the evolution of life on earth. That, too, is a chilling thought. The natives-only isolationists remind me, with their single-mindedness, of some of the hippies I knew during my college days. Their solution to the ills of the planet was to get back to nature. One girl I knew lived in a teepee deep in the forest and drove an old pickup into town. I never figured out how this was supposed to help the environment. She was deeply dedicated to living in a teepee, and I was constantly reminded of this because she smelled like a campfire.

My smoldering friend, however, never tried to ram her beliefs down another's throat. I wish her gentle nature would infiltrate the camps of the flower fundamentalists. Why turn gardening into an ideological battleground? I have never heard of a tulip escaping over the garden wall and knocking a rare wildflower out of existence. It would be a shame if one day the children of Minnesota knew tulips only from pictures in books.

Few bulbous plants are bent on world domination. Some of them seed too freely for some gardeners' tastes. I've run into people who dislike grape hyacinths because they get into their lawns. These are not people I would actually call gardeners. Nothing thrills me more than to have that sterile monoculture we call a lawn support a counterculture of crocus, snowdrops, squills, leucojum, or winter aconite.

Mild and semitropical climates seem most vulnerable to horticultural invasion: Kudzu vine ate the South. Tumbleweeds conquered the West. On a lesser

scale, Bermuda buttercup (*Oxalis pes-caprae*) has become the dandelion of California. Its buttery yellow flowers may charm the tourist, but gardeners curse its persistence. Three-cornered leek (*Allium triquetrum*) sometimes invades other golden state gardens; both are peskiest where the natural ecosystem has been seriously altered or damaged. Opportunistic plants often rely on a helping blade from bulldozers.

As well as safeguarding our own shores from real or imagined harm,

The tiny white parachutes of spring snowflake (Leucojum vernum) *enliven the boring monoculture of a lawn.*

we must look abroad as well. Loss of habitat, especially in southeastern Europe, the Near East, and South Africa, threatens many bulbs. Once-plentiful populations of native snowdrops, Grecian windflowers, tulips, and winter aconites in Greece and Turkey and many bulbs from the cape region of South Africa have been seriously depleted; apartment buildings sit where they once grew. Some of our most cherished American wildflowers, such as trilliums, also lose out to sprawling suburbs.

Agriculture wipes out a broad spectrum of plants. Overgrazing has long been an agent of destruction in southern Europe and the Middle East (not to mention our own western states). Fossil records speak of a much richer, more diverse flora than we encounter today. Bulbs managed to keep up with farming for thousands of years when horse-drawn plows created gashes only four inches deep. Modern tractors changed that, churning deep into the earth. Herbicides create a double whammy that few native plants can survive.

Some species have been driven to the brink of extinction by unscrupulous collecting from the wild, while others have gone over the edge. The lovely deep blue Chilean crocus, *Tecophilaea cyanocrocus,* appears to be gone from its native habitat and exists only in carefully guarded collections. Keen gardeners and botanical gardens keep the species alive in hopes that one day *azulillo,* as it was once known in its homeland, can be returned to the wild.

International agreements have helped to reduce this disgraceful practice (although the bulbs lost to overcollection are just a drop in the bucket compared to those lost through overgrazing, agriculture, and building). Few gardeners realized that the enrichment of their own gardens meant the impoverishment of the homeland of the bulbs they cherished. Although progress has been made, gardeners must be sure to purchase only from companies that guarantee that the species they sell are propagated in the nursery (hybrids and selected forms, of course, do not come from the wild).

My friend Panayoti Kelaidis, an esteemed plantsman, bought some bulbs of the common yellow golden chalice (*Sternbergia lutea*) several years back from a local garden center. He planted them here and there in the rock garden he shares with his wife, Gwen. She came in from a midwinter inspection of the garden to report, "Some crocus are blooming. They're white, and they're fragrant." Puzzled—since it was a month too early for the first crocus, which carry little or no fragrance—Panayoti went outside to check on the mysterious blossoms. He was surprised to find a patch of *Sternbergia candida,* a very rare species only discovered about 1975 on a remote mountain location in Turkey.

How strange that the bulbs would have fallen into the hands of one of the few people in the country who could identify it. He'd read a report about its discovery and the subsequent near-annihilation of it from the site by collectors. Panayoti contacted bulb experts in England to tell of the strange coincidence and was surprised to learn about reports of the rare bulbs turning up in Europe as well.

Piecing together the fragments of information, they concluded that a large bulb firm had sent collectors to plunder the bulbs in Turkey. Their timing coincided with the outcry from the international horticultural community to curb collection in the wild and promotion of international agreements to ban all but nursery-propagated stock of endangered species. The pressure was too much, and the company simply dumped their booty into mainstream markets. One sternbergia bulb looks pretty much like another.

The good news is that *Sternbergia candida* is making a comeback in its native environment. Tiny bulbils left in the ground by the collectors have reached maturity, and other colonies have been discovered. The pretty, scented white cups once again dot the mountainous cedar woods in southwest Turkey each January and February. In the meantime, its bulbs are being propagated, so that many gardeners will have the opportunity to enjoy it.

Conservation must be practiced. At the same time, the best way to ensure the survival of a rare species is for knowledgeable gardeners to grow, propagate, and share.

# Amazing and Adaptable

Every region of the country holds enormous possibilities to grow a wide selection of outstanding bulbs. Experimentation is a wonderful way to learn. A couple of this and a handful of that may not make a riveting picture to begin with, but it's better than spending a fortune only to discover that nine out of ten neighborhood voles prefer your garden. A few seasons will tell the tale of what's a good investment.

The adaptable nature of bulbs shouldn't come as a surprise. Their unique storage mechanism—whether it's a corm, rhizome, fleshy root, tuber, or true bulb—gets them through tough weather. In response to extremes, many species go dormant or nearly so, allowing us easy access to them. They can spend part of the year above ground without water and so can be easily handled and shipped. No other group of plants is as easily managed.

Many bulbs also possess a strong constitution—perhaps forged by the harsh climatic contrasts in which they evolved—that enables them to thrive under a wide

*A roadside garden in California's wine country bursts with signature plants of the region—canna, montbretia, and agapanthus.*

variety of conditions. Their strength is noteworthy, but there are limits. Sometimes we have to face the fact that a bulb we desperately wish to grow can't succeed under normal conditions in our climate. That's when we pull out the tricks and grow a bulb in an unconventional manner, such as in a pot, but that's another subject. The focus here is to thoroughly plumb our own garden resources as they exist to grow appropriate species, or to create lasting conditions where we can satisfy their needs.

Gardeners in the Northeast, mid-Atlantic, and Midwest may wish to concentrate on hardy bulbs that naturalize with native and exotic perennials in a variety of exposures, from full sun to dappled shade. Most of the traditional spring bloomers naturalize well in these areas, from crocus, squills, and aconite to narcissus and selected tulips. Their palette expands with charming pendant checkered guinea hens, shade-loving trilliums, Jack-in-the-pulpit, and fragrant lily-of-the-valley. The season continues with six-foot foxtail lily, native Turk's cap lilies, and fall-blooming crocus and leafless colchicums, called "naked boys" by the British.

West Coast and desert Southwest gardeners will also find a wealth of exotic bulbs from South Africa and South America that adapt readily to their climate, thrive with little care, and fit into their natural landscape. Showy blue lily-of-the-Nile, orange clivia, luscious pink belladonna lily, and fiery montbretia are complemented by butterflylike fortnight lily, colorful alstroemeria, and unusual species of iris and gladiolus.

Southern gardens may select from a wide range of tropical and subtropical beauties that bring blossoms throughout the year. Rain lilies pop up after a shower, show-stopping amaryllis bloom outdoors (to the envy of northerners), and brilliant *Gladiolus byzantinus* from the Middle East makes itself at home. Fragrant crinum, showy Japanese spider lily, and elegant calla lily find a permanent spot in these gardens.

Even Rocky Mountain and high-altitude gardeners everywhere will welcome the possibilities of introducing flowering bulbs to their gardens, from tough, adaptable Asiatic lilies to native camassia, avalanche lilies, and fairy lanterns, as well as many of the hardiest spring bloomers.

Consider height, bloom time, color, and hardiness as you select the appropriate species for your region and area within the garden. Some bulbs have more demanding requirements and take special conditions, while most thrive in a wide variety of situations. Most bulbs have carved out a specialized niche in their native environment. By mimicking the conditions in their homeland, it's possible to find any number of species to thrive in the setting of a woodland, meadow, lawn, perennial border, rock garden, stream bank, or waterwise garden. For the dedicated bulb enthusiast, no part of the garden is overlooked. Saffron crocus thrive in a sunny herb garden. Tiny species tulips and Grecian windflowers grow between cracks in a flagstone patio and along paths. The spring lawn becomes a sea of color—not with dandelions, but with crocus, species tulips, and sky-blue Siberian squills.

In addition to planting bulbs in a suitable site, it's nearly as important to make artistic judgments. The goal is to bring the bulbs into the garden in a naturalistic manner, to look as if they have sprung up of their own accord. Planting them with beautiful and beneficial companion plants—native and nonnative perennials, grasses, shrubs, trees, ground covers, vines, and herbs—will give immediate results the first year. The naturalized bulbs will continue to thrive with little care, giving a lifetime of continuing and increasing beauty.

# 2

# GROWING CONCERNS

Growing bulbs is simple. Some gardeners struggle too hard, fuss too much, and get so entangled in details that they forget the garden basics. If you get them in the ground right side up, that's pretty much it. As a general rule of thumb, most bulbs and corms need to be planted at a depth two to three times their diameter. A crocus corm, for example, may measure about an inch across. Three inches of soil on top the corm ought to be about right, but four won't be a disaster and two won't be a catastrophe.

Exceptions are few but important. The Madonna lily (*Lilium candidum*) grows best when its bulb is planted with just an inch or less covering its upper tip. Crinums, *Amaryllis belladonna,* and *Scilla natalensis* all but demand that the necks of the bulbs stay above ground. Plunging them deep in the soil invites failure.

Most rhizomes and tubers can be safely planted with two to four

*Scarlet* Tulipa linifolia *cuts an eye-popping swath through* Euphorbia seguieriana.

inches of soil atop them. Longtime growers of favorite plants, such as bearded iris, work out what is best for them based on observation and experience. It's worth paying attention to them. Most iris growers prefer to set their rhizomes right at soil level, and they recommend the period after flowering as the best time to divide and transplant. I agree, but our schedules don't always match those of plants.

I remember receiving some divisions of a choice heirloom variety from a friend in October. I was happy to get them, but I had other things on my mind—like how to get a couple thousand other bulbs in the ground before a predicted blizzard rolled into town. The paper bag of iris rhizomes stayed near the garage door, where I forgot them until spring. The roots broke through the crumbling paper into the soil and even produced a few flowers that season. This is not the recommended treatment for iris.

I've learned to exploit the forgiving nature of iris. I've planted them in clay soil and in sand, and I've never noticed the slightest bit of difference in performance. In some areas of my garden they receive regular irrigation and, in other parts, must make do with natural rainfall that averages a paltry fourteen inches a year. So willing are they to grow and flower, and so happily adapted are they to my climate, that I have to work very hard to spoil the iris display. If only every plant in my garden were as adaptable.

M*y challenge is to find suitable companions for bearded iris, such as annual, self-sowing* Papaver dubium *with velvety 'Superstition'.*

When a type of bulb grows particularly well, like iris or daylilies or crinums, the temptation is to concentrate on it, but the garden as a whole suffers. A space devoted to one type of plant becomes a mere collection, and the infinite possibilities for combining them with other plants in a garden setting are lost. An iris collection is an exhilarating spectacle for a few moments but quickly pales. The flowers are like colorful party dresses hanging on a department store rack. Their true potential isn't realized until they are seen at the dance.

# Grime on My Hands

Aesthetic considerations aside, each of us must learn what works for us. Soil type more than anything else affects bulb performance. Its composition varies widely, but soil falls into two categories: black, rich, nutritious, well-drained loam and what the rest of us have. There's no ideal soil for every type of bulb, but a sandy loam, liberally enriched with organic matter—the type of soil that grows tomatoes the size of softballs—will support the widest variety of bulbs in any region of the country. That's all well and good, but what about a plot of land most suitable for a quarry, a beach, or a pottery factory?

Much has been written through the years about soil—how to cope with it, how to enrich it, and how to make it. I've met gardeners who've spent a lifetime turning inhospitable ground into soil, endlessly composting, mulching, and planting cover crops. Then they die.

Making soil is not my life's ambition. Starting from scratch shouldn't mean from the beginning of time. I've been dragged to countless numbers of gardens for advice where "things aren't doing very well." Since I usually discover a bed of rocks, a sea of sand, or a pit of clay, I've come up with the answer: Buy it.

When I began to make my garden, I started with a sandy loam, heavier in spots, with little organic matter. The land had been cultivated in one form or another for a century, so I expected that it had lost some of its fertility. It was a start. A week after moving into the house, a truck dumped thirty yards of compost (by my request) in the lane leading to the house. Hauling this amount of compost around by wheelbarrow, spreading, and spading it in took all the grit I could muster, but tired muscles are just a memory. This soil, with regular top dressing and continuing enrichment where appropriate, will support my gardening needs indefinitely. If I'd needed to haul in enough topsoil to cover my acre site seven inches deep, I'd have done that

*Soil preparation pays off in my garden, supporting peach-toned lily 'Ariadne' with golden hops vine, variegated yucca, pink flowering tobacco, and too-bright rose campion.*

too. (I go by my own rule of thumb that 90 percent of plants can be grown passably well in seven inches of decent soil.) People willingly lavish money on carpets, furniture, and cars so sophisticated that they nearly drive themselves, but they won't cut loose when it comes to dirt.

Clay soil can be a death trap for bulbs. Roots grow in the spaces between the soil, and the fine particles of clay are difficult for the roots to penetrate. Compaction and overwatering make things worse. Roots need oxygen, and waterlogged clay suffocates all but those plants that evolved in swampy conditions. Fortunately, a great many bulbs colonize boggy ground, especially semitropical ones such as cannas, crinums, elephant ear, calla lilies, gingers, and Peruvian daffodils. Other bulbs that tolerate wet feet include many narcissus, *Gladiolus byzantinus,* rain lilies, Dutch iris, summer snowflake, and Naples onion. This is especially good news for southern gardeners, who must often deal with tight clay and rainy weather.

Having clay soil isn't the end of the world for gardeners in the West. Unless heavy equipment has compressed it relent-

*Southern clay soil presents no problem for muck-loving summer snowflake* (Leucojum aestivum) *and daffodils.*

lessly, a heavy soil still can support a huge variety of plants, even if the bulbs are somewhat limited. Species tulips actually prefer a clay-based soil. Darwin hybrid tulips cope well, as do most daffodils, crocus, colchicums, liatris, and daylilies. In milder parts, heavy soil supports agapanthus, montbretia, cannas, watsonias, clivia, and much more. The trick is not to water it too much. Terracing a garden with retaining walls, raised beds, and slopes improves drainage dramatically.

Sandy soil lends itself to amendment easier than the others. Well-drained and easy to dig, it needs liberal addition of organic matter to make it support more than the native plants than inhabit it. Drainage is a definite plus, but the incorporation of well-rotted manure, garden compost, and leaf mold enables sandy soil to retain moisture and, of course, provides nutrients.

Many novice gardeners confuse compost with mulch. The latter is a soil covering that protects the soil. Gravel is a form of mulch often applied to rock gardens or xeriscapes. A layer of loose pebbles an inch or so deep helps to prevent evaporation of soil moisture and keeps the crown—the basal area of the plant most vulnerable to rotting—high and dry. A gravel mulch works well for rock garden standbys like small bulbous and rhizomatous iris, crocus, and species tulips. Their natural habitat may often be on rocky slopes of the high plains and mountains of eastern Europe and western Asia, where the soil layer may be thin and the surface naturally mulched with gravel.

Bark nuggets or wood chips are another form of mulch, but I don't recommend their application. A layer of bark

*A gravel mulch like that in their natural habitat encourages grape hyacinths and* Iris reichenbachii *to prosper.*

decomposes slowly, and the microorganisms that cause the process need nitrogen, which they use at the expense of surrounding plants. I saw a garden once that was mulched with six inches of wood shavings. The owner couldn't understand why the plants hadn't grown an inch in three years. I told him to remove the mulch and apply fertilizer to his nitrogen-starved perennials and bulbs. The results were dramatic.

Other materials can be used for mulch. Ground pine and spruce needles make a good mulch in shade gardens, but extra nitrogen should be applied throughout the growing season to prevent its depletion. Don't worry about making the soil overly acidic if you live in a region where alkaline soils are the norm. A bit of acidity is often a boon to woodland perennials such as hostas, ferns, primroses, and bleeding hearts. Where overly acidic soil limits the variety of plants that can be grown successfully, add ground limestone to "sweeten" it. Check with local experts to determine how much and how often.

A newly planted shade garden benefits from mulch the first season before it begins to take care of itself. I remember using something called "forest litter," containing ground bark, pine needles, and leaves. The tiny pieces break down more rapidly than big hunks of bark "McNuggets." An inch layer keeps the soil cool and moist, but I don't know whether it's marketed anymore. Perhaps a bag of "forest litter" sounds like it would contain candy wrappers and picnic trash.

Gardeners who live near Hershey, Pennsylvania, often use cocoa bean hulls for mulch. Whether this does a bit of good for the plants is irrelevant; the hulls smell wonderful. As a chocoholic, if I had a supply of cocoa bean hulls, I'd mulch my living room floor with them.

Compost, on the other hand, is a soil amendment. It is organically based and can contain leaves, garden waste, kitchen scraps, or manure. All must be well rotted. Finished compost does not stink. If it does, it needs more time to break down before it is fit for use in the garden. Many gardeners make their own compost in piles or bins, but garden centers offer bagged or bulk compost, an advantage to a person starting from scratch. Compost is applied not so much for its nutritive value as for its high fiber content. A human needs a high-fiber diet; so does most soil.

It's a good idea to spread about three inches of compost in autumn or early spring to beds of traditional perennials and bulbs such as daffodils, hybrid tulips, or Siberian iris. (A light dusting of compost is virtually worthless.) The task can be accomplished every two or three years. For large gardens, many garden centers will deliver compost by the yard for a reasonable fee.

Take care not to bury the perennials in the bed or the smothered crowns may rot. After the chore is finished, the work is carried on by earthworms. Their burrowing activity helps to work the compost into the bed. This improves the tilth of the soil, whether it is clay or sand, and results in improved root action of the plants.

# Waterwise

Even in the semiarid West, more plants die from drowning than drought. The culprit? Overzealous gardeners with their hands on the spigot handles, or those who thoughtlessly set the automatic sprinkling system to pour on buckets of water without evaluating how much the plants actually require. Americans prize their manicured lawns and often base their watering schedules on what the grass needs. It is too much. Even turf doesn't require the gallons that are squandered on it. The majority of bulbs and perennials in any given garden require far less water than the lawn.

Most winter and spring-blooming bulbs are incredibly drought tolerant; some require a dry summer baking. Bulbs that originate in southeastern Europe, the Near East, the Mediterranean region, the western side of South Africa, and the central plains of America evolved to cope with a dry summer. The plants expend their energy early in the year, when moisture from rainfall or melting snow is plentiful. Shoots pierce the soil surface, buds emerge and open, hungry insects pollinate the flowers. As temperatures rise and showers taper off, the plant pumps nutrients and water into its storage tank below ground, be it bulb, corm, tuber, or rhizome. Seeds ripen and scatter, while the leaves—their solar-collecting task complete—wither and die.

The bulbous part survives the summer in a dormant state below ground. It rides out the desiccating winds and searing sun until the return of autumn rains or early snow trigger the roots to start anew. They refresh the bulb, and growth sometimes begins, although the shoots usually stay below ground.

A few plants, like grape hyacinths, lachenalias, many *Lycoris,* or *Arum italicum,* sprout in autumn and hold their leaves through the winter. New gardeners are often mystified and dismayed by this early sprouting, thinking that they have done something wrong. This habit can be put to good use. Old hands often group grape hyacinths around other spring-flowering bulbs. In autumn, when the whereabouts of dormant clumps of daffodils or tulips might be uncertain, the grape hyacinth markers prevent the errant spade from slicing through them during a planting frenzy.

Many bulbs from tropical and semitropical regions also go through a dry part of the year, often in the middle of summer but sometimes in winter. Some go completely dormant during the dry season, but often they persist, living off the stored water in their underground tuberous reservoirs.

A few bulbous plants have developed peculiar schedules of growth in response to their environments. Surprise lily, *Lycoris squamigera,* is aptly named for its habit of emerging from the bare earth in late summer. Like many autumn bloomers, such as crocus and colchicums, the surprise lily takes advantage of two seasons. It produces its leaves early in the season, abandons them when their work is finished, and produces its flowers late in the season. The schedule is the work of evolution, as the foliage benefits from the abundant early-season moisture. Its late-season flowers have less competition for the attention of bees—sort of like last call at a singles bar.

Because so many incredible bulbs originate in South Africa, it's worth boning up on its geography. The country has two distinct climates, one influenced by the Atlantic Ocean on the west and the other by the Indian Ocean on the east. On the western side, which includes half of the Cape Province, winter rains are followed by a dry summer. In the east, the pattern is reversed. Numerous microclimates with specially adapted plants also exist.

A ring of mountains and high terraces intercept rain-bearing winds and leave the high interior of the country relatively dry. Interest in the rich flora of South Africa—which holds a remarkable one-tenth of the world's species of plants—has largely centered on species from the mild coastal regions. These are, of course, most intriguing to gardeners in California, the Pacific Northwest, and parts of England. Recent expeditions into the mountains and interior parts of the land have concentrated on collecting plants that may demonstrate more cold hardiness. Some are previously unknown species, while others are high-altitude forms of favorite bulbous South African plants such as *Nerine, Kniphofia, Moraea, Dierama,* and *Gladiolus.* It will be a few years before these plants make their way into general commerce, but the next decade promises to be an exciting one for bulb gardeners.

# Too Darned Hot

One of the most persistent of all bulb-planting "rules" is timing. So pervasive is the phrase "It's still too hot to plant bulbs" in early autumn that most of us accept it without question. What it really means is that it's too hot for the gardener to feel like planting bulbs.

Having dug up numerous bulbs in late summer (usually not on purpose), I've had the chance to take note of the various stages of their development. In early September in my garden, there's not a sign of root growth and the bulbs appear completely dormant. About a month later, errantly disinterred bulbs show early root formation and, occasionally, emerging top growth. Cooler soil temperatures and sufficient moisture prompt the bulb to get busy.

When I am reminded that it's too hot to plant, I wonder why. The bulbs already in the ground don't suddenly disregard thousands of years of evolutionary programming and decide to bloom in autumn instead of spring. Why should newly planted bulbs behave any differently? They won't rot and they won't make a mistake. They'll simply sit where I plant them until conditions trigger their natural response.

A really quirky weather pattern can fool plants. An extremely chilly fall and mild winter can entice the cherry trees in Washington, D.C., to flower in December or January and the snowdrops and crocus to pop up prematurely. This always leaves gardeners scratching their heads, but the plants revert to normal behavior when weather patterns do. Bulbs will ride out a few years of irregular weather. If they couldn't, most bulbs would have become extinct long ago.

Late planting is a serious matter. Bulbs need a few weeks or a month, with sufficient moisture, to initiate root growth before the soil freezes. It is almost impossible to plant in frozen soil. Where the arrival of winter can be unpredictable, gardeners take precautions to keep their ground frost-free.

Sometimes wet weather delays the harvest of lily bulbs in the Pacific Northwest, where most commercial growers live. The soil in the northern third of the country may be under snow in late October and December. Gardeners who expect shipments of lilies cover beds where they intend to plant with bales of straw, or they dig holes and store the soil in the garage. This seems like a lot of work for what can still be failure. I think it's best to store the bulbs in the refrigerator and wait for spring. Even better, request that the company hold your order and ship in spring, since most growers have state-of-the-art facilities where lilies can be stored at proper temperatures and humidity. Properly stored lilies transplant well in the spring, even if it takes them another year to settle in and maintain their full stature.

A trick in the upper Midwest, where the Canadian Express can howl in suddenly with a devastating blizzard, is to soak spring-flowering bulbs for a day in tepid water before planting. They root more quickly this way.

This procedure is routinely recommended for snowdrop and guinea hen flower (*Fritillaria meleagris*) bulbs, as well as for Grecian windflower, winter aconite, anemone, and ranunculus tubers. The best candidates for a pre-planting soak are bulbous plants that ordinarily grow in moist climates. They will often have no protective covering, like a snowdrop. On the other hand, a tulip wears a thick brown tunic. It prevents the bulb from drying out during its dormant period and may also help to protect it from tunneling insects. It is no wonder that tulips can sit for six months, first in the warehouse and then in the garden center, and flower the next spring as if they'd never left the ground. On the other hand, snowdrops and guinea hen flowers have no protective covering and suffer when they are stored for a long time. The failure rate with these two "naked" bulbs is subsequently higher than that of other well-clad bulbs.

# Pesky

Logic dictates that bulbs native to parts of the world with climates similar to our own are the best bets for naturalizing. Plants from South Africa, the Mediterranean region, and the west coast of South America thrive along our own West Coast. Bulbs from tropical and semitropical Africa, Asia, and South America grow in our southlands. Bulbs from continental Europe and Asia fare well across our northern states. Geographic and climatic similarities don't always translate to success—some bulbs have carved out unique ecological niches and resist our efforts at their expansion—but it usually works.

Some bulbs demonstrate amazing adaptability far beyond what we might expect. The star flower, *Ipheion uniflorum,* inhabits moist meadows and woodland edges in temperate eastern South America. It comes as a delight that the pretty pale blue flowers thrive in such divergent climates as those of California, Colorado, and Connecticut. Not only does it demonstrate amazing tolerance to heat and cold, but the little charmer has one more ace up its sleeve: It's poisonous. Rodents and deer—the prime predators for most bulbs—find it unpalatable.

B*ecause of its adaptive nature, and because predators find it unpalatable, spring star flower*
(Ipheion uniflorum) *flourishes across much of the nation.*

If all other factors have been considered in selecting bulbs for a particular site, one more is essential: predators. My worst pests are a mere annoyance. I grouse about squirrels and slugs, an occasional vole or marauding raccoon, but my problems are few. I would dread facing the deer, rabbits, rodents, and snails the size of Volkswagens that some gardeners must.

The only deer not interested in your bulbs is headed down the highway strapped to the hood of a pickup. I live in a civilized city where deer do not have the run of the town, but it seems deer populations are on the rise. I remember waking up one morning in the Sheraton Inn in Northbrook, outside Chicago, to find deer nibbling on the foundation shrubs of the hotel. With their natural enemies—wolves, coyotes, and mountain lions—largely out of the picture, we face a national herd of deer with nothing to control their numbers but starvation and car collisions.

City gardeners who move to the country experience a shock. Sensitive, live-and-let-live types try scarecrows, repellents, guard dogs, and finally, violence. How you control pests is between you and your conscience; this is not a manual about pest control. Extension agents offer inconclusive lists of deer-resistant flowers, but

*Venerable stands of daffodil remain unbrowsed by marauding deer because of their toxic nature.*

most bulbs are not on them. Few, if any, bulbs may be considered completely deer-proof. Colchicums, jack-in-the-pulpit, spring star flower, sternbergias, and narcissus usually escape damage because of their toxic nature. Deer often pass up alliums (without an iota of proof, I theorize that the deer suffer from onion heartburn). Planning a garden based on a handful of plants, which may or may not survive marauding deer after a cold, snowy winter, doesn't present much of an opportunity. Some sort of control must be devised.

Some folks swear by a bag made from old pantyhose stuffed with human hair hanging from the branches. I would swear *at* it. When a method of deterrent mutilates the looks of the garden, I'd need to question it.

The tidiest and most efficient method of deer control is fencing. Deer jump—so it must be tall, over eight feet. Some companies specialize in deer fencing. If the garden is small and the fencing is much too visible (galvanized wire with green plastic coating is less intrusive), plant Virginia creeper or honeysuckle to strangle it. Deciduous and evergreen shrubs planted inside will also disguise it. Other gardeners, taking advantage of deer's natural distrust of enclosed spaces, string two sets of fences, only four feet tall but five feet apart. The animals feel trapped when they hurdle the first barrier and avoid going farther.

Dogs rank second in terms of deterrence. I know several country gardeners that get good protection from their canine friends, who live most of the year outdoors. I met a man in Montana with an extensive, unfenced garden that is all but immune to deer attack. When he started the garden, he bought a puppy. Several times a day, he and the youngster took a tour of the property line to "take care of business" at key rocks and stumps. By the end of the first month, the dog—a creature of habit— knew exactly what was expected of him. Every few weeks, the owner takes the stroll with his pet, not only to reinforce the dog's routine, but to reintroduce his own scent. The smell of humans and dogs is a powerful deterrent. This method, however, may prove unpopular or embarrassing in more densely settled areas, not to mention wreaking havoc on one's electrolytes.

Deer are wary of unsure footing. Short, coiled rolls of chicken wire set end to end can encircle a garden, with grasses and other plants allowed to grow through and obscure them. The deer's instinct to avoid boggy soil or quicksand kicks in when it sets foot on the springy concealed wire. Old wooden pallets offer similarly unsure footing. Placing them might present an artistic challenge, yet I can imagine a boardwalk theme to a pallet-encircled garden.

Motion detector alarms and lights initially work wonderfully, and gardeners congratulate themselves prematurely. Deer head for the hills the first few times the lights blaze or the sirens scream, but like people who live near airports or freeways, the deer learn to adapt. They get over the racket soon enough since it carries no further consequences, and deer may appreciate bright floodlights, the better to see what's on the menu.

Alternate methods employed with varied results include sprays of hot pepper or garlic (which must be regularly reapplied after rain), the aforementioned hair bags, blood meal, and unwrapped bars of soap drilled through the center and strung up throughout the garden. I can't imagine that these soaps-on-a-rope could contribute much to the artistry of a garden, but they do make the best of an overabundance of Father's Day gifts. Too bad deer aren't afraid of gaudy neckties.

## City Mouse, Country Mouse

Rodents do the most damage out of sight. Squirrels forage in recently disturbed soil, undoing the planting work of the gardener who's stepped inside to wash his hands. Mice forge trails beneath mulch and snowbanks in winter, feasting on newly planted bulbs while the unsuspecting gardener stays warm and blissfully un-aware inside. Voles, shrews, and ground squirrels tunnel underground. I've heard horror stories of tulips in full bloom disappearing below ground before a gar-dener's eyes.

It's a war. Humans have been fighting rats and mice forever. The battle with rodents runs from traps and baits to hand-to-hand combat. Gardeners plunge hoses down tunnels in an attempt to drown the critters. An experienced Connecticut gardener told me how she dropped poisonous castor bean seeds down the holes of shrews with good results. Temporary but effective results come from soaking bulbs in a commercial deterrent such as Ropel or Deter before planting. A big, hungry cat—what's known as a mouser—keeps rodent populations down. Too many Amer-ican cats live the champagne-and-caviar life to be effective at chasing mice.

Softhearted people trap squirrels and drive them across town. Not only is this scenic ride a total waste of time—squirrels move in waves and distribute themselves evenly around food supplies—but in some areas it is illegal. Rodents are rodents, no matter how furry the tail. What you decide to do on your property should be up to you, as long as you employ recognized humane methods.

## Slugging It Out

As squeamish as many people may be at killing rodents, most have no such com-punction when it comes to slugs and snails. Everybody hates them. A slug is essen-tially a snail without a shell, classified scientifically as *Limax*. I've heard them called worse. A number of different species are found throughout the world.

I feel compelled to put in a plug for slugs. They are nature's recyclers, and there is a place for them in an ecologically balanced garden. They usually feed on decaying vegetative matter, but it irks me when I catch one with an entire hosta in its mouth. Then the armistice is over. There's no such thing as complete eradication, so it seems wise to fight selective battles, protecting the rare or young plants or those prone to constant attack. If slug and snail damage chronically makes Swiss cheese of a plant despite your best efforts, the plant can hardly be considered an asset to the garden.

Most gardeners complain about their slug problem and, when pressed, will sometimes tell of their secret ways to combat them. In a society where pulling the wings off of butterflies is considered the first step toward being a serial killer, gardeners only talk slugs with fellow gardeners, with whom they get positively maniacal when it comes to their favorite methods of killing them. They all assume—wrongly—that I want to hear about it. But that's my job, to pass decades of tactical knowledge on to a new generation of warriors.

In a totally informal survey of my gardening friends, two methods came out as favorites for killing slugs. The first involves a flashlight and a pair of scissors. The second involves the aforementioned flashlight and a salt shaker. Salt crystals pull moisture from slug bodies and dehydrate them, but unfortunately, salt is nearly as deadly to plants. Snipping and salting the night-feeding gastropods may be emotionally satisfying, but other methods exist for long-term control.

Most bulbs are vulnerable to slug and snail attack when their tasty young shoots first emerge. Lilies are a case in point. As they grow, their stems become tougher and thicker and they become increasingly unpalatable, like old asparagus stalks. Some gardeners encircle their most vulnerable plants with sharp sand or gritty wood ashes that the soft-bellied slugs choose not to crawl over. Diatomaceous earth—the scratchy silica skeletal remains of microscopic algae called diatoms—is used similarly. Rings of copper strips have also been tested. The copper holds a small electrical charge that shocks their moist bodies and discourages slugs from crossing the barrier.

One time-honored method of control is to leave half a grapefruit or cantaloupe rind upside down on the ground or patio. At dawn, after a busy night, the slugs congregate underneath to get some rest. Lift the rind in the morning and stomp them. I recommended this to my friends Susan and Ronda, who are concerned that their dog, Violet, would eat slug bait. It turns out that Violet has a taste for grapefruit and cantaloupe, so they're going to plan B, which involves stale beer.

Saucers of beer, embedded at ground level, tempt slugs for a drink, and the tipsy ones fall in and drown. The bodies must be removed daily, and new beer added. It's a disgusting business, and I never thought the assortment of lids and saucers, full of dead slugs, did much for the aesthetics of the garden. I gave it up, fearing that slugs from miles around would spread the word that I threw a nightly kegger, and the influx of party guests would never end.

A report in *The Wall Street Journal,* however, disclosed the results of an important study for those who still favor this method of control. Various beer brands were tested to see which attracted the most slugs. The overwhelming favorite was Budweiser. I'm surprised the advertising department of Anheuser-Busch has not parlayed that fact into a big promotional campaign. Imagine this slogan: "When we say this Bud's for you, we don't mean the primrose." What gardener could resist?

Susan rejected the idea of slug saloons. The important thing is that Violet not develop a taste for beer, since it would doubtless ruin her trim boxer physique.

Plan C will probably involve a spray bottle of vinegar. This is one of the most environmentally friendly, completely horrifying slug terminations I've ever heard of. Spray the vinegar (which won't harm plants in small amounts) directly on the slugs, who apparently imitate the Nazis being liquidated by divine wrath in *Raiders of the Lost Ark.* It's low-budget Spielberg without the dramatic John Williams score.

I don't have pets, so I go directly to plan D. Give me Corry's Slug and Snail Death any day. I like a product with such a promising name. I've tried many brands of slug bait over the years, but I've had the best results with Corry's. It looks like dry instant oatmeal. My friend Diane, a professional gardener, gave me a great birthday present: a used parmesan cheese container with a handy shaker top for even, nonclog spreading. (Only a gardener would be thrilled with a birthday haul that included a kink-free rubber hose, some weird species of mullein, and an old cheese container.) I sprinkle bait happily under the (remaining) leaves of the slug's favorite foods during dry periods, because metaldehyde baits are quickly deactivated by rain or watering.

Most commercial slug bait contains metaldehyde and must be used intelligently. If Susan and Ronda go to plan D, what about Violet, who has the culinary discretion of a goat? The answer is an old hose. As a matter of fact, I've got the old one in the potting shed waiting for them. We'll cut it into ten-inch pieces, sprinkle slug bait inside, and roll them under shrubs and hostas. Slugs crawl in, but they don't crawl out. It's easy to empty the bodies into a plastic bag and dispose of them. We hope Violet won't develop a taste for rubber.

# Arachnophobia and Other Things to Get Over

A long list of insects and diseases that might plague bulbs is scary. Don't worry. Only a few constitute a real problem. One theory puts forth the idea that weak plants are most vulnerable to attack. It's nature's way of weeding out the weaklings. Strongly growing, healthy bulbs are not at much risk. Spring-flowering bulbs do their thing and depart before most infestations rear their ugly heads.

It takes a few seasons for a new garden to work out a balance, where plants, birds, insects, and humans live in harmony. I'm a firm believer in natural remedies. Ladybugs, praying mantis, green lacewings, predator wasps, spiders, and birds know what to do if given a chance. I was never heavily into the use of garden pesticides, but I largely gave them up many years ago out of laziness. The garden thrived without them. I remember waking early one fine June morning and venturing outside: The first rays of the sun illuminated a million tiny dewdrops strung on the fine strands of spiderwebs throughout the garden. I was amazed. It dawned on me that I hadn't faced a serious outbreak of aphids, whiteflies, or spider mites for several seasons. The garden had worked out its own balance without my intervention.

If a plant requires constant attention to keep it pest free, the question must be asked: Is it worth it? Those of us who tend large gardens are frequently forced to face facts, and the answer is usually no. My friend Lauren Springer popularized the phrase "Darwinian gardening." This survival-of-the-fittest approach is not as hard-hearted as it sounds.

Give a plant the best chance for survival by planting it where its requirements of sun, shade, soil, and water can be met. If it fails to thrive, move it and try again as many times as your patience allows. Some of my friends garden by baseball rules: Three strikes and it's out. Then move on; some things were not meant to be. There are thousands of plants that can be grown in any given region. Give up on the ones that are chronic sicklings and expand your gardening horizons. I tire of gardeners who make trips to the East Coast and come back raving about the rhododendrons or whatever is in blatant bloom at the moment and then yearn to grow them in the worst way, which is exactly what they do.

Among the insects that may target bulbs, only a few are a cause for alarm. Pests vary from region to region, but the most troublesome include spider mites, thrips, Narcissus flies, borers, wireworms, cutworms, whiteflies, Japanese beetles, and nematodes. Have a professional diagnose your problem by showing her or him an infected part; it's difficult to make a diagnosis on the phone. Extension agents, county agricultural commissioners, garden centers, and botanical gardens and arboretums have programs to help gardeners make ecologically responsible choices in pest control.

Tiny spider mites multiply during hot, dry weather. They form webs on the undersides of leaves and feed by sucking plant juices. Leaves lose their green coloration and look dry. Mites can be easily controlled by spraying leaves with a strong blast of cold water, followed up by a soapy spray. Insects hate soap nearly as much as eight-year-old boys. The soap softens the hard casings of the insect bodies and they basically melt away.

Two types of thrips—gladiolus and onion—are common on some bulbs. The former are most damaging to gladiolus, on which they cut through the outer layer of skin cells to get to the juicy bits. The symptoms are somewhat similar to those left by spider mites. Onion thrips cause white patches, brown tips, and distorted leaves on species of *Allium* and occasional other bulbous plants. Because thrips attack the center of the leaves, they don't succumb to sprays. Systemic insecticides—sprays absorbed into the leaves, or poison granules that are taken in by the roots and distributed throughout the entire plant—can be most effective.

Narcissus flies lay their eggs in the necks of bulbs such as amaryllis, snowdrops, leucojums, and narcissus as the foliage withers. They hatch and the larvae eat the center of the bulb, a particularly rude shock for the gardener since they won't find out until the following spring when the bulb fails to make an appearance. Narcissus fly is not widespread; where it occurs, dust bulbs with Diazinon as they wither.

Borers, cutworms, and wireworms usually aren't detected until they've done their dirty work. Bearded iris, lilies, dahlias, and gladiolus are sometimes attacked by borers, especially in the eastern part of the country. They burrow into the base of the stalk or rhizome and gut it. Controls range from inserting coat hangers in borer holes to spear the caterpillars to spraying with Sevin or using systemic insecticides. Wireworms are the larvae of beetles that can eat the roots of bulbs, causing the entire plant to collapse. Control them by removing the infested plants and dusting the hole with Sevin. Cutworms are the larvae of moths that usually favor young vegetable shoots, but they will sometimes attack bulbs. Adult moths emerge from the soil in spring and lay eggs that quickly hatch into caterpillars. They earned the name *cutworms* for their despicable habit of sawing off young plants at soil level. Protect vulnerable plants with a collar around their stems. I cut the bottoms out of wax-coated paper cups. If stuck firmly and deeply in the soil, they will present cutworms, which operate on and directly below the surface, with a barrier.

Like mites, whiteflies feed on plant sap; they are more distressing than life threatening. Soap sprays at weekly intervals (to combat periodic egg hatching missed by the last spray) work well. Japanese beetles infest many areas in the eastern half of the country. Of the bulbs, cannas and dahlias are preferred by the beetles. Hand-picking is the preferred method of control, even if most of us would prefer not to touch the beetles. Nematodes can cause roots to rot; symptoms include deformed and split leaves. Because they are microscopic, only a soil sample can pinpoint a nematode problem. If severe, soil fumigation is the only recourse.

Ants are a minor problem. Their presence usually indicates a bigger threat—aphids. Ants sometimes "farm" aphids, milking them for the honeydew on which the ants feed. A flurry of ant activity on a plant usually includes their farm hidden under leaves or in leaf joints.

Aphids are dangerous. It's not that their feeding on the juices of any one plant poses a particular problem, it's their mobility. Flying aphids travel freely about the garden and can spread a virus from one plant to another. Viruses abound, but the most common and serious is the "breaking" or "mosaic" virus that attacks both tulips and lilies. In tulips, the symptoms are easy to see: a formerly red tulip may be garishly splashed with "lightning" strikes of white or other colors. In the 1700s the Dutch prized these color "breaks." The bulbs often continued to live and prosper for a time, and with no knowledge of microscopic virus, breaking was much anticipated and appreciated. Fortunes were made and lost in tulip "futures," as schemes were laid to propagate the most beautiful broken tulips. The framework eventually collapsed like a house of cards.

Broken tulips should be grown only in seclusion, if at all, as the virus is spread by aphids to other tulips and lilies. In lilies the symptoms include distorted buds, mottled flower coloration, irregularly streaked leaves, and general loss of vigor. There is no cure, and infected plants should be destroyed, not composted. A late but not quite fatal spring freeze can also do the same thing, so don't go pulling up all the lilies if they don't look quite right on the first of June. I tend to segregate lilies from hybrid tulips (most small species seem almost immune). Some lily species such as *Lilium regale* are also quite resistant to the virus. Tiger lilies (*L. tigrinum*) carry the virus but are seemingly unaffected by it. It's a sad fact that we must choose between the tiger lily and the rest of the clan. Like a dysfunctional family, they can't coexist.

Other viruses sometimes infect other plants like iris and freesia. Off-color leaves and distorted flowers signal the presence of the disease, especially if the damage can't be blamed on extremes of weather or insect damage. Dispose of the plant posthaste.

The fungal disease botrytis attacks bulb foliage during cool, damp weather. It starts as small yellow or orange patches that eventually engulf the leaves in gray mold. Lilies, tulips, and dahlias are frequent targets. Some species and cultivars are more susceptible than others. In areas where botrytis is a major problem, situate frequently attacked plants where air circulation is best and start a spraying regimen recommended by experts in your area. Give up on varieties that persistently fall prey.

Most gardeners have some sort of mildew problem. In fact, many of us jokingly compete for the dubious distinction of mildew capital of the world. Both downy mildew and powdery mildew can affect the foliage of bulb leaves in especially bad years, usually when temperatures are low and humidity is high. Mildew spores are spread by wind, so it's important to curb an outbreak early. Where mildew can be expected, start dusting with sulfur-based remedies before symptoms occur.

I've simply eliminated the most mildew-prone plants from my garden. If a plant comes down with mildew, I tell visitors it's a rare silver-leaf form. It then goes on my "hit list," which means it is next in line to go when I need space for my newest infatuation.

The ugliest plant disease has to be corn smut. It gives me the willies. Fortunately it does not affect bulbs. Onion smut, which can attack any alliums, is recognized by dark blisters on the leaves. It is fatal to the bulb; destroy it. The disease is prevalent in some areas in the northern part of the country and thrives in wet years. Check with your regional experts before investing in hundreds of dollars of ornamental onions.

Writing about diseases is depressing; reading about them must be more so. It's with a sigh of relief that I conclude this section with the cheerful summation that there are very few other bulb diseases of much consequence, and with the earnest assessment that if a bulb needs excessive pampering and gallons of spray just to survive, it can hardly be said to have naturalized.

# Myths

A garden visitor once asked me, "How large is your staff?" After a speechless moment, I replied that I don't have one. She still wanted to know how I keep up with the dividing, mulching, staking, dead-heading, fertilizing, and soil cultivation. "I don't do any of that," I told her. "The perennials, bulbs, shrubs, and self-sowing annuals pretty much take care of themselves." From the look in her eyes, I don't think she believed me. I'm sure she thinks my "staff" arrives at the crack of dawn each morning and slaves until they drop. Occasionally my neighbors may catch a glimpse of me in my pajamas, weeding and puttering at dawn, but my phantom staff never arrives. I switch into jeans and get my daily gardening chores finished in about an hour.

People make gardening much too difficult on themselves. Although it is certainly not maintenance free, my garden is most demanding in May and early June, as well as fall bulb planting. In midsummer, I'm coasting. Perhaps it's because I don't subscribe to the old horticultural practices. Let me debunk a few myths about bulbs:

- **Bulbs require frequent division.** Wrong. The only bulbous plants that should be divided regularly are bearded iris, which I divide every four or five years. The only other reason to divide clump-formers is to increase their numbers.
- **Deep planting discourages tulips from splitting.** Not in my experience. Some varieties are simply prone to split into nonflowering bulblets after the first year. They are to be avoided. A tulip bulb reinvents itself every year. The best varieties (discussed in chapter 6) remake themselves into a single bulb or sometimes two. This slow multiplication is fine. Plant tulips slightly deeper in sandy soil (six to eight inches is sufficient) and higher in clay soil (five or six inches of soil above them is plenty). The good varieties are nearly indestructible; the poor ones would split if they were buried in the Grand Canyon (backfilled with Mt. Rainier).
- **Bulbs need plenty of fertilizer.** They don't. Too much fertilizer promotes lush, rank growth that flops in the rain and breaks in the wind. Grow plants lean and mean, the better to cope with the vagaries of weather. Feed only to help a plant with an obvious deficiency. Some bulbs, such as lilies, do best in organically rich soil that is regularly top-dressed, but this is different from applications of standard granular or liquid fertilizer. Bulbs that are on the decline—demonstrated by poor flowering—often benefit from a fertilizer high in potash, such as is formulated for tomatoes. Make sure that the cause is a nutritional deficiency, not the shade of a tree. I've often investigated a "mysterious" decline in vigor of a group of lilies or peonies, only to discover that they're trying to flower in almost total shade. Twenty years ago, when the tiny sapling ash tree was planted, there was plenty of sunshine. Gardens change.
- **Bulbs need to be mulched.** Not really. I used to mulch lightly with ground bark but gave it up since the decomposing bark steals nitrogen from the plants. Tightly planted perennials planted with bulbs shade the soil and reduce evaporation.

A mulch of small gravel, however, is appropriate for rock gardens and hellstrips (the area between the sidewalk and street, so named because it is hot, dry, and devilishly difficult to grow all but dryland plants in it). Shade gardens under deciduous trees are largely self mulching. Some leaves, such as cottonwood, sycamore, and Norway maple, form thick, smothering mats that need to be removed in autumn, but most leaves make a good natural protection. Some will begin to break down in winter and, as the first crocus or snowdrops emerge, the excess can be raked off and consigned to a compost pile.

- **Bulbs need the soil around their feet cultivated.** No. Cultivation disturbs their roots. Plant appropriate perennials and annuals tightly together above the bulbs to cover every inch of earth. They'll squeeze out most weeds. Throw those cultivators away; I've yet to run into the plant that responds favorably to having its roots disturbed weekly.

- **Bulbs can only be planted in autumn.** No. While a vast majority of hardy spring-bloomers are fall planted, bulbs have varying schedules. Some can be transplanted from containers at any time during the year as long as the soil is not frozen.

- **Bulbs can only be transplanted when they're dormant.** No again. Who remembers in autumn what seemed so obvious in spring? Finding elusive dormant bulbs is a hassle and I always miss a few. The few stragglers look pitiful. It takes a little extra effort to transplant bulbs while they are actively growing, but it's often worth the effort. Dig slowly and carefully, endeavoring not to break or injure the underground stem. Water thoroughly. Pot-grown bulbs forced for bloom indoors are easily planted in the garden when the foliage is still green; it's easier to determine how they'll look and combine with other plants. Since bulbs are customarily planted at or near the top of the pots, set them deeper in the ground.

- **Bulbs need preventative spraying for pests and diseases.** No. Use environmentally friendly remedies, such as a soap spray for aphids and spider mites, when outbreaks occur. Never underestimate the power of ladybugs or predator wasps to control pests, but they'll never have the chance in a pesticide-soaked environment.

- **Bulbs need to be cut to the ground after flowering.** Wrong again. This is the worst mistake possible. Let them die down on their own schedule, disguising unsightly withering foliage where possible. Remove stems of spent flowers to promote more blossoms or prevent seeding on some bulbs such as hybrid tulips and lilies. Lighten up about most dead-heading; enjoy the beauty of the seed heads and allow your bulbs to seed themselves.

- **Bulbs should be cut to the ground in autumn.** No. In nature, there are no little elves running around with mini weed-whackers, leveling the bulbs and perennials each fall. Let nature take its course, protecting plants from winter harm with their own frosted foliage. Pulling up the stalks of lilies invites problems, creating a funnel for water that can drown the bulb.

Gardening shouldn't be a form of punishment. Follow your own rules. I look back at the spring, remembering my damp, muddy clothes, raw hands, and throbbing, sore muscles. Autumn planting is no picnic either. A staff would come in mighty handy, but bulb gardeners wear their dirty fingernails and calluses like badges of valor. I'm more than willing to pay the price for the untold pleasures the blooming bulbs bring me.

# 3

# THE LAY OF THE LAND

Many gardeners live and die by the USDA Zone Hardiness Map. That's too bad. It takes one variable into account—minimum winter temperature—and that's simply not enough to predict plant hardiness. Gardeners from different states ask, "What's your zone?" the way people used to ask, "What's your sign?" Hardiness maps and astrology have plenty in common: There is probably something to them, they are not exact sciences, and some people get more out of them than others.

Plants can't read. They have no idea what zones they occupy. They continue to live or die because of a combination of factors, most notably exposure, soil type, precipitation, humidity, and of course, temperature. Maximum summer temperatures are often as important as minimum winter temperatures. How low it doesn't drop in winter is also extremely important when it comes to bulbs,

A *blue and yellow pastiche in shade features wood hyacinth* (Hyacinthoides hispanica), *leopard's bane* (Doronicum caucasicum), *and heartleaf* (Brunnera macrophylla).

since most traditional spring-bloomers won't perform without an extended cold period of at least six weeks. Its conclusion triggers them to flower; without it, they won't. *Crocus chrysanthus* brushes off a cold, snowy Salt Lake City winter but fails in a balmy, warm Miami winter. Plants are not like people.

People who attend horticultural seminars are a suspicious lot. If a noted expert comes from a zone that stays ten degrees warmer in winter, they cross their arms in defiance; the speaker can often hear some grumbling that sounds like "doesn't know what he's talking about" or "he should try getting that through the winter here."

As my hero, Henry Mitchell, once pointed out, "It is not nice to garden anywhere. Everywhere there are violent winds, startling once-per-five-centuries floods, unprecedented droughts, record-setting freezes, abusive and blasting heats never known before. There is no place, no garden, where these terrible things do not drive gardeners mad." Mitchell, who took two weeks off each June just to admire his iris, also advised that real gardeners go on despite disasters. They make gardens "so that all who see it say, 'Well, you have favorable conditions here. Everything grows for you.' Everything grows for everybody. Everything dies for everybody too."

Don't sweat the zone thing. Use it as a helpful tool, but consider other information. This book breaks with tradition in *not* utilizing the USDA Zone Map. Practically every garden book published in the last decade has that map stuck in the back, and most gardeners know their zone number better than their ring size. This book has its own map. It considers summer temperatures, humidity, regional weather patterns, and corresponding similarities within distinct regions. These have names, not numbers.

Don't take it as gospel. As gardeners know, conditions vary from state to state, county to county, and door to door. Of course there's a big difference between gardening conditions within a region, such as between Green Bay and Madison, or between Austin and New Orleans, but the plant palette for each city within the upper Midwest or the South is quite similar. The tables in chapter 8 provide extensive lists of plants that are good bets for each region. It takes into account the adaptability of plants and their track record in any region. Every site has its quirks, but if yours are extreme—say you live at the top of a mountain or at the northern or southern boundary of a region—use your own good judgment in determining how you fit into the grand scheme of things. Turn on the Weather Channel. Do your temperatures and readings continually exceed or lag behind most of the major cities in your region? Plan accordingly.

Topography, elevation, proximity to moderating elements (such as oceans, lakes, and giant apartment buildings) give every gardener the task of learning the limits of his own personal zone. Don't believe everything you read (here or elsewhere), and make determinations for yourself. If I relied on the zone assignments given to my plants, I'd have to chuck out half of them.

# Intimacy

An experienced gardener knows every foot of his or her land intimately. He knows where the water collects and stands. He knows where the last patches of snow linger. He knows where the clumps of crocus first emerge.

Even a typical, square yard contains several distinct microclimates. Beds on the north side of buildings are cool and shaded. Hot spots may be found against brick walls, near patios, or along walks. Evergreens and fences form windbreaks and provide protection and shade. No formula exists that declares where a certain species should be planted, but an educated guess by a gardener who knows the lay of the land is the best place to start.

Cool, shady areas on the north sides of buildings, fences, and evergreens thaw slowly as the sun rises in the sky. It's a pleasure to experience two months of crocus. The ones on the north side of my house emerge just as the crocus in the south-facing borders finish. If these cool areas stay relatively shady and moist throughout the rest of the summer, they're likely spots to plant dicentras, trilliums, arums, erythroniums, and Solomon's seal.

Hot pockets try the patience of many novice gardeners. The reflected heat of a brick wall might fry delphiniums or turn roses into instant potpourri, but it might be ideal for an early display of crocus, *Iris reticulata,* and early tulips planted amid clumps of herbs like sage, thyme, horehound, and artemisias. Turkish onion (*Allium karataviense*) and gayfeather (*Liatris spicata*) continue the show, while saffron crocus and blackberry lilies close the season. The heat of the wall can also be moderated by trellises of vines.

The topography of a garden offers opportunities and drawbacks. Daffodils might fare poorly on a steep, dry slope in a semiarid region but thrive well in a moist, low-lying area at its feet. In a similar situation in the Pacific Northwest, the daffodils may be perfectly accommodated on the hillside, while the lowland is best planted with trout lilies, arisaemas, and camassia.

Any garden can hold many more bulbs than most people would think possible. I'm continually finding and creating more room. When I told a friend, a novice gardener, that I was planting about two thousand bulbs last fall, she raised her eyebrows in amazement and asked simply, "Where?" If I had the use of visual aids, like sheets of acetate demonstrating the layers in the soil where bulbs and perennials of various sizes root, I could have done a better job of explaining. I tried to tell her how bulbs grow and flower at different times of the year and that the soil is like a layer cake, with the larger bulbs at the bottom and the small ones near the top and lots of roots of perennials poking down through. I pointed out that I have a wide range of conditions, from dry, sunny areas to a rock-terraced slope to shady, moist conditions along an irrigation ditch. I ended with the lame generalization, "Oh, there's plenty of room out there somewhere."

Eventually I will run out of room, but I'm not terribly concerned about it now. It takes imagination to see the possibilities. Even a burgeoning, overstuffed perennial garden has an unexploited layer a few inches below the surface where myriad so-called minor bulbs can find a home. Early in the growing season, between those emerging perennials, under those shrubs just showing buds, and even among those

sprouting tulips, there's plenty of bare earth. It's crying out for a hefty order of crocus, snowdrops, Siberian squills, bulbocodium, Grecian windflowers, Michail's
flower *(Fritillaria michailovskyi)*, grape hyacinths, *Puschkinia,* meadow squills, and
many more.

When planting larger bulbs, such as lilies, tulips, or hyacinths, plan to include
minor ones at the same time. It takes effort to dig major holes, so you might as well
get double the reward. After the larger bulbs go in, fill the hole all but two inches
deep. Add a layer of smaller bulbs to time-share the space. They will not get in one
another's way, nor will they interfere with most perennials plunked in on top.

Some aggressive perennials, such as obedient plant and plume poppy, don't make
good companions for bulbs. They gobble up space quickly and don't leave much
opportunity for bulbs to burst through their tight mats of roots and stems. Tap-
rooted plants, such as Oriental poppies or gas plant, make good bulb neighbors since
their roots go straight down and rarely forage into the top few inches of surrounding soil. Perennials with shallow, fibrous roots, such as creeping veronicas, creeping
Jenny, and carpet sedums make ideal companions for any bulbs, especially the small
ones, since their roots can easily be penetrated by sprouting bulbs. The advantage is
that the bulbs show more beautifully against a foliage backdrop rather than bare
soil, and there's no gaping hole when the bulbs go dormant. Self-sowing annuals
serve the same purpose, with California poppies or love-in-a-mist providing a
frilly framework of foliage, which grows to disguise the bulb's own foliage as
it matures.

# On the Rocks

Minor bulbs can enhance almost every area of any garden. Rockeries are natural
places for small bulbs since they provide so many mini-microclimates. Just one big
rock creates a warm southern exposure for snow iris and a cool north face to protect
snowdrops. Rock gardens provide accelerated drainage, which is usually a benefit.
In humid climates, the air close to rocks heats up and dries out, aiding plants from
the Mediterranean region that resent damp conditions.

Much has been written about rock gardens over the years. Their construction
can become an art form. The greatest ones both mimic and enhance nature, recog-
nizing the beauty in seeing plants in a naturalistic habitat while remembering that all
forms of gardening are interpretive. The selection and placement of stone is the

foundation to any rockery. For authenticity, experts choose either native rock (or add to existing outcrops) or select stone that is most like that in which the majority of plants they grow evolved. Most rock gardeners agree that the stone should be homogenous, otherwise the garden looks like an accumulation of summer vacation souvenirs.

Like other gardens, those made of stone are personal creations. Everyone has to start somewhere. My sister and I, blessed with indulgent parents, built rock gardens all over the place as children. We did indeed use rocks that we hauled home in the family station wagon from trips to the mountains. Our efforts became increasingly sophisticated over time, and we thought they were splendid. In retrospect, our little rock gardens must have appeared to be the result of a rash of unexplained pet deaths. That's why, to this day, I remain very indulgent of the efforts of fledgling rock gardeners.

Rock gardens vary to suit their makers' interests and obsessions, evolving over time through experimentation and inspiration. Even naive first attempts provide wonderful pleasure and eventually become more sophisticated after the "edelweiss phase" wears off. My rock gardening friends are not only among the most passionate of gardeners but have also become very intuitive, artistic ones as well.

I don't have a proper rock garden, although I built a retaining wall from lichen-covered native stone on the west side of my house. I lugged stone for several days for this project, which allowed me to level a modest slope so I could lay a brick dining patio. The wall is about forty feet long but only about three feet tall. When I picture what hell must be like, I imagine hauling rock for a stone wall that never ends.

I left plenty of room between stones and filled it with well-drained sandy

*An audacious rock garden combination features* Tulipa vvendskyi, *purple rock cress, and yellow* Alkanna orientalis.

loam. There are bound to be trouble spots where two rocks meet and soil does not stay in place. Plug these immediately with hens and chicks, the super glue of the plant world. I plant my flowering wall with whatever strikes my fancy, although I keep in mind that a stone crevice suits some plants and not others. Some plants seem at home in a setting between rocks, while others appear to be out of place. Prim bedding plants look downright silly, but a wide range of plants combine well in the wall.

I use my wall to showcase smaller plants, including bulbs, that might otherwise be swamped in my borders of rambunctious perennials. I can get a close-up view of tiny pink *Bulbocodium vernum,* which looks like a small spring colchicum; milk squill (*Scilla tubergiana*), a lovely white species with larger flowers than its Siberian cousin; and small narcissus such as yellow 'Sundial', white and yellow 'Minnow', and 'Jack Snipe', with its golden swept-back petals. Many species tulips have created small colonies in a short time. The black-throated, wine red cups of *Tulipa pulchella* look dramatic against the red leaves of *Bergenia* 'Redstart'. Bronze *T. altaica* pokes through yellow violas. *T. vvedenskyi* may have a cumbersome name, but its blossoms are unforgettable. Deep orange-red (shocking with purple rock cress) and the size of a coffee mug, they seem oversize for the wavy, ground-hugging leaves that accompany them. *T. sprengeri,* the last of any tulip to bloom, waits until early summer to display its long-stemmed vermilion flowers. It is the purest red of any flower in the garden—no cast of orange, no hint of blue—and makes a thrilling climax to tulip time.

# The Hills Are Alive

Many homeowners consider a steep slope, or even a mild one, a problem. Sometimes they carpet them with lawn (if you've ever been a ten-year-old and had to mow one of these, you know this treatment borders on child abuse). Sometimes they wrap them in black plastic covered with bark nuggets, girdle them in railroad ties, or bury them in concrete. The effect is rarely gratifying.

A really steep slope may need support to keep it from sliding down the street during a wet season. Retaining walls of stone, stucco, or recycled concrete suffice. Aggressive, colonizing plants help to control erosion, such as snow-in-summer or creeping liriope. Even rather bland ground covers spring to life with a progression of bulbs interplanted with them.

No plant rots on a hillside. Depending on the exposure, a slope offers wide open opportunities. Plants that ordinarily fail in a damp climate may thrive on a hill. Tulips, lilies, many alliums, and some varieties of iris come to mind. Even when too much rain is not an issue, a hillside changes through the seasons with sequential planting. Even states and cities—especially on the East Coast and in the South—get into the act, planting slopes against freeway ramps with daffodils followed by daylilies. This can't be copied everywhere. My own city tried it with mixed results: The daylilies have been great, but Denver is not daffodil country, at least not on a dry slope. Darwin hybrid tulips would have been a better choice.

Where rainfall provides, daffodils turn any hillside into a spring paradise. They compete well with grass (be it bluegrass or rough meadow grasses), need no protection from animals, and grow in beauty each year. Early, mid, and late season varieties extend the show for as much as two months. Even one variety, planted en masse, may be so splendid that the gardener feels no compulsion to improve upon it by introducing other kinds.

A woman I know saved up and ordered ten thousand daffodils to glorify the slopes in her garden. She neglected to budget for labor and decided to take a week off and plant them herself. The first day, she dug neat holes in artistic shapes and worked in

R*ivulets of daffodils flow down a Chicago hillside.*

*F*iery Chasmanthe aethiopica *makes a dazzling display in California.*

bone meal and compost. The second day, she used the "mass grave" method, dumping as many as possible in hastily dug furrows. By the third day, she resorted to simply throwing the bulbs on the ground and sifting a few spadefuls of dirt over them. She laughs about it now, the memory of calluses and an aching back having faded. "You know what?" she exclaimed. "Five years later I can't even tell the difference—they look glorious!"

Gardeners have the luxury of planning intricately composed groups of plants that don't need to look great from a speeding car. In the South, a hillside planting might well include daffodils but be punctuated with clumps of daylilies and Dutch iris. Several dozen bulbs of *Ipheion* might turn into several hundred over the years, producing a pale blue flow of flowers as they seed themselves down the hill. In autumn, *Sternbergia lutea* does the same, only in golden yellow.

On a West Coast hillside, any number of succulents take to life on a slope. In spring, purple babianas, tawny homerias, and sweet-scented yellow *Gladiolus tristis* pop up through them. For more dramatic results, *Chasmanthe aethiopica* in orange or yellow performs well. I have a vivid recollection of a stone wall in Berkeley planted with chasmanthe at the top. The tall, grassy foliage is rather handsome to begin, but when it erupts into fiery bloom, the result is fabulous.

Agapanthus are an obvious—perhaps too obvious—choice for mild slopes. These easily grown plants are planted in vast groups on street medians with endless rows of stiff stems, and gardeners sometimes dismiss them as too common. Perhaps, but they're tough, drought tolerant, low maintenance, and gorgeous. The commonplace can still be beautiful (and they're a far cry from lawn or rock mulch). Gardeners in cold climates covet them and their lovely blue flowers. The right companions make all the difference: Romping nasturtiums disarm their stiffness, the way a pair of tennis shoes dresses down a tux.

# Tapestries

Imagine your garden without leaves on the trees, where sunlight will penetrate bare branches in spring and coax the bulbs from the earth.

Even I am having trouble envisioning this. I need to think back beyond the heat of summer, to the chilly, damp spring that I thought would never end. I remember one of my most successful bulb plantings, where eight hundred *Crocus chrysanthus* sprang up through the circular lawn in the middle of the shade garden on the east side of the house. It took about two hours to plant them one fall, but they give me nearly a month of pleasure each spring. The yellow ones bloom first, soon joined by pale lavender and creamy white. These give way to deep golden yellow and purple. Not bad for an investment of a few hours and seventy dollars, but the lawn looks unkempt for a month while I resist the urge to mow. (Actually, I rarely have a burning desire to get out the lawnmower, but waiting for the crocus foliage to ripen makes a good excuse.) Because crocus leaves expand from the base, it's not too hard on them to set the mower at the highest level and nip off the tops.

If you decide to naturalize crocus in a lawn, choose a thin one beneath deciduous trees. The crocus will compete better with the grass, forming big clumps after just a few years. To achieve a natural look, it is often said, toss the bulbs by the handful and plant them where they fall. This sounds terribly liberating and adventuresome, so by all means do it, wind in your hair and brimming over with nature's artistic guidance. Me, I'm down on my hands and knees stuffing that lawn with what seems like a bottomless bag of corms. I cover the space I can reach and move on, forgetting where I've been soon enough. The results are plenty random enough, believe me. Planting goes relatively smoothly with a dandelion digger. Simply stab the tool a couple of inches deep into the turf, rock it back and forth to open a small hole, push the crocus corm into it (pointed end up), and firm the soil. A few fall in sideways or upside down; they all manage to come up. Turn on the sprinkler for an hour. This is the only work you will ever need to do again for the crocus. They take care of themselves.

I've always been entranced by that famous Flemish tapestry "The Unicorn in Captivity," which shows the legendary beast encircled by a lawn of grass and tiny flowers. A pastiche of small bulbs imitates that look, including not only crocus but winter aconites, snowflakes (*Leucojum vernum*), and glory-of-the-snow. I've added patches of each to my crocus lawn for variety and an extended period of interest.

Creeping perennials such as bird's eye veronica (*Veronica filiformis*), violets, and bronze ajuga also colonize the circular lawn surrounded by perennial beds. I've avoided the temptation, however slight, to plunk a unicorn sculpture in the center, opting instead for a large Italian clay pot fitted with a fountain head that sprays water over polished stones.

# Grasslands

From the eastern forest to the foothills of the Rockies, much of our country once was a sea of grass. Several species dominated the plains and prairies, while a diverse collection of native perennials and bulbous plants found niches within their domain. Winter and spring moisture turned the land green, and sheets of brilliant blossoms spread across it.

Summer sun and wind sucked the moisture from the land. Trees rarely encroached—fire saw to that. Lightning set off blazes that swept across the land. A unique flora adapted to the alternate cycles of growth and burn. Much of it disappeared as settlers turned grassland into farmland. Gardeners seek to reintroduce the native plants and flowers, creating a microcosm of an ecosystem that has almost vanished from view. The central part of the nation is not renowned for its wealth of native bulbs (as a whole, our country takes a definite back seat to central Asia, the Mediterranean region, and South Africa). Nevertheless, a few standout bulbous plants evolved on the plains and prairies.

One signature plant of the region is *Liatris*. Several species of these so-called gayfeathers or blazing stars command attention for their rigid stems studded with small, rosy purple flowers. A uniquely American member of the daisy family, it has flowers opening from the top downward. This flies in the face of tradition, since spiky flowers like *Delphinium, Eremurus,* and *Digitalis* inevitably open their lowest flowers first.

The rich purple, blue, and pink hues of various species of spiderwort (*Tradescantia*) bloom throughout the plains. Though some gardeners might classify them as perennials, they are included here because of their rhizomatous roots, much like those of agapanthus or daylilies, that allow them to survive and thrive despite extremes in weather or, in rare instances, fire. They grow and flower in spring and often go dormant when hot, dry conditions prevail. Other grassland perennials with similar rhizomes include white, spring-flowering Canada anemone (*Anemone*

*The charming natural flora of the southern plains—pink* Allium drummondii, *spiderworts, and bluebonnets—needs no additional plastic floral tributes.*

canadensis); that favorite food of the Monarch butterfly, milkweed (*Asclepias syriaca*); brilliant orange butterflyweed (*A. tuberosa*); and moisture-loving wild iris, such as purple *Iris versicolor* and violet blue *I. shrevei*. Great Solomon's seal (*Polygonatum canaliculatum*) also prefers moist sites where its graceful arching stems produce tiny dangling white bells.

Nodding onion (*Allium cernuum*) is widely distributed across the country, from the upper Midwest down to New Mexico and into Oregon and Washington. The city of Chicago, once the site of a massive expanse of these pendant pink flowers, is said to take its name from the Ojibwa tribe's words "she-kag-ong," meaning "wild onion place." Several other noteworthy ornamental onions grow across the country, such as small, soft pink *Allium drummondii,* which flowers on the Texas plains in spring, forming pools of color with bluebonnets and spiderworts.

Wild lilies delight us but often defy attempts to cultivate them. A moist meadow situation suits swamp lily (*Lilium superbum*) with its July display of striking golden-orange, chocolate-spotted Turk's-cap flowers. *Lilium canadense* ranges in the wild from Ontario to the Appalachians. In moist summer fields, its willowy four-foot stems bear exquisite bells of cinnamon-sprinkled yellow or, occasionally, maroon red. Small bulbs from a lily specialist make a good investment, or seed can be scattered in autumn as it would naturally.

A meadow-in-a-can is not the answer. These seed mixtures usually contain European wildflower seeds that, while pretty, are about as representative of our wildflower heritage as one of my lectures is of the great tradition of kabuki theater. To truly re-create a native habitat, it's necessary to kill off introduced weeds such as thistle and quack grass. Layers of black plastic or the vigilant application of herbicides such as glyphosate (Roundup or Kleenup) take a hot summer to be effective. Then you can plant.

Low-growing grasses such as little bluestem (*Andropogon scoparius*), sideoats grama (*Bouteloua curtipendula*), prairie dropseed (*Sporobolus heterolepis*), or other native grasses should be seeded or transplanted with a "wildflower meadow." Attractive in their own right, these grasses squeeze out true weeds but work in harmony with the flowers with which they evolved. Fall or spring seeding is possible; regular irrigation and a light covering of straw prevent erosion while the seeds germinate and take hold. While fire is still the preferred (and no doubt exciting) method of prairie management by aficionados, an annual or biennial autumn burn may be unpopular or illegal in your neighborhood. While fire does provide nutrients, beat back encroaching weeds and tree seedlings, and open the prairie garden up for spring growth, you may need to resort to autumn mowing.

# The Dryland Garden

Beautiful gardens have nothing to do with the amount of water that is required to maintain them. They are created from imagination and good horticulture. Each of us may adopt, in our own way, water-saving practices. Unfortunately, many gardeners see only the bad examples of low-water landscaping—gravel and a few starved-looking plants. Ironically, the use of vast expanses of rock may reduce water consumption, but the rocks heat up in the sun and raise the air temperature around a house. More electric energy is needed (requiring water to generate it) to cool the interior of the home.

The best examples of dryland gardens are so colorful and lush that it would be hard to imagine that they require very little water. Exploring the rich and diverse palette of natives and adaptable non-natives, gardeners create landscapes of great beauty and originality without draining the well. They may build on the traditions of the past (adapting a style such as the cottage garden) or create their own interpretations.

When I visualize most of the eastern half of the nation, it's largely green. When I think of the West, other colors come to mind. More than ever before, gardens where rainfall is scant or unpredictable don't copy the green gardens of another region. Flowers and foliage echo the natural landscape. Blues and purples are borrowed from the sky and mountains. Pink, peach, and brilliant scarlet come from the native stone and setting sun. Silver, white, and cream are picked up from the clouds or snow. Shades of sage green, straw, gold, and maroon are found in the native grasses and shrubs.

It doesn't matter whether the plants come from far away, as do star of Persia or Grecian windflower. The important thing is that they grow as if they were native. The western garden isn't defined by what can't be grown, but rather by how many wonderful plants thrive under our blue skies.

What does a true western garden look like?

It's filled with an abundance of amazing plants. It blooms from the first spring crocus to the last autumn crocus. It changes through the seasons and rolls with the punches. It can be subtle and serene or wild and bright. It reflects the influence of our Spanish, English, Italian, German, and Japanese roots, among many others. Most of all, like good gardens everywhere, it reflects the person who made it.

There's only one style of gardening in the West that gets my goat—the manufactured look that has variants in every state. In California, it's the palm stuck in a bed of mulch with a few globes of boxwood. In New Mexico and Arizona, it's yards of gravel (underlain by plastic) with holes punched through for a specimen of cactus or ocotillo. In my own state, Colorado, it's the pile of lichen-covered rocks topped by a thicket of aspens tethered to a conspicuous forest of stakes. I have nothing against palms, ocotillo, or aspen, where appropriate, but such plants are often used by landscapers who are too lazy to learn about the countless plants, native or otherwise, that can be grown.

# Where the Buffalo Roamed

Throughout the West, gardeners continue to question the validity of the standard bluegrass lawn. That extensive stretch of water-guzzling turf seems like a relic from the fifties, when every family aspired to imitate the Cleavers on *Leave It to Beaver.* Ward and June don't live here anymore. Instead, western homeowners redefine their properties to reflect the beauty of their natural landscape. These new "front yards" reflect a varied palette of plants in tune with the unique growing conditions of the West.

One alternative to standard turf is buffalo grass (*Buchloe dactyloides*), native to the western Great Plains. Of its many advantages, it needs little or no fertilizer, irrigation, or mowing. It grows well in either clay or sandy soil. Buffalo grass stays short naturally, about six to eight inches tall, although it can be mowed periodically if a more formal appearance is required. It has a lovely blue green color during summer—a foliage tone echoed over and again in the West—and a tawny sheen in winter. Best of all, since it breaks dormancy late, it makes an ideal habitat for early spring bulbs.

This western version of the classic meadow fits in rather well in the city. It has none of the tall prairie look that scares the dickens out of uptight suburbanites in the Midwest. A buffalo grass bulb lawn explodes with color without being threatening. Minor bulbs that grow naturally in Asia Minor, the Middle East, and central Asia thrive as never before in this turf. Since it stays short, even the smallest bulbs show well. Gardeners may mow the grass very short in autumn, allowing the bulbs an even more prominent position the following spring. Since buffalo grass thrives on scant rainfall, the bulbs get the hot summer baking they prefer.

The fine-textured turf provides a soft gray-and-gold backdrop for the blossoms of *Iris reticulata* and *I. histrioides* in shades of blue, purple, plum, and white. They accent crocus, especially *Crocus ancyrencis, C. sieberi,* and *C. chrysanthus* and its many cultivars. Small tulip species adapt well, including deep rose *Tulipa humilus,* yellow *T. kolpakowskiana,* scarlet *T. linifolia,* yellow-and-white *T. tarda,* apricot or yellow *T. batalinii,* and yellow *T. urumiensis.* They all multiply by division or seed, forming incredible bunches with ten to thirty flowers from each original bulb in as little as five years. The results are nothing if not stunning.

The bulb foliage fades just as the late-season buffalo grass begins to green up in late spring. The lawn can be mowed then and again every month or so if it is to be used as a family wrestle-with-the-dog-play-croquet-torment-your-little-sister type

A*n initial handful of bulbs turns into a traffic-stopping display of* Tulipa batalinii
*in a never-irrigated buffalo grass lawn.*

of area. If not, many other bulbs can be added for summer and autumn pleasure. In
late spring and summer, this short meadow supports patches of dwarf and standard
bearded iris, thick colonies of gayfeather and butterflyweed, tall stands of *Eremurus,*
and alliums like *A. jesdianum* and *A. caeruleum.* Many native and adaptable perennials
such as gaillardia, prairie coneflower (*Ratibida columnifera*), and blue flax also grow
willingly and add drama in the short dryland meadow. This, of course, begins to
frighten neighbors who do not possess enlightened artistic standards. In autumn, late
rains coax crocus to bloom, including lavender *C. speciosus,* purple saffron crocus (*C.
sativus*), red-violet *C. medius,* and pale pink *C. pulchellus.*

# Wet and Wild

A stream, pond, or lake presents marvelous opportunities. Banks and edges are
unique planting areas where specially adapted plants sink their roots into the oozing
earth. White calla lily is a classic "ditch plant." In its South African homeland, calla
lily grows so abundantly along streams and boggy ground that it's called ditch lily or

pig lily. It blooms in winter when rain fills the streams. If the streams slow to a trickle in a dry summer, the lily goes dormant while its tubers stay cool and moist below ground. Many bulbous plants that colonize moist ground use this method to cope with drought, from cannas of tropical America to the cammasias of wet meadows of the mountainous West.

Low-lying areas are not the curse that we've been led to believe by builders who can't wait to fill them up. Those constantly moist "hog wallows" can expand what we grow to include a treasure trove of flowers. I know of a suburban garden where the developers managed to route the entire drainage pattern of the block into one unlucky gardener's lot. Everything rotted in the back third of her yard until she decided to work with it rather than against it. Splendid stands of Japanese and Siberian iris, Solomon's seal, skunk cabbage (*Lysichiton americanum*, a perfectly lovely plant despite its dreadful name), and summer snowflake now complement astilbes, primroses, and ligularias. This is the horticultural equivalent of making lemons into lemonade.

# Into the Woods

Woodland plants take advantage of optimum conditions. Just as the bulbs of the plains and mountains emerge as the snow recedes, bulbs living beneath a canopy of deciduous trees initiate growth when sunlight temporarily illuminates the forest floor. The soil that nourishes them is the product of one autumn after another, blanketing the ground with leaves that crumble into deep, rich loam.

The success of a shade garden starts with good soil. A bag of bark nuggets can never compensate garden-grown woodland plants for the organically rich soil in which they evolved. Nor do the best shade gardens rely solely on an endless variety of hostas, no matter how impressive the individual plant. With so many textures and colors of foliage to play with in a woodland garden, the word *boring* need never be heard again.

Early bulbous plants native to the eastern woods charm more than electrify. Our native Jack-in-the-pulpit (*Arisaema triphyllum*) may be the most beguiling flower of the shade, although it has stiff competition from its relatives, such as native green dragon (*A. dracontium*), fragrant white *A. candidissimum* from China, and *A. sikokianum* from Japan. Another Japanese species, *A. ringens,* has very large leaves and helmet-shaped blossoms with prominent purple-brown and white stripes. It comes from southern Japan and grows best in our own southern states.

*S*hade gardeners covet the double form of blood-root (Sanguinaria canadensis 'Multiplex').

The blossoms of bloodroot (*Sanguinaria canadensis*) appear to be made of fine white porcelain until they shatter after a few days. The double form is saddled with the unfortunate name 'Multiplex', sounding more like a theater than a flower, but it's one of the most coveted stars of the shade garden.

The perfect harmony of trilliums, with three leaves, three sepals, and three petals, puts them in the forefront of shade plants. Some are grander than others—like *Trillium grandiflorum* of eastern American woods, with its magnificent double form—but all are lovely. *Trillium ovatum* grows in redwood forests of California and the Pacific Northwest, and its white flowers resemble those of its eastern cousin. *Trillium luteum* grows in woods from Kentucky and Missouri south to Alabama and Arkansas. Its foliage, splashed with pale markings, accentuates the greenish-yellow flowers. The patterned leaves of *Trillium sessile,* also native to the eastern woodlands, are similar, but the flowers are smoky maroon. Trilliums settle in easily where conditions mimic those in the woods. The same can be said for the erythroni-

*T*he silver-etched leaves and yellow blossoms of Trillium luteum *unfold beneath the textured trunks of river birch.*

*E*legant Trillium grandiflorum *thrives in moist shade with a support group of wood hyacinth and sweet woodruff.*

ums, known colloquially as trout lilies, dog-tooth violets, avalanche lilies, or fawn lilies. Good-looking leaves, often marbled with a dark stain, set off delicate blossoms that endear them to collectors.

Dicentras steal the gardener's heart with their lacy leaves and pendant flowers. Three American species, squirrel corn (*Dicentra canadensis*), ever-blooming bleeding heart (*D. eximia*), and Dutchman's breeches (*D. cucullaria*), are overshadowed by bleeding heart (*D. spectabilis*) from China, but all deserve a place where conditions allow. Grace and refinement are the hallmarks of Solomon's plume (*Smilacina*), merrybells (*Uvularia*), and Solomon's seal (*Polygonatum*). They contribute throughout the season with flower, form, foliage, and fruit.

A great favorite of shade gardeners is the variegated form of European *Polygonatum odoratum,* growing two feet tall and bearing twin sets of tiny, scented white flowers. Great Solomon's seal, *P. canaliculatum* from the eastern United States, is sometimes called David's harp. In moist, super-duper soil it is said to grow as tall as seven feet, but usually it grows about four feet tall with large clusters of white bells.

*Variegated Solomon's Seal sports a complicated name:* Polygonatum odoratum *var.* thunbergii *'Variegatum'. Its simple flowers and white-edged leaf complement white tulips in Cole Burrell's Minneapolis garden.*

The graceful curve of the top is characteristic of the genus but is all the more impressive on a grand scale. There's no need to interfere with these plants, as they will increase steadily by creeping rhizomes just below ground level.

# City Living

There are cities and then there are cities. I suppose bulbs could be persuaded to naturalize even in the concrete canyons of Manhattan, but my mission is not necessarily to line Park Avenue with narcissus. Every little patch of ground might become home to a handful of persistent snowdrops or clump of daylilies, but a city environment is demanding on bulbs.

When I lived in the heart of old Denver, I gardened in a courtyard. My back porch, and those of all my neighbors in the venerable old row houses, opened onto our own private oasis (even though a thoroughly modern, thoroughly hideous apartment building loomed twenty stories above us to the east).

The courtyard baked under the noon sun but was shaded much of the rest of the day. The soil was testament to more than a century of habitation. Digging in it yielded parts of very old cars, ancient pet graves, and the concrete foundations for a dozen pairs of successive wooden clotheslines.

The surrounding brick walls were both a blessing and a curse. They made a protected winter microclimate that heated up like a sauna in summer. In time, wisteria, grapes, and Virginia creeper scrambled up the buildings and made it more hospitable for people and plants. We'd set a television, my neighbors and I, under the grape arbor on hot nights for a lawn chair version of a drive-in movie.

The garden became home to innumerable bulbs. Sapphire blue squills, *Chiono-doxa* 'Pink Giant', and spring starflowers abounded. Snow crocus multiplied at an astounding rate, with single corms increasing to clumps with up to fifty flowers after six or eight years. My favorite early tulip was the Kaufmanniana hybrid 'Ancilla', which opens its creamy white petals flat on sunny days to reveal its red-ringed yellow center and closes them at night into a thin red point. The heavy soil was never a problem for this tulip, and it multiplied slowly without diminished flowering. I also grew indestructible 'Shakespeare', another Kaufmanniana hybrid, its salmon red petals streaked and tipped with yellow (although I was never fond of the color), and

*While the movers loaded the van, I shot these hand-me-down iris with clematis and wisteria on the last day I spent in my inner-city garden in 1993.*

*Capable of holding its own—even in the city—martagon lily dazzles with yellow foxglove* (Digitalis grandiflora) *and meadow sweet* (Filipendula vulgaris *'Flore Plena'*).

'Sweet Lady', a Greigii hybrid with coral red blossoms and purple-mottled leaves that looked sensational with the deep maroon leaves of *Lysimachia ciliata* 'Rubra' emerging through it. It continues to be a favorite.

One of my biggest successes was with the Darwin hybrid 'Golden Apeldoorn'. I bought the bulbs at the market a few blocks away, and they became the most faithful tulips imaginable, multiplying and blooming better each year. When I'd move a perennial, it seemed like a bulblet often hitched a ride. 'Golden Apeldoorn' colonized the garden, and I assume they still do.

Indigo blue *Iris reticulata* 'Harmony' bloomed at the base of the leathery leaves of heartleaf bergenia still wearing their winter shades of plum and brown. Grape hyacinths came up with yellow *Iris bucharica,* its jointed stems holding waxy leaves as green as Granny Smith apples. The early summer show was stolen by heirloom bearded iris handed down through the family. Most of them have lost their names through the years, so I know them only as "Aunt Ola," "Aunt Norma," and so forth. Aficionados break bearded iris into many groups such as standard dwarf, border, intermediate, and tall, but they forget one important group: the dead-relative iris. They've been overshadowed by a flood of new hybrids with pert, outfacing falls and trim, tiny standards, but I like the droopy old-fashioned ones with their pretty pastel colors and sweet scents.

The heavy soil didn't suit most lilies for long, but the martagons settled in for the long run. I love the waxy petals of their pendant flowers and the somber shades of dusky pink and plum. The curious old hybrid 'Bendick' has deep brick-red flowers and persists for decades. The apricot-yellow flowers of 'Mrs. R.O. Backhouse' might appeal to a broader audience, speckled and flushed with rosy pink. The best of the Asiatics proved to be the old variety 'Yellow Blaze'. I imagine its sturdy five-foot stalks still light up the courtyard with its canary flowers in July. My friend Mary Hoffman in Portland calls it "the tree of lilies." I missed it in my new garden and finally found it offered one year by the Pacific Northwest Lily Society (of which I'm a member despite the distance) and feel quite content to see its pretty if not elegant flowers once again.

A protected city garden has its limitations but opens up new avenues of exploration. Big expanses of brick, concrete, and asphalt moderate winter weather, sometimes enough to make growing otherwise out-of-reach exotics feasible. I can't say that they naturalized for me, since I'd lose them during a really harsh winter, but I took great pleasure in keeping montbretia, yellow calla lilies, and even ixias blooming for two or three years.

I still remember my courtyard garden in intricate detail. On the advice of friends, I haven't returned since I moved away. Gardeners who do visit their former gardens often come back broken-hearted upon seeing weeds choking their former flowers—or worse, the roses, iris, and lilies they cherished ripped up and replaced by sod. I hear that my courtyard blooms on in the hands of new gardeners. I prefer to revisit it in old photographs and memories.

# 4

# AUTUMN
## *Beauty and the Beastly Chores*

The calendar may say that the year is three-quarters spent, but in most ways, the bulb gardener's year begins in autumn. It's an exhilarating, exasperating, exhausting season. Schizophrenia reigns. On one hand, with the temperatures moderating, one is more inclined to face the garden with a fresh view. Fall-blooming perennials swing into action, while annuals, perceiving the cooling air and shortening days, bloom with renewed enthusiasm to set as much seed as possible before it's too late. Late-season bulbs are the icing on the cake. Even when one knows that they're coming, their appearance delights a gardener like a cooling shower.

On the other hand, every imperfection of a garden—the mistakes, the experiments that failed, the ravages of heat and insects, the chic color combinations that clashed—has been on display

*Sometimes fantastic combinations fall from the sky, as when my peach tree decided to decorate (or pummel) the autumn blossoms of* Colchicum *'Violet Queen'.*

for much too long. A gardener sometimes comes close to wishing a hard frost would come prematurely and put him out of his misery.

I never feel that death wish. If parts of the garden have gone awry, I get busy. I grab a shovel and begin to refine an area. I take notes during the spring and summer and act on them in fall. If plants have not met expectations, or if I've erred in judgment when it comes to color or height, it's time to move or compost them. Sometimes this "refinement" wipes out an entire area before I'm finished. I must look like a dog hunting long-lost bones, heaving hunks of perennials over my head in a frenzy.

I prefer to get the perennials sorted out before starting on the bulbs. I look forward to the arrival of postal and air freight trucks at the curb containing the boxes of bulbs I ordered during late summer. If it's been a hot summer, it's difficult to get in the bulb-ordering mood. When it's 95 degrees, I can't work up any enthusiasm for tulips. Panic sets in about the first of September, when I realize that the really choice stuff is probably in danger of being sold out. Really diligent gardeners order the moment the catalogues arrive in late spring and summer; they probably worked on their term papers in advance, too, instead of waiting until the night before they were due. Old habits, good or bad, die hard.

While admitting my weakness, I'll confess that catalogues mesmerize me. I order without thought of where I'm going to plant what I buy or whether other bills will sit on my desk unpaid. If bulbs ever come to the home shopping network, I will end up like those compulsive shoppers that find they've run themselves tens of thousands of dollars into debt. A new species of *Fritillaria*? I'll order five. No, with a couple dozen I can try it in more areas to see how it does. . . . *Tulipa pulchella* 'Alba'? I only have a handful in the hellstrip, and it's so pretty that fifty more would really be great. . . . The blue wood hyacinths look fabulous in the east shade garden, so maybe I should plant a couple hundred pink ones along the irrigation ditch. . . .

I make endless lists, draw red circles on the catalogue pages, put question marks where I'm undecided and a big *X* when I'm absolutely positive that I must have something. Sometimes I wonder if it's time to seek professional help (not in the garden, but on a couch).

After the packages arrive, I slit the packing tape to reveal the treasures inside. I inspect each mesh and paper bag, leaving a trail of fine wood shavings behind me as I finally take them to the basement to store for the time being. I pull out yellow legal pads, draw crude sketches of each area, and walk around the garden looking for obvious holes and trying to remember what things looked like last spring. I consult the previous year's legal pad maps and photographs to jog my memory.

# The Late Show

Inspiration for planting more bulbs comes from the splendid show that surrounds me. The late lilies come from the Oriental division, which includes hybrids derived from species native to China and Japan, such as the gold-band lily (*Lilium auratum*) and the rubrum lily (*L. speciosum*). Neither of these two species is especially difficult to grow if their requirement of moist, well-drained soil (neutral or slightly on the acidic side) is met. Sandy soil liberally enriched with compost fits the bill. The natural habitat for these species is at the edge of woodlands, often on hillsides at the base of shrubs through which they intertwine.

Gardeners with heavy soil need to do something drastic. Plop a big pile of sandy, friable topsoil on the east side of the house or a tall hedge and work in plenty of compost. If your soil is alkaline in nature, amend with aluminum sulfate, mulch with pine needles, and add a couple of teaspoons of vinegar to the watering can every month or so. Resist overwatering.

I grow these Oriental lilies best in bright shade (with a few hours of direct sun) on a slight slope where excess water never stands. Protection from the afternoon sun is preferable in all but the mildest climates. Lilies of all sorts enjoy the same cool root run that they do in the wild, so I plant a jumble of perennials to shade their feet, such as Jacob's ladder, granny bonnet columbines, prunella, and astrantia. Fairy candles (*Cimicifuga racemosa*) makes an elegant partner with its tall cream-white spires of fluffy flowers.

An excellent selection of *L. speciosum* var. *rubrum* is 'Uchida', which grows up to about four feet tall with as many as twenty deliciously scented flowers. Each rosy red petal, edged in white and sprinkled with darker red spots, curls back from the center to reveal six long, delicate filaments bearing anthers coated in cinnamon pollen. Florists routinely remove the anthers since they've permanently stained too many lace tablecloths through the years. I prefer mine not to be mutilated, so if I cut them for bouquets (leaving plenty of leafy stem to replenish the bulb), they are displayed on a marble or wooden table with no frilly doily. These lovely "rubrum" lilies, sweetly but not overpoweringly scented, persist and multiply for decades where conditions suit them.

The flowers of *L. auratum* measure eight inches in diameter with a wide band of pale yellow running down each crimson-flecked white petal. It is intensely, exotically fragrant, especially at night. The gold-band lily cast such a spell on American gardeners during the first part of the century that millions of bulbs were imported

*The legendary beauty of gold-band lily* (Lilium auratum) *is accentuated by the fluffy spires of fairy candles* (Cimicifuga racemosa).

from Japan. A 1906 catalogue from Child's Nursery in New York lists the common species and three variants, including a robust form called 'Macranthum' for seventy-five cents, as opposed to the normal twenty cents, and a variety with an additional red band down the petal center for a whopping dollar each. We can only hope that clients of Child's got their money's worth but, for the most part, the bulbs of that era spent far too long on poorly ventilated ocean freighters and arrived in terrible shape. The rotting, mushy bulbs fared poorly in gardens, and this lily—in fact, all lilies—were branded as difficult.

*L. auratum* needs a cool spot in deep, loamy soil, where it will grow as tall as six feet. While it is not the easiest of lilies, it is not impossible. Recent hybrids like the 'Imperial Gold' and 'Golden Discovery' strains closely imitate its striking beauty but are much easier to please. 'Lemon Meringue' and unspotted 'Ardaty' reach only about four feet.

'Stargazer' has captured the cut flower and pot lily market. This petite beauty, introduced in 1975, was the first up-facing Oriental lily. It grows less than three feet tall and usually bears four to eight raspberry red flowers with darker marks and a thin white edge on the petals. 'Stargazer' is proving itself as a garden plant as well. Since I can't resist having them all over my patio, engulfing the late summer evening in sweet perfume that smells a lot like Juicy Fruit gum, I order more each year. In autumn the pot-grown bulbs get transplanted to my shade gardens (which have several hours of direct sunlight) where they prosper and multiply with little attention from me. The aroma must be perceptible blocks away. I revel in it.

'Black Beauty' debuted in 1957. Its parentage involves *L. speciosum* and scentless *L. henryi;* its recurved flowers resemble those of a tiger lily but are deep bloodred, with each petal outlined in white. This is one tough lily, very resistant to disease, and established plants zoom up to nine feet tall and bloom with as many as fifty flowers. A tetraploid form with extra chromosomes is said to be even more vigorous, although I can't imagine how. A good group is a riveting sight and carries a light perfume like that of violets. It blooms in mid to late summer (depending on local conditions), but I mention it here because of its close ties to the usually late-blooming Oriental tribe.

Classic Oriental hybrids that have stood the test of time include pure white 'Casa Blanca,' crimson pink 'Journey's End', the 'Imperial Pink' and 'Imperial White' strains, white 'Allegra', 'Red Jamboree', the coral pink–striped 'Coral Bee' strain, and rose-banded 'Pink Ribbons'. Try them first, ordering from a lily specialist. These varieties are the standards, usually four to six feet tall, blooming in August and September, and always fragrant and lovely. Staking spoils the effect of their elegant flowers, but if they're grown in half sun, no staking should be necessary.

Frankly, these flowers are not suitable for every garden, but it's worth every effort to satisfy them. Oriental lilies flourish for the most part in the Pacific Northwest, northern California, parts of the Rocky Mountain states (usually with deep snow cover or major mulch), the mildest part of the northeast states, and the coolest parts of the mid-Atlantic states. Botrytis, basal rot, and virus are their worst enemies.

# Surprise Lily

Surprise lily is completely irresistible. The pink trumpets of *Lycoris squamigera* appear on strong, leafless stems in late summer, just when a weary gardener needs a good shot in the arm. Three to seven blossoms crown its two-foot stalk. Resembling small pink

**L**eafless surprise lily (Lycoris squamigera) *springs from the earth in late summer, with its naked stems disguised by German statice and sea kale foliage.*

trumpet lilies with a hint of apricot in the throat, these lilies are at their best when they pop through a spray of fine, gauzy flowers like those of German statice or *Origanum laevigatum* 'Hopleys'. The contrast of blue foliage, such as blue oats grass or sea kale, sets off the flowers well. It's a disservice to grow surprise lily without company, simply ignoring the obvious patch left by the disappearance of the foliage in June. Flowers never look their best against bare earth.

Surprise lily is sometimes called resurrection or magic lily because of its unusual growth cycle of growing its leaves in spring and then rising up, seemingly out of nowhere, with blooms in late summer. This Japanese genus is, for puzzling reasons, named for Marc Antony's mistress Lycoris, an actress who surely never played Tokyo. It demonstrates a hardier constitution than its beauty suggests. I've seen several old vegetable gardens in the countryside north of the city where elderly women grow their surprise lilies in rows like onions. They make enormous clumps. The garden loam is rich and sandy, a hint in growing it successfully. On the other hand, a friend gave me a division from a clump that had been growing for decades in thick, sticky clay. My friend is also very stingy with water, so the bulbs rarely sat with wet feet.

The bulbs resemble those of narcissus with a slender neck that should be planted just a few inches beneath the surface (but deeper in sandy soil or in cold winter areas). They usually go in the ground during autumn after flowering, when they are dormant and commercially available. They take a couple of years to settle in this way, just sending up a few amaryllis-like leaves and no flowers the first few seasons. They can also be transplanted while in active growth in spring, making sure to fill the hole first with water. It's a muddy mess, but most bulbs moved during active growth settle in better this way.

# Autumn Onions

Few ornamental onions seem to have captured the public's imagination like that big purple lollipop of spring, *Allium giganteum*. The late ones are hardly noticed, but several make fantastic garden plants. Chinese chives, *A. tuberosum,* has been cultivated for centuries in China. Normally consigned to the herb garden where it's called garlic chives, it also makes a great addition to the border. Vigorous and floriferous, Chinese chives blooms in late summer and early autumn with tight umbels of small chalk-white blossoms held on thin stems about two feet tall.

Because of its late flowering time, it gives a lift to late combinations with

*Autumn isn't all fiery tones, as with the wiry stems of garlic chives* (Allium tuberosum) *in the feathery embrace of* Artemisia x 'Powis Castle' *and felty gray* A. ludoviciana 'Valerie Finnis'.

artemisias, ballotas, marrubiums, dianthus, sea kale, and any other perennials with silver or blue gray leaves. Easy to grow in any soil as long as it receives plenty of sun, a clump increases and lasts forever. Established plants hold up well to periodic drought. Whack a clump in half or thirds to increase.

From a grassy mound of thin leaves rise the fragrant flowers of Siberian garlic (*Allium ramosum*). Up to two feet tall, the color varies from white to white with purple stripes to purple. It seeds but not to excess. Siberian garlic does not yet have a wide following, but its late bloom season recommends it for a place in the late border, alongside colchicums and pink or crimson asters and chrysanthemums.

German garlic (*Allium senescens*) grows in the wild from central Europe to northern Asia. With such a wide geographic distribution, it's to be expected that several forms have been brought into cultivation. The most commonly grown type has round, rosy pink heads of flowers over tufts of thin green leaves. The form 'Glaucum' is noted for twisted blue green foliage that appears to be swirling down the bathtub drain. (Some plants are said to bring a sense of motion to the garden; this little whirlpool is a perfect example.) It, too, bears pink flowers of a softer shade. The stems are usually less than eight inches tall, and the foliage is crisp and blemish free throughout the season, so German garlic makes an ideal edging plant for herb garden or herbaceous borders. It's a great favorite in the upper Midwest and Northeast for bordering paths. Silver foliage, like that of lamb's ears or achillea, also compliments the flowers to advantage.

Mid- and late-blooming onions hold their leaves throughout the growing season, unlike the early bloomers that go completely dormant after flowering. These clump-formers tolerate more moisture since they remain in active growth. Even so, they can't tolerate spongy soil. *Allium thunbergii* 'Ozawa', the latest onion to flower in temperate regions, is a show stopper. The two-inch-round flower heads of this Japanese species bloom bright violet with red highlights as if fresh from a henna rinse. At just over a foot tall, they're lovely with a symphony of similar colors or contrasting splendidly with golden chrysanthemums and the glowing scarlet leaves of sumacs and burning bush. The autumn garden never had it so good. Despite what most books recite, this species is very hardy, growing perfectly well in Minneapolis, which is not noted for its mild winters.

# Naked Boys

Colchicums have three minor drawbacks: The bulbs aren't cheap. The long straplike leaves die a horrible death. Slugs can make the mess even worse. Knowing that, it still takes a hard heart to ignore the beautiful flowers, especially arriving as they do in autumn, when a gardener's spirits are at their lowest. It's surprising we don't see more of them, but I suspect that the typical midsummer let-down prevents despondent gardeners from planting the bulbs when they're available in late August and September. Sometimes you'll see a bushel basket at the nursery that has erupted into pink bloom before the bulbs get a chance in the soil. This uses up the bulbs' reserve strength. Perhaps some gardeners imagine that such a lovely thing must be difficult to grow. They are wrong. After all, they'll flower in a bushel basket.

The few "common" names for colchicums are unsatisfactory and not widely used. "Autumn crocus" doesn't work since colchicums are not crocus and true autumn crocus bloom at the same time. "Meadow saffron" may be more lyrical but is equally misleading since colchicums have nothing to do with saffron, which is plucked from a true autumn crocus, *Crocus sativus*. The best folk name comes from the British, who in their own inimitable style coined the name "naked boys." The plump, opening buds could easily recall a group of very pink young lads after a chilly late-season dip in a pond.

The flowers of some colchicums are shaped like cups, others like vases, and still others like floppy magnolias. Three species and their hybrids make up the bulk of commercially available plants: *Colchicum autumnale* is smallest, just four to six inches tall, with six lavender pink petals. It is dwarfed by *C. speciosum,* pale to deep rose-purple, at almost twice the size. *C. bivonae* falls somewhere in the middle but is distinguished by heavily tessellated petals, meaning that they display checkered markings like those of the guinea hen flower (*Fritillaria meleagris*). Selections and hybrids are somewhat of a muddle. Some show checkerboard marks of varying intensity, some have deeper tones, others have white throats. Bulbs of 'Violet Queen' planted one year don't always match others shipped the next season, but it doesn't really matter. They're all pretty.

Selections of *C. autumnale* include tiny 'Album' and a captivating double white form called 'Alboplenum'. Just to confuse us, there's a larger white goblet-shaped form of *C. speciosum* named 'Album'. (Music is so much easier to keep up with: To Beatles fans, there is only one White Album.)

*C. bivonae* has been crossed with the other two species to produce 'The Giant', a nearly one-foot-tall amethyst flower with a white throat, and 'Violet Queen', also on the large side with deeper violet-pink petals and white center. The same parentage is apparent in 'Princess Beatrix', checkered ruby violet, and 'Princess Astrid', with a light purple check pattern on a white background. The aptly named 'Lilac Wonder' multiplies and blooms abundantly and is thankfully not named for royalty.

One variety is unmistakable. 'Waterlily' looks like its namesake, with scores of

*Pristine goblets of* Colchicum speciosum *'Album' emerge through a silver symphony of* Artemisia canescens *and variegated licorice plant* (Helichrysum petiolare).

Colchicum *'Waterlily' floats in a shining pool of cotton lavender* (Santolina chamaecyparissus).

lilac pink, overlapping petals. I normally dislike double flowers of any kind, but I make an exception for this one. It is especially winning as it appears in autumn through a carpet of tiny gray leaves such as woolly thyme or Serbian yarrow. Lavender cotton makes a perfect backdrop. 'Waterlily' has become a bit pricey, but being long lived, it's worth it. If I had to choose only one colchicum for my garden, this would be the one.

Colchicums grow in meadows, light woodlands, and scrubland throughout much of Europe into the Middle East. They tolerate a wide range of soils and exposures. While moisture must be supplied in spring when the leaves grow, they can dry up somewhat through the summer, just as a meadow bakes dry under the summer sun. Brown, stiff tunics like those of tulips cloak the bulbs, an indication of built-in drought tolerance. A dry summer especially seems to benefit 'Waterlily'. The stems hold the heavy flower heads upright without breaking if they have not absorbed an excess of moisture.

One of my reference books makes a point of telling us gardeners to use caution when planting *C. autumnale* around grazing livestock, as it contains the poison colchicine. This would never have dawned on me since I have a strict rule about not admitting cows to the garden.

# Afternoon Delight

As I write this in the first week of December, balmy weather prevails. The temptation is to put work aside to visit the autumn crocus. Five species revel in the late autumn sunshine. Not all early Decembers can be counted on to bring such delight, for a foot of snow could easily blanket my Denver garden. Even so, such snows melt almost as quickly as they come under the intense sun over the mile-high city. The crocus pop through, sometimes lingering as late as the New Year. What gardener can resist playing hooky to see them?

The tiny lavender goblets of *C. goulimyi,* found in olive groves in southern Greece, appear in concert with its leaves. I'm quite certain I couldn't grow an olive tree, so it comes as a pleasant surprise to be able to satisfy this flower. *C. medius* also belies its roots in northwest Italy and southern France, flowering in a pleasing shade of wine red. Bulbous plants often possess reservoirs of hardiness that can be exploited through careful placement. Planting the corms of autumn crocus in exceedingly well-drained soil—perhaps on a slight slope—greatly enhances their chances to settle in for the long run. A south-facing wall has long been employed as a heat trap and shelter for marginally hardy plants. These species from the Mediterranean region prosper in the more similar climate of coastal California.

*Crocus pulchellus* from Turkey produces graceful cups of silver pink with purple veins. The larger form 'Zephyr' is a bleached, pearly blue. *Crocus kotschyanus* (formerly known as *C. zonatus*) is a tiny treasure from Turkey and Lebanon of pale lilac with a yellow throat. The squirrels decimate my populations, but its corms multiply so speedily that the crocus manage to keep up, even if I can't be certain where the flowers will appear. The corms turn up by the hundreds when I dig within a couple of yards of the original planting.

Almost all autumn-flowering crocus bloom without leaves, taking advantage of the moist spring to grow them. Saffron crocus (*C. sativus*) is an exception, displaying its foliage and flowers simultaneously. This species is not known in the wild, having been cultivated for thousands of years in the Middle East for its long, red stamens that produce the dye and spice of the same name. Somewhere along the line, the saffron plant

also lost its ability to reproduce from seed; its flowers are sterile. It does know how to multiply by offsets, so a well-situated corm eventually makes a thick, showy clump of deep lavender flowers. Purple veins etch the petals, and the shocking red stamens and yellow pollen attract attention. Millions of gardeners plant saffron crocus each fall, but it only sticks around when grown in very well-drained soil that is positively incinerated during the summer. Imagine the heat that these corms have become accustomed to in the world's saffron centers of Spain, India, and the Middle East.

The best autumn crocus for most of the central and northern states is *Crocus speciosus*. Extremely adaptable, it blooms like crazy—sometimes corms send up two or three blossoms in succession— and multiplies well by division. The bright lavender flowers open from thin, elegant buds six inches or more long. They open under sunny skies, revealing a tracery of purple veins and golden orange stamens. They are very pretty poking through mats of sedums, marrubiums, and plumbago. It's lucky indeed when the loveliest plant of a genus is the one that performs the best. More often it seems the showiest species barely limps by in the greenhouse or stays alive only in some remote Irish garden.

Autumn crocus (Crocus speciosus) *pokes through maroon-tinged foliage of plumbago.*

Scattered across a wide area that includes Russia, Iran, and Turkey, *C. speciosus* displays some lovely variations. 'Conqueror' is large and deep lavender blue. 'Aitchisonii' has exaggerated venation on its pale lilac petals. 'Albus' is, of course, white but is not high on my list since I doubt it would put on much of a show against melting snow. 'Cassiope' is lavender with a yellow throat and, perhaps because it was selected from a population toward the southern extreme of the species' range, performs well in the mid South.

# Pigs, Sprites, and Corkscrews

Cyclamens may look as dainty as ice skater Michelle Kwan, but they're as tough as Hulk Hogan. In nature, they inhabit semiarid lands, where they often colonize shady spots beneath small, spreading trees and outcompete all comers. Their tubers grow as big as a giant cinnamon roll, which brings to mind (or the other way around) the folk name *sowbread*, from the pigs that forage for the dormant tubers.

The most common and adaptable of the hardy cyclamens is *C. hederifolium,* native to Turkey and mountainous parts of southern Europe. Its tuber sends up a flurry of lovely blossoms like hovering pink sprites just inches above the ground. They often start to appear in late summer before the foliage does. As the silver-frosted, pine-green leaves spread their ivylike carpet (*hederifolium* means "leaves like ivy"), the effect is superb. The species is variable, and seedlings exhibit a variety of pewter- and silver-splashed leaves and flowers ranging from white to shell pink or rose. After the flowers set seed, the stem coils into a corkscrew that, if tugged gently, springs back into shape.

It seems an advantage to plant *C. hederifolium* beneath shrubs and in hammocks between major tree roots, as the greedy tree roots soak up excess moisture, keeping the tubers in a dry state of summer dormancy. Autumn rains and cooler days trigger the flowers to push through the soil. The exact time varies a bit from year to year and certainly from region to region. Where suited, the tubers increase steadily in size, and seedlings sprout. Complementary companions include all manner of woodland creepers—veronicas, moneywort, brass buttons, and small ferns—and larger perennials like liriopes, bronze-leaf heucheras, and epimediums.

This is the most successful cyclamen for naturalizing throughout most regions, although winter- and spring-blooming species such as *C. coum, C. persicum,* and *C. repandum* perform better either in the South or on the West Coast.

# Other Autumn Surprises

There's a little bulb with a big future. It's a big hit in the upper Midwest and is making its way around the northern part of the country. It shows enormous potential. I first encountered it one September at the Minnesota Landscape Arboretum, outside Minneapolis. Beneath shrubs in light shade spread a carpet of rosy lavender, like a patch of pink muscari nearly a foot tall. They call it *Scilla numidica,* and it was introduced to the region by the first director of the arboretum, Dr. Leon Snyder.

This vigorous, foot-tall species is somewhat of a mystery. *S. numidica* is native to northern Africa and is described as small, pale pink, and rather insignificant. That doesn't sound like the beautiful species I saw and have since introduced to my own garden. It more closely matches the description of *S. scilloides* from China and Japan, but it still must be considered a superior form and could possibly be a hybrid. If it is related to *S. scilloides,* that would explain its affinity for Minneapolis, where many Chinese and Japanese plants such as hostas and daylilies grow like gangbusters in the moist, humid summers.

Whatever its true identity, the pink squill is a dynamite bulb for the autumn garden. Airy, graceful, and colored an eye-catching shade of pink, it invites artful combinations with contrasting foliage plants such as silver-splashed lamiums and blue spruce sedum, or at the feet of ornamental grasses like the bronze-leaf *Pennisetum setaceum* 'Cupreum'.

*Scilla numidica/scilloides* might make a lovely pool of color around the base of an old favorite that is ready to make a run at the fall market: Re-blooming bearded iris have been on the verge of renewed popularity for several decades. Hybridizers work

*An impressive stand of* Scilla numidica *expands in the dappled shade of a Minneapolis garden.*

Hardy Begonia grandis *puts a flourish on the waning season in Joanna Reed's garden in Malvern, Pennsylvania.*

furiously to make the promise a reality. The first time I saw an autumn-blooming iris, I was driving down a busy street in Denver and noticed them growing along a sidewalk. At first I assumed they must be made of silk, but upon closer inspection (with much horn honking and many gestures directed toward me), I determined they were the genuine article. I straightaway ordered some for myself, and although they bore perfectly nice purple or gold flowers in the spring, I could never coax them to re-bloom. I assume the fault is mine, so I'm prepared for another go at it. One day in the not-so-distant future, autumn iris may be nearly as common as their early summer counterparts.

The small pink, tropical-looking blossoms of *Begonia grandis* come as a delightful surprise in late summer and bloom all the way up to frost. Its green leaves are veined with red and the flower stems are red as well, making the foot-tall (or taller) plants a vibrant addition beneath red-berried or red-leafed shrubs. Most begonias come from tropical lands and wither with the first touch of frost, but *B. grandis* grows wild in light woodlands of southern temperate China. It is hardy at least as far north as Philadelphia, and thrives in moist, humus-rich soil in light shade across the mid-Atlantic states into the South, as well as the Pacific Northwest into California. Tiny bulblets develop in the leaf axils and pop up in the spring around the base of the mother plants, from which an extensive colony can spring.

# Berries and Pods

Flowers are not the only pleasures of the season. Flaming crimson and golden leaves lure leaf peepers into the countryside and mountains. Gardeners never need to leave home to explore the autumnal splendor.

It's been ingrained into us that the passing of a flower is a sad thing. Phrases like "the bloom is off the rose" or "gone to seed" have become such powerful metaphors in our language that it takes an effort to see beyond the flowers. It's been a long time coming, but many of us have begun to appreciate the fruiting and seeding of plants.

Rivaling rose hips in showiness, the berries of *Arum italicum* turn from bright green to tomato red as autumn approaches. The prominent spikes of berries spring from an inauspicious beginning. The May flowers require a search, as their ivory color is camouflaged among the spring foliage. The blossoms are constructed much like calla lilies, but whereas the latter appear as brazen as showgirls on the garden stage, those of arum seem ready for the convent. The British, ever able to turn a phrase—albeit a sexist one—dubbed the plants "lords and ladies." The lords, of course,

Golden morning light illuminates the brilliant berries of Arum italicum, *with unexpected apple accompaniment at Joy Creek Nursery in Scappoose, Oregon.*

*Like polished onyx, blackberry lilies* (Belamcanda chinensis) *burst from their pods among the autumnal show of gloriosa daisies.*

stand ramrod straight and bold, the ladies shy and retiring.

The variety or subspecies 'Pictum' (sometimes called 'Marmoratum') makes especially handsome leaves. Triangular in shape, they are veined in white or cream, somewhat resembling the popular houseplant arrowhead (*Syngonium podophyllum*). They emerge in autumn and carry through winter despite their tropical appearance. They may disappear during summer drought or hang on to complement the berries if enough moisture is available. Lords and ladies are quite adaptable to sun or partial shade and to most soils but need sufficient heat to produce a good display of berries.

*Arum maculatum,* native to Great Britain, grows in hedgerows and is known as cuckoopint or lords and ladies as well. It looks like a miniature form of *A. italicum* and thrives in cool, moist shade gardens. Other pretty fruit or pods on bulbous plants include scarlet asparagus berries, inflated pods on martagon lilies, red berries on *Smilacina racemosa,* deep blue berries on great Solomon's Seal (*Polygonatum canaliculatum*). Woodland gardeners rely on fabulous foliage after the main flush of spring flowers to keep their interest during summer. Their efforts are rewarded in autumn (if they've avoided the trap of planting hordes of gaudy impatiens) by these appealing fruits and berries as counterpoints.

Blackberry lily (*Belamcanda chinensis*) gives double pleasure. Its starry yellow, orange-freckled flowers bloom heavily in summer. The pods expand and change from green to golden brown, finally splitting to reveal their contents. The hard black seeds, the size of a small pearl, shine like polished onyx. They are great favorites of flower arrangers but make dramatic pictures in the garden as well, combined with late-blooming rudbeckias, zauschnerias, and 'Golden Fleece' goldenrod.

Native to China and northern India, the plants produce tubers and foliage very much like an iris. A sunny position, moisture during the growing season, and well-drained soil suit them well. Self-sown seedlings perpetuate the clumps. It may seem obvious that the flowers, which only last for a day but are produced abundantly for many weeks, should not be dead-headed if the lovely blackberries are to follow. Long ago, when I was a tidier gardener who didn't always think for himself, I removed the spent blooms in my constant sweeps of the garden and deprived myself of the payoff. Sometimes lazy is good.

# A Well-Traveled Bulb

Gardeners on the West Coast who grew up in colder parts of the nation may feel a twinge of homesickness when they remember the vivid fall colors from their youth. Every region has its moments, and brilliant autumn flowers still mark the season in the Pacific Northwest, California, and the desert Southwest. A plethora of bulbous plants continue their long season of bloom from summer into autumn, while new ones burst forth.

*Nerine bowdenii* sends slender stems skyward just as its leaves wither at the end of the growing season. The South African bulb comes from the southeastern part of Natal, where summer is relatively wet and winter is dry. Another marvel of adaptation, *N. bowdenii* sits out the winter, grows its leaves through the summer, and flowers at the transition between seasons. If it sounds like a perfect plant for most of the western coastal states, it is.

Six to fifteen brilliant pink flowers form a ring at the top of the two-foot stem. The six wavy petals, about two inches long, are striped deeper pink down the center. With their protruding filaments, the flowers might be said to possess a spidery elegance, although that compliment is usually paid to the red flowers of spider lily (*Lycoris radiata*), with which this genus is often confused.

Clumps of *N. bowdenii* are very showy but still light and airy. Easy to grow, this is the hardiest of the so-called Guernsey lilies, surviving a winter chill to perhaps as low as 5 degrees. The main cause of failure is too much water during its dormant winter period. Avoid planting the bulbs in low-lying areas.

The true Guernsey lily, *N. sarniensis,* survived a 1659 shipwreck to root on the sandy beach of the island of Guernsey, off the east coast of England. The bulbs were intended for Holland, en route from a trip to the Far East that had stopped in South

Africa. Because the original point of departure of the Dutch East India Company vessel was Japan, it was assumed at the time that the bulb was native to somewhere in the Far East. Flower-loving locals brought the flower into their gardens, and the flame red "Guernsey lily" became a hit through their cut-flower trade with the mainland.

A century would pass before the mystery was solved. The bulbs of *N. sarniensis* were finally rediscovered flowering on the slopes of Table Mountain in the Cape Province. It's amazing it took so long before anyone noticed the brilliant spikes of up to ten iridescent flowers crowded at the top of strong, two-foot stems. The petals share the same shimmering "gold-dusted" quality as many daylilies.

Selections and hybrids have been produced through the years, so the color range now includes white and pink forms. Like its cousin *N. bowdenii,* the Guernsey lily blooms in late summer and autumn. Its long, amaryllis-like leaves appear in spring, persist through summer, and wither as the flowers bloom. Both species, of course, make lovely cut flowers.

Other species and hybrids of *Nerine,* usually with similar, easy-to-accommodate requirements, can sometimes be seen on the West Coast. *N. undulata* looks like a shorter, paler version of *N. bowdenii. N. filamentosa* is also short and bears pink flowers with dark red or purple anthers, while the flowers of *N. crispa* are thin and delicate with wavy petal margins. *N. duparquetiana* is white with a pink band. Five of its twisted petals are arranged in a fan shape, with one lone petal protruding with the stamens. Good late hybrids, all two feet tall or so, include red purple 'Ancilla', rose 'Elvira', and vermilion 'Fothergillii Major'.

# Spider Lilies

The red spider lily, *Lycoris radiata,* is easily confused with the Guernsey lily, but this bulb really does come from the Orient, namely the subtropical regions of China. The spider lily looks like a Guernsey lily that's been on a stringent diet. The flowers are longer and slimmer, and its graceful red filaments protrude several inches. Migrating butterflies are often attracted by its brilliant color. The golden spider lily (*L. aurea*) is unmistakable with its similar, bright citrus-orange flowers. Spanish colonists may have introduced the golden spider lily, native to China and Japan, to this country. It is still found in autumn blooming around ruins in St. Augustine. Floridians call it "hurricane lily."

Spider lilies bloom in late summer and autumn and follow growth cycles almost identical to those of the Guernsey lilies, letting the leaves do their work in winter. When winter rainfall is scant, provide supplemental moisture. In very hot areas, spider lilies grow best with shade and humus-enriched, moisture-retentive soil. The bulbs look much like those of daffodils and take several years to settle in. Where frost seldom visits, they can be planted with the neck at the surface. Plant deeper in colder areas, but remember the foliage must survive the winter to continue to bloom.

An heirloom variety of red spider lily blooms vigorously in old gardens in the South. Seemingly identical in appearance to imported bulbs sold in catalogues, it exhibits incredible tenacity. A genetic investigation determined that this old clone is a triploid, meaning it has an extra set of chromosomes that give it extra strength. It was widely available in the South before World War II but was supplanted soon after by less expensive imports without the extra chromosomes.

A similar genetic inconsistency is also apparent in the old-fashioned oxblood lily (*Rhodophiala bifida*). Bulbs planted early in this century still send up their leafless stems in autumn, bearing small trumpets the color of old red books. Even where a house no longer exists, rows of oxblood lilies mark garden beds that have all but disappeared. Clumps of amaryllis-like leaves mark the spots in winter. These survivors also have an extra set of chromosomes that their relatives in modern-day Uruguay and Argentina, to which *R. bifida* is native, do not.

Southern bulb expert Scott Ogden loves unraveling a mystery. He believes that among early German immigrants to the Texas hill country, a bulb enthusiast named Peter Henry Oberwetter traded native bulbs with collectors around the world. During the Civil War, Oberwetter sided with the North and exiled himself to Mexico, where he continued to collect and export bulbs. The super-duper form must have fallen into his hands at this point. Austin is still the world capital of this superior form, although gardeners have spread it throughout the South, where it thrives in any type of soil with little care.

# Red Flags

Crimson flag (*Schizostylis coccineus*) grows near and at the edges of streams and ponds in the Natal Province of South Africa. Its clumps of evergreen leaves resemble those of iris, so the gladiolus-like flower stalk appears a bit incongruous at first. Six-petaled, vivid orange-red flowers open in late summer and autumn. Selected forms

*Crimson flag* (Schizostylis coccineus) *waves in front of billowing* Aster sedifolius.

also bloom in shades of pink, white, rosy red, and salmon. These invite combinations to fit the "last fling" gaudiness of the season, such as with white wood aster (*Aster divaricatus*), vigorous lavender *A. sedifolius,* or any complementary late-season hybrid ('Purple Dome', for example). The fluffy clouds of purple and lavender showcase the brilliant spires of crimson flag. Autumn is no time for restraint.

I envy gardeners who grow crimson flag well by planting it in organically rich soil near a water source. I've killed this lovely plant several times by keeping it too dry, despite the fact that it demonstrates remarkable hardiness, often to temperatures well below zero. A streamside clump in a garden a half-hour drive from my house has been spreading and flowering for twenty-odd years. Gardeners in naturally moist climates often succeed with this flower in normal border conditions.

# Small Autumn Bulbs for the West Coast

Crocus and colchicums that occur naturally around the rim of the Mediterranean Sea often take up permanent residence along our West Coast. Why should northerners have all the fun growing late-season crocus and colchicums? In addition, a couple of unusual autumn ephemerals can be successfully naturalized along the coast.

Most of the widely grown species—*C. speciosus, C. medius, C. kotschyanus, C. goulimyi,* and *C. pulchellus*—thrive in all but hot desert areas. The list increases with *Crocus serotinus,* which grows on stony hills in Spain and North Africa; its flowers and leaves appear together and thrive in light shade. Subspecies *salzmannii* has deep lilac flowers held on graceful white stems, while subspecies *clusii* differs by having darker veins and, remarkably, fragrance. *C. longiflorus* from southern Italy, which also carries a pleasant scent, is quite attractive with light violet petals that turn to bronze with purple veins on the exterior side and a bright red stigma.

Pretty purple *C. banaticus* from Romania also naturalizes in the shade of deciduous trees. *C. cancellatus* grows on rocky Grecian slopes and forms colonies of almost white flowers with delicate lavender veins. *C. niveus,* another Turkish beauty, offers pure white petals, a yellow throat, and showy red anthers. *C. caspius* grows on the shores of the Caspian Sea, and its flowers are white or blushed with pink.

None of these corms is likely to jump out from the supermarket shelf. It takes determination to track them down. My computer stores a long and growing list of plants that I've seen and lusted after. I order every catalog I can find in hopes of spotting them. The library at a public garden or arboretum is a great resource, since many dealers regularly send their catalogues to them. It's also possible and easy to obtain bulbs by mail from England, the Netherlands, and, increasingly, central Europe, where thousands of species and varieties that never reach most American sources are sold. (I've included a few excellent international and domestic sources starting on page 230.) Plant societies are another good source of unusual bulbs or their seeds.

Several colchicums are a good bet for most parts of California, Oregon, and Washington as long as the gardener doesn't drown the bulbs during their summer dormancy. Besides the many hybrids, *Colchicum speciosum* and *C. variegatum* from Turkey and the Aegean Islands can be relied upon. The latter may be only four inches tall, but it bears many checkered deep lilac flowers, and its foliage is smaller and tidier than the rest of the lot. *C. cilicicum* from southern Turkey is a very floriferous species that produces its leaves in winter after the many (up to fifteen per corm) deep lilac-pink flowers bloom.

Where snow rarely arrives, autumn snowflake (*Leucojum autumnale*) survives. It inhabits rocky places in Portugal, Spain, Sicily, and northern Africa. Suited to sandy soil in sun, autumn snowflake resembles its spring cousins but is even more delicate in appearance. At just six inches or so in height, autumn snowflake gives a late lift to the rock garden. The pendant flowers are not quite so inflated as those of the spring species, and they hang from tiny dark filaments above very thin, reedlike leaves. A maroon cap at the top of the flower bell sometimes streaks down the crisp petals like a watercolor dissolving in the rain. In some ways, it reminds me of miniature Venus' fishing rod (*Dierama*). The leaves, which grow through winter, sometimes don't emerge until after the flowers.

*Moraea polystachya* is just one of the many peacock flowers of South Africa but perhaps the only one commonly available that blooms in late autumn and into winter.

Most of its cousins inhabit the Atlantic side of the country and grow and flower during the rainy season of late winter and spring (see chapter 6). *M. polystachya* is but one species of a very lovely genus with irislike flowers, but it is all the more valuable in the garden for its late display of lilac blue or blue blossoms with a yellow center. The corm is very tough and goes into a long dormant period during drought. For best bloom, however, plant it in full sun among other plants that receive regular summer moisture. The grassy leaves grow between one and two feet tall. Because of their toxic nature, they are rarely browsed by deer, nor are the corms bothered by rodents.

Another late South African bulb, *Spiloxene alba,* is endearingly called little star. It's a perfect description of the white flowers that grow only two inches high. Its six thin petals, tinted purple on the outside, open flat. This species comes from damp, marshy areas of the Cape Peninsula, so it grows readily near water features or in a moderately moist border. It also performs well in much of the South, where it naturalizes in short grass. Bright fall-blooming *S. canaliculata,* also native to the same region, is distinguished by a dramatic maroon eye in the center of its golden flower. Growing up to eight inches tall, the flowers have wider petals and measure two inches across above thin, grasslike leaves. Golden star, *S. serrata,* is named for the tiny serrations along its leaf edges, but it's the flowers that make it a valuable late-garden addition, starting in late autumn and continuing well into spring.

# Return of the Rain Lilies

Autumn doesn't arrive in the South with the blast of cold fronts, blustery winds, and threats of the first big freeze. The change is subtle. The heat loosens its stranglehold on the land by degrees, and rain clouds push up from the Gulf. Cooling rains quench the thirst of the parched earth and coax dormant bulbs to bloom.

Rain lilies truly mark the transition to autumn. Just as northern gardeners anxiously wait the arrival of snowdrops that telegraph the first impulses of spring, southerners look forward to the first flush of rain lilies. Their simple yet elegant blossoms signal that the oppressive heat is on the wane. Hot days may still be in store, but the garden begins to change. Gardeners count to five after the first major autumn deluge: It takes that many days for the trumpets to burst from the soil and open in shades of pink, yellow, or white. Some waft a dusky sweet perfume in the air.

Rain lilies belong to the genus *Zephyranthes,* which translates to "flowers of the west wind." Other folk names include fairy lily and Atamasco lily, but that's usually reserved for the spring-flowering Florida species (covered in chapter 6). As many as a dozen species of wild rain lilies inhabit the South, while gardeners also cultivate others from Mexico and South America. It's difficult to keep up with the fluctuations within the group since, according to some experts, it now includes bulbs formerly classified as *Cooperia, Habranthus,* and *Pyrolirion* (but don't hold your breath, since taxonomists' favorite game must be musical chairs).

White rain lily (*Zephyranthes candida*) is a favorite southern wildflower, though it is actually native to Argentina. The La Plata River was named not for its silver rapids or its association with the precious metal but for the gleam of white rain lilies lining its banks. The star-shaped flowers, with six anthers brushed with golden pollen, have made themselves as much a part of the southern landscape as jonquils and azaleas. They grow about six inches tall and are accompanied by thin evergreen leaves something like that of grape hyacinth. White fairy lilies multiply readily but can hardly be considered too aggressive. They are very pretty naturalized at the edges of ponds or streams, or tucked into the front of borders. They put up with the worst extremes of soil as long as they don't get fried to a crisp during the heat of summer.

Another Argentinean species, *Z. flavissima,* is one of the prettiest golden yellow rain lilies. Like the white rain lily, it is easy to please on moist streamsides, damp low places, or moisture-retentive borders. It blooms over a long period from spring until fall if kept damp. Additional fall-blooming yellow rain lilies include brilliant gold *Z. pulchella* from the western Gulf Coast of Texas and golden yellow *Z. citrina* from Mexico. The former prefers a damp spot, while *Z. citrina* manages to seed and spread even on poor, dry clay.

Another foreign rain lily that has been embraced with open arms is satin pink *Z. grandiflora*. Nobody knows the secret of this pretty flower for, although it is found natu-

The return of the rain lilies such as Zephyranthes flavissima, *accented by purple-tinted leaves of* Sedum x 'Vera Jameson', *spells the beginning of the end of oppressive summer heat in the South.*

ralized far and wide in the South, the plant is sterile and cannot set seed. It multiplies by division and needs a helping human hand to move from town to town. We can only speculate that it is a very old hybrid of unknown origin that once caught the fancy of a gardener—spiritual kin of Johnny Appleseed—who aided in its spread. Perhaps the largest rain lily, the showy blossoms of *Z. grandiflora* are the size of a small daylily flower and are held on stems up to a foot tall. The long, thin leaves reinforce the image of a miniature pink daylily or perhaps of a tiny amaryllis.

*Z. rosea* from Cuba is sometimes confused with *Z. grandiflora* because of its pink autumn flowers, but it's less than half its size. This bright gem, deep rose-pink with an apple green throat, grows remarkably well in Florida, clustered near paths or at the edge of borders. Its flowers carry the peculiar but delightful scent of hot cocoa. The small white flowers of *Z. insularum* might easily be taken for an albino form of spring star flower (*Ipheion*) if it weren't for their late-season bloom and affinity for southern Florida. It, too, is native to the Caribbean islands but imparts a rare breath of springlike freshness. My sister, who lives in Florida, misses the small bulbs she grew up with in the North but finds solace in the sweet simplicity of the rain lilies.

# A Champion of Adaptability

Hundreds of miles north, the golden chalices of *Sternbergia lutea* sparkle in grassy fields and ancient lawns of old homesteads from Atlanta to Richmond. It might be easy to mistake it for a crocus (which it resembles in almost all respects) unless you count the stamens and find it has six while a crocus has a mere three. This fall beauty, native to much of southern and southeastern Europe, also makes itself at home at least as far north as Philadelphia, across and through Tennessee and Kentucky to Texas, and—remarkably—into coastal California and the Pacific Northwest. That's adaptability.

One key to its long survival is that it is somewhat poisonous to most wildlife and thus is usually left alone. Most bulb companies ignore it as well. Although I've seen pots of the bulbs available at a few local nurseries, such as in Fredericksburg and Austin, this bulb is almost totally absent from today's bulb catalogues. That's a shame, since new homeowners could do a lovely favor for future generations (not to mention themselves) by planting a couple dozen of the graceful golden chalices. If they can be found through mail-order sources, plant them in early autumn. Perhaps the bulbs are best spread from neighbor to neighbor, since they are easy to dig and transplant while the leaves are still green during winter.

It doesn't take much to suit sternbergias. Most any soil, unless it is under water, accommodates the little bulb. In its native habitat, the bulbs are often found on hillsides and sometimes in light shade in the hottest regions of its distribution. Despite the small size of the bulb—about two inches in diameter—planting them rather deep (about six inches) protects them from extreme heat in the South. Sternbergias would probably conquer the hearts of northerners as well, except the foliage is produced in winter and won't survive extended periods of frost. A very protected microclimate, such as against a stone wall or foundation, often helps the winter leaves make it through the cold season.

*Sternbergia clusiana,* native to the Middle East, is just as pretty but can be identified by its slightly larger size, longer petals, and gray green leaves that appear after flowering.

# On Toad Lilies

Gardeners who know toad lilies either love them or hate them. Those who don't know them probably don't want to get within a mile of something with that name. Put aside any preconceived notions; they're lovely plants. (I was going to say something about them leaping into the gardener's heart, but I've thought better of it.)

Toad lilies (*Tricyrtis*) grow from creeping rhizomes and produce small, rather waxy flowers that rest on the broad, pointed leaves like toads on a lily pad. If someone had not told me this, it would never have occurred to me since the flowers remind me of orchids. Some gardeners are too imaginative for their own good.

Yellow toad lily (*Tricyrtis flava*) grows beautifully in lightly shaded gardens across much of the South. Oblivious to heat and humidity, this Japanese species makes arching stems up to twenty inches long with alternating six-inch-long leaves. A purple-speckled yellow flower emerges from each leaf joint in late summer and into autumn. Spotted toad lily (*T. macropoda*) from China grows up to three feet tall, and its cream or pale yellow flowers are heavily spotted with purple. Light shade, organically rich soil, and a constant supply of moisture assure a fine late show from it and the rest of its relatives. Slugs are their worst predators.

Purple toad lily (*T. formosana*) from the semitropical island of Taiwan is considered by many to be the loveliest of the genus. Its red buds open to reveal spotted, rosy purple flowers of a heavy waxen texture. They are all the more showy since they are not perched in the leaf axils but held in clusters at the tops of maroon stems.

*P*urple *toad lily* (Tricyrtis formosana) *forms a spreading colony that waits until fall to brighten a moist, shady Pennsylvanian planting.*

These upright stems are clad with shiny, dark green leaves. Growing as tall as three feet, this species forms vigorous colonies with its stoloniferous rhizomes.

Hairy toad lily (*T. hirta*) sounds dreadful but is not. Native to Japan, it is found growing in woodlands, often among rock outcrops. Its white flowers wear a pattern of plum purple spots, while the graceful, arching stems, buds, and leaves are brushed with fine silver hairs. This species probably figures in the parentage of the popular upright hybrids 'White Tower', with pure white flowers, and 'Lavender Tower', with lavender-spotted white flowers.

This is the hardiest of the toad lilies and persists well as far north as Denver, Chicago, and Boston. As might be suspected, *T. hirta* and the rest of the clan also grow vigorously in the Pacific Northwest. It always takes a little fiddling or adjustment when it comes to making a particular plant perfectly at home, but I'm continually struck by the adaptive nature of so many plants. In an age where some gardeners compartmentalize themselves into little regional cliques, it's important sometimes to recall how much we have in common.

# 5
# WINTER

*Lands of Winter Warmth and
Awakenings in the North*

I t takes a while for northern gardeners who move south to adjust to the rhythms of the seasons. Those who think winter is a dull one in the garden are in for a surprise, and those who wait until April to begin planting are in for a shock. Winter and early spring is the time to get your ducks in a row. Gardeners treasure these cool days to work in the soil and to enjoy the bulbs that highlight their gardens. Nowhere else in the nation is the distinction between "cool season" and "warm season" so important. Paperwhites, cyclamens, and ranunculus join pansies, snapdragons, and ornamental kale in making winter a flower lover's delight.

There are frustrations and disappointments as well, when cold fronts barrel down from the north, frosting flowers ill-prepared for the drop. My friend Diane Peace, from central Texas, calls winter the menopausal season in her garden, where temperatures fluctuate

V*ivid Persian buttercups* (Ranunculus asiaticus) *consort with snapdragons, larkspur, pentas, pansies, and society garlic in a late winter Texas garden.*

wildly from below freezing to the nineties. Still, she and her husband, Tom, cherish the winter flowers that cope with the vagaries of weather, and they both taunt me with photos and descriptions of the pretty bulbs in their garden that I must grow on my sunporch.

Gardeners everywhere decorate for the winter holidays with paperwhites. They are almost universally esteemed for their piercingly sweet fragrance, except by a group of people who perceive the scent differently from the majority. To them, paperwhites are the "dirty sock" flowers. Being in a closed room with even a single stem makes them gag.

One advantage to living in the South or West is growing paperwhites outside, catching only a faint whiff on the breeze. Throughout much of the South, California, and into Oregon, paperwhites flower in abundance during early winter and midwinter. *Narcissus tazetta* var. *papyraceus* is native to Spain, Italy, and southern France and is naturalized in mild climates throughout the world. The common, heavily scented paperwhite is so named for its pure, papery petals, described in its variety name *papyraceus*. The texture of paper is more apparent as the flowers fade. They don't drop their petals but instead hang on to them as the breeze dries them to a crisp.

Carrying a more delicate fragrance, the Chinese sacred lily (*N. tazetta* var. *orientalis*) is a close relative of the common paperwhite. Bulb merchants made a big fuss about it during the late Victorian era, when all things Oriental, from carpets to pagodas, were in vogue. This was an exotic introduction from the mysterious Far East, with clusters of blossoms with white petals and small orange cups. The Chinese sacred lily does indeed grow along small sections of the coasts of Japan and China, but it is not a native. These colonies are relics of early ocean trade with Mediterranean merchants, who brought bulbs from their homeland. Oddly enough, this variety no longer exists in the wild in the Mediterranean region, if it ever did. Varieties and selections have long been valued—there were hundreds during their heyday in the seventeenth and eighteenth centuries—and it's just a quirk of fate that this one was sent around the world.

The variety 'Grand Monarque' is very much like the Chinese sacred lily but blooms a month later. It has long been a southern favorite. A double form called 'Constantinople' or 'Double Roman' also has deep roots in the South. The miniature 'Canaliculatus' is a lovely little clustered narcissus with a soft, pleasant fragrance. About half the height of standard paperwhites at about ten inches, it displays tiny white flowers with a short, butter yellow cup.

Despite their ease of culture, growing and flowering down to about 10 degrees, the bulbs have a tendency to split in some gardens, especially in heavy soil where they tend to work themselves right up to the surface. Although one alternative is to dig, divide, and plant them deeper every few years, another is to try some varieties that require little maintenance.

Gardeners who treasure heirloom plants hold the variety 'Grand Primo' (a member of the *italicus* branch of the paperwhite family) in high regard. The flowers open a tawny cream color and fade as they age. Accompanied by a light scent and a strong constitution, this nonsplitting bulb persists for generations. A similar variety is found in California, called 'Minor Monarque' with white petals and a yellow cup. It, too, may be found in gardens in old neighborhoods. An antique variety that lost its name (although some claim it was the legendary 'Seventeen Sisters') has come back reincarnated as 'Avalanche'. Modern gardeners are giving it rave reviews for its large white petals, yellow cup, good scent, and robust performance.

Recent paperwhite introductions also hark back to the glory days, with various degrees of scent and a wider range of heights, color, and forms of flowers. 'Bethlehem' is only eight inches tall, and its delicately scented flowers are pale yellow petals with bright gold cups. 'Nazareth' is a bit taller, and its similarly toned flowers carry a heavier perfume. 'Galilee' grows as tall and is pure white with a somewhat moderate fragrance. Soft-scented, pale yellow 'Israel' is set off by a sulfur yellow cup and grows up to twenty inches high. These new selections come from breeding work in Israel, where the next selections are rumored to be 'Golan Heights' and 'Occupied Territories'.

'Erlicheer' is a double paperwhite sold by Dutch merchants to northerners as a novelty: They can use it for summer bedding. This sounds dreadful to me, as unappealing as chrysanthemums in the spring, but nurseries sell a blue million of those every year, too. 'Erlicheer' is not hardy for northerners, but it has become a good winter paperwhite in the rest of the nation.

The hoop petticoat narcissus (*N. bulbocodium*) has settled in wonderfully through much of the South and mid-Atlantic states. The flowers are constructed quite differently from most narcissus, with the unpleated cup turning into a wide, inflated cone, and the surrounding petals shrinking to a few pennants seemingly blowing in the wind. Variants of the species and related ones bear white, cream, or darker yellow blossoms. Native to Spain and southern France, it seems to naturalize best on slight hillsides or in acidic sandy ground, a testament to its need for good drainage. In some ways, it's a symbol of southern gardening, with the tiny inflated flowers resembling the hoop skirts of another era. I can imagine generations of little girls dressing little dolls in this golden finery. While a display of the six-inch-tall flowers is not quite as grand as masses of their bigger cousins, it does come in the middle of winter. Because they can sow themselves (an advantage for an "unimproved" species), colonies spread over time.

The Lent lily (*N. pseudonarcissus*) has the same advantage and also blooms in winter where temperatures don't plummet much below 15 degrees, and later in colder regions. Introduced during colonial times, the yellow Lent lily is sometimes found growing along ditches and country roads where it has escaped from garden captivity. Native to western Europe, it has been treasured for a very long time despite its relative dowdiness compared to many highly bred daffodils. While its stems are only six inches high, the flower cup is nearly that long, so it is actually quite showy. It blooms as early as January in some areas, but usually later depending on conditions.

# French-Roman Hyacinths

Hyacinths don't top the list of bulbs that naturalize well, especially in the South. Some can live for a very long time in northern gardens but the wind quickly goes out of their sails. Their top-heavy, flower-studded stems diminish in size and number of flowers and begin to resemble their wild ancestors. Long before Dutch breeders gussied them up like Las Vegas showgirls, hyacinths were as simple and lovely as the girl next door.

Across the rocky hills of northern Spain and southern France, wild hyacinths bloom each spring in shades of white, pink, and blue. They carry a spicy, sweet scent with a hint of cinnamon. French-Roman hyacinth (*Hyacinthus orientalis* var. *albulus*) is one of the nearly wild varieties that have been cultivated in Europe since the time of Napoleon. Its flowers are much smaller than modern hybrids and are spaced farther apart on the stem. Each bulb produces multiple stems. While not as showy as the buxom beauties most of us know, French-Roman hyacinths possess a strong physical nature and, when planted in well-drained loam in a sunny spot, thrive for decades. The white form appears to be the toughest, as well as the most readily available. They survive extremes of southern heat as well as northern cold and can sometimes be found naturalized in lawns and short grass around older homes.

# Superstars

*Ipheion uniflorum* may be the best bulb for naturalizing across much of the country. It is adaptable in its soil, sun, and water requirements, needs no attention whatsoever, is rarely if ever bothered by pests, and its lavender blue flowers complement its companions. Last but not least, the foliage withers away inconspicuously. Spring star flower simply does not get the respect it deserves.

Perhaps the pale stars don't jump out from the catalog pages like a flashy double daffodil or an orange crown imperial. I see lovely patches of it wherever I travel in late winter in the South and on the West Coast, and in spring in northern latitudes. There are limits to its endurance. Although spring star flower should do well as far north as Boston, a sheltered position, gritty soil, and perhaps a winter mulch may benefit it. Its flowers cast a gauze of dusty blue across a lawn just springing to life or cluster at the feet of anemones or daffodils. It is especially pretty, to my mind, combined with the classic silvery *Narcissus* 'Thalia'.

*I. uniflorum* is a subtle, unassuming plant native to Argentina and Uruguay, growing in fairly moist ground in light shade or sun. Each bulb produces a single flower on a slender stem three to six inches long. Its pale, thin, blue green leaves smell of onions when bruised. The six-petaled flowers open flat on bright days to reveal a cookie cutter–perfect star. Variable in color by nature, spring star flower is represented by several selections in commerce. 'Violacea' tends more toward the purple end of the spectrum, and 'Froyle Mill' is the deepest blue available. 'Album' is the large white form, while 'Rolf Fielder' has a white throat on a dark blue background. Some authorities say 'Wisley Blue' is dark blue, but the specimens I've seen with this name are rather pale and not much different from the commonly seen garden form.

# Ranunculus and Anemones

The jewel-tone flowers of *Ranunculus asiaticus* appear in the deep South and on the West Coast after the New Year. Flowers in shades of red, yellow, pink, orange, and white make a dazzling display. They've been in cultivation for many centuries, beloved by the Persians who selected the best forms from their native wildflower. This heritage is recalled in the folk name *turban flower*, suggested by the tightly overlapping petals of the double forms. The French carried on the breeding tradition. The whimsical common name *fair maids of France* may have been evoked by the resemblance of the flowers to the skirts of cancan dancers.

Cool, humid conditions promote the best flowering. Dissected leaves emerge in autumn, followed by stems a foot or more tall, depending on variety. Flowers come in both single and double forms, some more tightly "wrapped" than others. Where temperatures drop much below 20 degrees, the display of flowers may be ruined by frost. Excessive summer moisture, coupled by poor drainage, may rot the tubers.

Poppy anemones offer some of the most sumptuous colors of the late winter and spring garden, or any other season for that matter. Simple in design, the rounded petals often frame blue black stamens. This dramatic center underscores the shades of velvet red, pink, white, and lilac purple. Several strains, such as the single de Caen and semidouble St. Brigid, have been selected over the centuries from *Anemone coronaria,* native to the Mediterranean region. The handsome foliage emerges in fall and is followed in midwinter by flowers on straight, hollow stems about a foot tall depending on the variety.

Novice gardeners often confuse anemones with ranunculus. Look for a frilly collar of leaves on the stem below the flower that is part of the charm of poppy anemones. Both plants belong to the buttercup family, rather than the iris or lily families that so many bulbous plants do. Buttercups have great leaves. It's a lucky break for gardeners, who often exert a great deal of energy designing around typical linear bulb foliage.

Freezes destroy the filigreed leaves that must be preserved if the plants are to prosper, while sticky clay often rots the dormant tubers. Where frost rarely threatens, plant the tubers about two inches deep in well-drained soil to ensure long-term survival. If success eludes you, fear not: The tubers are inexpensive, and there is no shame in replanting each autumn to enjoy these lovely flowers for winter and spring.

*Anemone apeninna* is widely distributed across southern Europe. It blooms in shades of lavender blue, pink, and white on six-inch stems. It competes well among short grasses or in an open woodland and makes sheets of color once established. It flowers in late winter in the South and on the West Coast and later in the northern extent of its climatic limits (to about Philadelphia). Wood anemone (*A. nemerosa*) shows its pretty white, blue, or pink flowers over a long period from November to May in a moist, shady position. It is found in woods throughout Europe and into Asia. Good-looking foliage, reminiscent of that of Virginia creeper, sets off the short, rounded petals and yellow centers of the blossoms. Grecian windflower (*A. blanda*), a favorite across much of the country, is suitable for naturalizing in the

South only in the upper and mountainous parts. Even so, it is best in a cool, shady spot beneath deciduous trees, although it performs best in sun farther north.

Enchanting the gardeners who take them in are the neglected native anemones, including Carolina anemone (*A. caroliniana*), a tiny winter bloomer ideal for lawns in shades of white, pink, blue; and *Anemone heterophylla,* native from Texas to Alabama, which also bears blossoms in the same trio of colors with long, thin petals above a tuft of parsleylike leaves. It, too, is short—about six inches tall—and naturalizes in lawns and blooms from February into April. Stems elongate as the thimblelike seed head grows and finally bursts into a flurry of cottony seeds. Neither makes a suitable addition to the typical rectangle of manicured grass, but both are delightful in a laid-back lawn.

# Wood Sorrel

The handsome cloverlike leaves and delicate blossoms of wood sorrel grace winter gardens in both the South and West. The plants are sometimes sold as "shamrock plants" but *Oxalis,* native mainly to tropical and subtropical North and South America and Africa, is not related to the true Irish shamrock. Northerners make do with the bulbous plants in the windowsill, but some species come into their full glory in mild winter states in midwinter and carry on well into summer. The overlapping flower petals spiral to a point when the flower closes at night and on cloudy days, but they unfurl quickly on bright days, even in shade. *Oxalis crassipes* comes from southern Brazil and makes an impressive but not invasive mound of celadon green leaves topped by sprays of pink blossoms. *O. regnelli,* also from South America, sports large, deep maroon leaves accented by white or pale pink flowers. 'Iron Cross', with its bronze patches on the inner third of the green leaves, is the most popular form of Mexican *O. deppei*. Coral pink flowers add the finishing touch.

*Oxalis purpurata* var. *bowiei* is noted for its pale green leaves, a profusion of lavender pink flowers, and its fine performance in southern gardens. Hybrids such as white, large-flowered 'Grand Duchess' and white-striped red 'Candy Cane' expand the range of these ground-covering bulbs; specialist growers offer many more. While a sandy loam suits them best, some—especially *O. purpurata* var. *bowiei* and *O. crassipes*—grow well in stiffer soil. Light shade is usually best. They are delightful planted next to pathways or steps and beneath taller perennials. During very hot, dry weather, the bulbs go dormant to await more favorable conditions.

# Cyclamens

Winter windowsills across the northern half of the country display the showy red, coral, pink, lavender, white, and bicolored blooms of *Cyclamen persicum*. Dazzling in color and variety, these "florist cyclamens" have been selected over many years from the single species indigenous to Cyprus and Tunisia. Books regularly warn against trying them outside, but gardeners in the deep South know better. The white-marbled leaves emerge in early winter, and the swan-necked flower stems appear a few weeks later. The flowers make pretty accents beneath trees open to the winter sun, alongside lamiums, ornamental kale, and oxalis, all of which complement the attractive cyclamen leaves. When summer heat returns, the tubers begin to go dormant. Tree roots help to sop up excess moisture that can rot the tubers.

Southward from Virginia, *Cyclamen coum* may be found in bloom throughout the cool winter months, even through light dustings of snow and into spring. A

*Cyclamen repandum from Greece naturalizes easily beneath trees, where the roots soak up excess moisture that might rot the cyclamen during its summer dormancy.*

tough plant, native across a wide range from Bulgaria to the Middle East, this so-called Persian violet blooms with the crocus in northern latitudes.

*Cyclamen repandum,* native to Greece, Italy, and southern France, makes a lovely show in West Coast gardens. Its pink or rose flowers are held about six inches high above the silver-veined leaves that have reddish undersides. The flowers appear beneath shrubs and trees in late winter and often bloom well into summer.

# Cape Bulbs for the Coast

A wealth of South African bulbs, mainly from the Cape of Good Hope, highlights a West Coast winter. Much of coastal California and southern Oregon provides climatic conditions that mimic the winter rains and relative warmth of their homelands, so the bulbs respond in a spectacular manner. Since rainfall often comes a bit later in the season (and may be more erratic) in California than in South Africa, gardeners keep a watchful eye for the emergence of the winter bloomers' foliage, providing extra moisture if the sky does not.

Some bulbous South African plants demonstrate an unusual survival technique: Despite what appear to be favorable conditions, a few plants of a group simply sit out a season. This "ace up the sleeve" strategy is an adaptation that leaves a few survivors in the event that disaster strikes, such as prolonged drought, fire, or decimation by animals.

Winter is a thrilling season for West Coast bulb fanciers. There are many hundreds of species that can only be touched upon here, so I've selected those that are most readily available. Most of these bulbs grow easily from seed, and gardeners who fall under their spell should consider joining organizations of other like-minded gardeners, such as the International Bulb Society. You will never have a boring winter.

The small flowers of *Lachenalia,* sometimes called leopard lily or cape cowslip, are displayed in quantity along straight stems above attractive leaves. The effect can be bold, such as from the scarlet, yellow, and olive three-toned tubular flowers of *Lachenalia aloides* var. *quadricolor,* or subtle as in the case of the butter-and-lavender blossoms of *L. pallida. L. bulbifera* is tomato red, *L. viridiflora* is an unusual shade of turquoise green, and *L. glaucina* is the color of opals. Established bulbs send up thick, glossy leaves—sometimes spotted—and many racemes (generally from six to twelve inches tall) of long-lasting flowers. About a hundred species of *Lachenalia,*

*The pale bugles of* Gladiolus tristis *hover above a handsome colony of* Lachenalia pallida.

all indigenous to the Cape, make this a very popular plant for collectors.

*Spiloxene capensis* begins to bloom about the same time as the lachenalias. The flowers display the classic star shape that is the hallmark of the genus. On stems about eight inches tall with grassy leaves, they are usually white—sometimes yellow and white and rarely pink—strikingly accented by a chocolate brown patch with an iridescent green eye. After heavy, prolonged winter rains on the Cape in 1990, the display of *S. capensis* was said to be spectacular, with the flowers popping up in many places where they'd never been seen before. Gardeners may wish to use this to advantage, providing additional irrigation or praying for a rainy December.

Fortnight lily, *Dietes iridiodes,* can come into bloom at any time of the year but is almost always in flower at the opening of the New Year. It makes a commanding presence in a sunny garden with spiky, rigid leaves about two feet tall. The main attraction is the procession of white flowers, like those of iris, that open for a single day. (I'm surprised we don't call this plant "dayiris.") No matter their duration, there are always fresh flowers—exquisitely formed and marked with lavender and yellow at the center—for an extended period.

*Chasmanthe aethiopica* produces an imposing stand of long, bright-green leaves up to four or five feet tall that puts most ornamental grasses to shame. It then proceeds to crown itself in winter with flaming orange or yellow flowers. These are tubular and thin with a flaring lip and protruding hood, displayed alternately along the stem. The whole stem looks like it's been in a book press for a few days. One spike may produce as many as thirty flowers, providing a long show. The corms are easily satisfied in most soils in either sun or partial shade, as long as they receive sufficient water during their growing season. This ease of culture and perhaps a general prejudice against orange flowers sometimes keeps chasmanthes out of "refined" gardens. That's just fine, because they look wonderful in the gardens around the bungalows in old neighborhoods of California towns, such as in Berkeley and Walnut Creek. They are dazzling combined with striped New Zealand flax (which emphasizes the architectural qualities of both plants) as well as purple princess tree (*Tibouchina urvilleana*) and glowing orange and gold calendulas.

The color orange may also play against the popularity of *Clivia miniata,* simply called clivia. It is native to the broadleaf evergreen forests along the eastern coast of South Africa that stay relatively moist throughout the year. Clivia is, nevertheless, somewhat drought tolerant because of thick, fleshy roots and tough, evergreen

*Brilliant clivias are as at home in this shady setting in Los Angeles as in their native South African woodland.*

leaves. A favorite houseplant of the Victorian era because it would grow and flower in dim, cold parlors, clivia makes a grand statement in the winter garden. Strong stems support clusters of a dozen or so flowers above the foot-tall clumps of broad, shiny leaves. The clear orange petals fade to white in the interior of the blossom, accented with a dash of bright green.

A yellow form of clivia has been coveted by gardeners for decades and is becoming increasingly available, even if it still commands a high price. A selection with variegated leaves is exceedingly rare, and the lucky gardeners who have it must keep it under lock and key. There is no trick to growing a clivia except to keep the afternoon sun off the leaves or they will burn. Since the foliage is held for several years, the damage is slow to repair. I should know—one of my plants took years to recover from the careless scalding I gave it on the patio. With the most minimal of care, a clump increases steadily by offsets and should be considered, for all intents and purposes, immortal.

I have a problem with calling this plant "kaffir lily," as it is sometimes known, for several reasons. First, clivia is a perfectly good name, and several other South African plants are occasionally called kaffir lily, including *Schizostylis coccinea.* Second, the word *kaffir* is a derogatory term in South Africa for people of color; it has no place in gardening. (Yes, political correctness comes to horticulture.) I don't think most people who innocently use the term *kaffir lily* would choose to do so if they understood its vulgarity.

Winter red-hot poker (*Veltheimia*) was another Victorian parlor favorite. *V. bracteata,* sometimes called forest lily, grows in South African coastal woodlands. A rosette of attractive broad leaves, wavy along the edges, emerges in autumn (although it will stay evergreen or nearly so in a moist shade garden). From it rise pale stems up to two feet tall, spotted with maroon. They support dense clusters of chalky pink, tubular blossoms about two inches long. The effect is strikingly similar to that of red-hot poker (*Kniphofia*), which explains the common name.

*Veltheimia capensis* grows on well-drained hillsides around the Cape and into the semiarid regions along the Atlantic coast. The nose of the bulb can be left slightly above soil level at planting time, since the bulbs eventually push themselves halfway out of the ground. Its leaves have a blue cast, its stems are a few inches shorter than its cousin, and its flowers are smaller. In compensation, the flowers are shaded a brighter pink. Like clivia, the leaves of either species are likely to scorch in hot sun, so light shade and moist, well-drained soil during the winter months are preferable.

Cape tulip (*Homeria*) is, I suppose, about as close as any South African bulb comes to looking like a tulip, but it possesses a charm all its own. The six petals flare away from the cup-shaped flower, which measures about two inches across. Each corm usually sends up one long, relaxed leaf and a thin stem, slightly more than a foot tall, that produces a handful of flowers over several weeks. Warm shades of salmon and honey mark those of *Homeria collina,* while flowers of *H. ochroleuca* var. *aurantiaca* are golden yellow with tangerine overtones. Where cape tulip settles in successfully, such as on a rocky slope, its seedlings can be expected to pop up, perhaps even to the point of becoming a nuisance. Some southern gardeners grow cape tulip well—one of the few South Africans that persist there—in raised beds and rock gardens.

Few gardeners expect the sweet fragrance from the flowers of *Tulbaghia simmleri* (formerly *T. fragrans*). One of South Africa's society garlics, it is native to the east Transvaal Province and blooms in winter with clusters of mauve pink or white flowers shaped like those of hyacinths. (Perhaps I draw that comparison because their perfume reminds me of hyacinth). Don't bruise the long, glaucous leaves as you stoop to inhale, or you'll get a whiff of onions as an unwelcome bonus. The plant, slightly less than two feet tall, stays evergreen unless severely drought stressed and may bloom sporadically throughout the year if kept relatively moist. *T. violacea,* native to the eastern seaboard of the Cape Province in forests (although it grows fine in sun), begins to bloom in winter but saves its best show for spring and early summer. It is distinguished by smaller pink flowers above tufts of thinner leaves that grow about a foot tall; the selection 'Silver Queen' is variegated.

Chincherinchee is the strange name carried by *Ornithogalum thyrsoides,* given by the eighteenth-century botanist Carl Thunberg trying to describe the rustling sound made by wind blowing through the dry flower stalks on the cape. The plants have never played this song for me. The long-stemmed white flowers are common at the florist, where they are sometimes called star-of-Bethlehem, although that name is usually reserved for the small, white-flowered *O. umbellatum* from Israel.

*O. thyrsoides* grows robustly and multiplies steadily in most West Coast gardens, providing a good show of eighteen-inch stems topped by dense clusters of white, green-eyed flowers for about a month in winter. Giant chincherinchee, *O. saundersae,* comes from an area east of the cape that receives summer rainfall, so it is on the opposite growing schedule. In summer, its four-foot stems provide similar white clusters of flowers. It is relatively hardy (even I have had limited success with it outdoors) and may be grown in the Pacific Northwest.

# As Snow Recedes

Plants that bloom in late winter and early spring are often characterized as brave or stalwart. These may be attributes we admire in people, but they have nothing to do with plants. Plants bloom when their genetics prompt them to do so, even if we are somewhat surprised by their timetables. The flowers that push up during what we call inclement weather couldn't care less about our big faces hovering above them, but we find them endearing. We dote over them (I make my doting quick if it's cold) and call them snowdrops, winter aconites, snow iris, snowflakes, snow crocus, Siberian squills, and glory-of-the-snow. The operative word is *snow.* They are a tough bunch.

Whenever a break in cold winter weather occurs, gardeners look for the first signs of life. To many of us, even the tiniest sprout is encouraging, but the first flower is a party. Throughout much of the northern portion of the nation, the imminent demise of winter is signaled by a snowdrop.

It's taken me a long time to truly appreciate the common snowdrop (*Galanthus nivalis*). It's a big deal to some people, especially in England, where innumerable forms with almost imperceptible variations elicit extraordinary interest. Snowdrops demonstrate variability due to their extensive range from the eastern Mediterranean region into Russia. In addition, several species have been hybridized with the common snowdrop. Very few of these forms and hybrids appear in American catalogues, perhaps because many gardeners feel the way I do. As sweet and welcome as the white pendant flowers might be, I have little interest in chasing after 'Lutescens' (with yellow markings on the inner petals instead of green), 'Viridapicis' (its three outer petals are also tipped with green instead of being pure white), or 'Magnet' (with long pedicels that dangle the flower far away from the stem).

Whenever I see a big fuss about them, I think to myself, "Hey, it's just a snowdrop." To me, that's enough. On the other hand, I do covet 'Atkinsii', a robust hybrid with stems nearly double in length from the normal five inches or so, and I also find the double forms of snowdrops intriguing. Although several other species besides the common snowdrop are sometimes grown, the best may be the giant snowdrop *(G. elwesii)* from Turkey. It is distinguished by its size—up to ten inches in height—and its wide, gray green leaves.

Giant snowdrop is a better choice for gardeners in semiarid regions, as it demonstrates better drought tolerance, while the common snowdrop colonizes best where moisture is constant throughout the year. Neither settles in easily after being first

*Snowdrops emerge from a bed of crumbling leaves at the first hint of spring weather.*

planted, since the bulbs tend to dry up in storage. Don't expect a 100 percent return on your investment initially (unless you get them "in the green," since they divide easily while in bloom). Those that do survive will seed themselves in quantity. A few snowdrops eventually become an avalanche of flowers.

# Winter Gold

I sometimes watch people when they shop for bulbs. We all try to stretch our dollars as far as we can, so we don't buy everything we'd like. We think to ourselves, I could get these early yellow daisylike things, or I could wait and have a bunch of really red tulips later. The tulips often win, and the winter aconites sit on the shelf.

Winter aconites bloom nearly as early as snowdrops—sometimes concurrently— and their simple yellow flowers pierce the brown debris of the winter garden. Native to much of Europe where it inhabits moist woods, *Eranthis hyemalis* holds its flowers just above the soil. The flowers look like a tiny version of the single 'Father

*W*inter aconite and Siberian squill weave themselves through a late winter tapestry of ivy.

Hugo' rose, albeit four months early. Their golden yellow color has olive undertones. The blossoms are borne singly, surrounded by a lacy bract of dissected leaves.

*Eranthis cilicica,* a similar species from the mountains of southern Turkey, may be recognized by the bronze tone of the "clown collar" encircling the blossom. This seemingly unimportant, nit-picking detail may be the only major difference between the two species, but it's an indicator of performance. *E. hyemalis* naturalizes best in moist climates, while *E. cilicica* performs best where summers are dry. Most every gardener can scatter these little yellow charmers around the shade garden under trees and shrubs and in the lawn, but gardeners in the West will fare better with the latter, which also performs well in a sunny position. A hybrid between the two, called 'Guinea Gold', bears larger flowers than either of its parents, with a telltale bronze ruff. It is sterile but vigorous and long-lived. Rock gardeners, who often regret letting self-sowing plants loose to seed themselves in inconvenient little crannies, prefer well-mannered 'Guinea Gold.'

# Snow Iris

Snow iris is sometimes a bit too "brave" for its own good. The buds poke through a layer of melting snow without damage, but open flowers sometimes get smashed by a new layer of snow. A late blast of really arctic air also ruins them. Nevertheless, the gamble usually pays off. Several species are included in the group of snow iris, including *Iris reticulata,* native to meadows and rocky hillsides across a wide area from Turkey into Iraq and Iran; *I. histrioides,* from a single mountain in northern Turkey; and *I. danfordiae,* also from high altitudes in Turkey.

Most of the bulbs we grow are hybrids and selections from the first two species. There is no such thing as an ugly snow iris. The colors range from deep blues and purples to pastel shades and nearly white. The standards (the three upright petals) and falls (the three lower petals) of these iris are tiny and slender compared to those of their giant cousins but no less lovely. The falls have no beards but often bear a patch or stripe of vibrant orange or yellow. The common form of *I. reticulata* is a clear,

*Snow iris (Iris reticulata 'Pauline') multiply in a seemingly inhospitable border of prickly pads and silver cushions.*

deep blue. It is a perfectly lovely plant and should not be overlooked, although its many forms are equally good: pale blue, orange-blotched 'Cantab'; reddish plum 'J.S. Dijt'; deep bluish purple 'Harmony'; sky blue, orange-striped 'Joyce'; white-blushed powder blue 'Natascha'; deep purple, orange-blotched 'Hercules'; and navy, orange-blotched 'Edward'.

Dozens more are available, led by 'George', an offspring of *I. histrioides,* which is slightly larger in all respects than most snow iris, with lavender blue petals highlighted by a prominent white patch on its falls. It is said to be fragrant—as are several others, such as 'Edward' and 'Harmony'—but I confess that as my back has become less flexible with time, I rarely prostrate myself on cold, damp ground and can't vouch for the scent.

Some snow iris increase very vigorously by division ('Harmony' may be the champion), but my advice would be to order a dozen of as many varieties as possible and compare their progress for several years. Then go hog-wild with a few that succeed brilliantly in your conditions. Snow iris grow in almost any type of soil and in any exposure as long as they receive sun on their pencil-thin leaves in spring. A hot, dry summer doesn't faze them. In fact, bulbs planted in my hellstrips that get little summer moisture and bake to a crisp outperform the ones in more moderate conditions.

The only snow iris that drives me to distraction is the freckled yellow one, *Iris danfordiae.* It is notorious for its habit of splitting into smaller bulbs that often refuse to bloom the second season. The bulb in commerce is a triploid form (with extra chromosomes), selected by bulb growers for its rapid multiplication. A fertilizer high in potash and low in nitrogen may persuade it to commence flowering in the third season, but by then I've often forgotten about it. The normal diploid form would probably make a better garden plant, as it relies more on seeds than splitting for reproduction. Alas, it is not for sale as far as I can tell. The best advice I can offer is to treat *Iris danfordiae* like a self-renewing biennial: Plant it in the same sunny, well-drained spot two years running, set the bulbs about six inches deep beneath a ground cover like *Sedum spurium* 'Red Carpet', and feed the foliage religiously. Or give it up.

# Parachutes

Inside most sophisticated, grown-up gardeners there's the lingering wonder of little kids. We never forget the thrill of our childhood springs when flowers seemed like fragile toys. I feel quite deprived that I never saw a spring snowflake (*Leucojum ver-*

*num*) bloom until after I had already voted in several presidential elections. The first thought that popped into my mind, however, was, "Wow, it's a parachute!"

That's as a good a reason as anyone needs to grow spring snowflake. Its inflated white bells have green-tipped, serrated edges, and although it bears a superficial resemblance to a snowdrop, no imaginative child would ever confuse them. Spring snowflake grows about six inches tall, bears a half dozen or more flowers on solitary stems from a well-established bulb, and usually flowers a few weeks later than the snowdrops. Native to southern and eastern European woodlands, *L. vernum* multiplies and thrives in light shade or sun in most any moist soil. It is very pretty combined with winter aconite and hellebores.

# Crocus

Two species of crocus dominate spring. The first is *Crocus chrysanthus.* So many selections of this small, widely distributed species (from the Balkans to Turkey) are available that a gardener can spend many years experimenting with them. One of my favorite catalogues lists twenty-seven varieties. To be fair, some are reputed to be hybrids derived from crossings with *C. biflorus,* indigenous to the southern and western Mediterranean region. Still, that's a whole bunch of crocus, so to speak, with colors ranging from white and yellow to purple and every shade and combination possible. Contrasting patterns of deep bronze or purple veining vary their looks even more.

This group of short, early crocus are often called bunching crocus or snow

*Crocus 'Snow Bunting' blooms as perennials stir to life.*

crocus. They revel in a cold winter but often perform acceptably as far south as Tennessee, Kentucky, and Georgia. The only way to kill them is to drown the corms or shade them out. They are suitable for myriad uses, including lawns, shade gardens under deciduous trees, borders, hillsides, cottage gardens, and rock gardens.

One of my favorite plantings of snow crocus is in my front garden. It used to be an ordinary lawn until I bought the house. Then, stripped of grass, it turned into my version of a cottage garden, stuffed to the gills with every plant that appreciates a sunny, relatively dry summer. In spring, snow crocus bloom in waves of color that roll into one another. The way to achieve this casual look is to buy four or five varieties in lots of a hundred. Start with any color, such as straw yellow 'Moonlight', and overlap into the next variety. Plant all but about fifteen of them, and then mix them into 'Gipsy Girl'; with its yellow petals feathered bronze on the outside, it leads the eye deeper into the bed, where it meets 'Blue Bird', which has violet blue outside petals and a cream interior. This is a natural invitation to start a wave of 'Cream Beauty', which in turn could lead into yellow and purple 'Advance', and so forth. Waves of color can also be created in a large lawn. With at least twenty-seven choices, the possibilities are nearly unlimited.

The second dominant species is usually called Dutch crocus. These plump jumbo crocus are selections from the European species *Crocus vernus.* The Dutch have been playing around with it for a very long time but seem to have stopped; there hasn't been a new variety introduced for ages. Most of our current cultivars and hybrids have been in commerce since well before I was born. They truly qualify as classics: pure white 'Jeanne d'Arc' from 1940, purple 'Remembrance' from 1925, white-striped lavender 'Pickwick' from 1925, pale lavender 'Grand Maitre' from 1924, light purple 'Vanguard' from 1934, and brassy yellow 'Giant Yellow' from all the way back to 1600. This venerable clone, possibly a hybrid with or between *C. angustifolius* and *C. flavus,* masquerades under several names. Whether called 'Giant Yellow', 'Dutch Yellow', 'Golden Yellow,' or 'Flavus Giant Yellow', this is probably the same corm, vegetatively propagated by the millions, that bloomed in the gardens of Ottoman emperors, that bloomed in Thomas Jefferson's garden at Monticello, and that bloomed in the royal gardens of Czar Nicholas. It's a piece of living history.

Snobs are hard on these reliable old crocus, criticizing their size and lack of refinement. Don't take any notice. Plant them to enjoy the lovely sheen of their bold flowers, nicely accented by a prominent fluff of gold or orange stamens. They're "good doers" in sunny border positions in both light or heavy soils, although they rarely increase rapidly or bunch up like snow crocus. They are fine in lawns if the foliage isn't mowed drastically or prematurely.

Other species are too good to ignore, although there are far too many to cover here. One advantage in growing true species is that, where acclimated, they produce seed rather than multiply simply by offsets. *Crocus tommasinianus* is a favorite for naturalizing in lawns for this reason and is said to be less attractive to nosy squirrels. The standard species from Bosnia and Croatia—soft lavender with no yellow in the throat of the flower—blooms early and gracefully. To top it off, it performs well in most of the South, except for the most tropical sections along the Gulf. Forms selected for their pleasing colors include rich purple 'Barr's Purple', violet 'Ruby Giant', silver lavender 'Roseus', red violet 'Whitewell Purple', and self-explanatory 'Albus'.

*Crocus sieberi* from Greece and the Balkans is ordinarily white with a yellow throat and purple on the exterior of the petals. Several selections are variations on this theme, such as 'Firefly', 'Tricolor', 'Hubert Edelstein', 'Violet Queen', and the subspecies *atticus,* found around Athens, which is white with purple outside streaks. 'Bowles White' lacks the purple pattern on the outside petals and has a red stigma and orange throat. This species and its selections also perform admirably in much of the South and West. Sustained high winter temperatures inhibit flowering, but where it drops into the low fifties and forties with regularity, some other crocus flower well. This includes the aforementioned *C. tommasinianus* (dubbed "tommies" by some southern gardeners), the ancient 'Giant Yellow', some of the snow crocus varieties in the upper South, and cloth of gold and golden bunch crocus.

Cloth of gold (*C. angustifolius*) comes from southwestern Russia, the Ukraine, and Armenia and has been in cultivation since the seventeenth century. Its interior is golden yellow, while the outside is dramatically veined with maroon. Golden bunch crocus (*C. ancyrensis*) from the region of Turkey around its capital, Ankara, lives up to its name by bearing up to five vivid golden-orange flowers per corm. Despite the tiny size of the two-inch-tall flowers, they bloom early and are impossible to miss. Italian crocus (*C. etruscus*) comes from light woodlands in the northern part of the country. Subdued lavender petals are complemented by a silver cast on the outside with a few purple stripes, and by a pale yellow throat. Though usually a failure in the South, it's a good bet along parts of the West Coast.

To my knowledge, there's no such thing as a true pink crocus. That's why I'm surprised why more gardeners don't grow little *Bulbocodium vernum,* an early pink gem with all the charm of crocus and more. Closely related to the mainly autumn-flowering colchicums, *B. vernum* is a true alpine plant native to high slopes and meadows of the Pyrenees and Alps. It blooms in early spring, its small but elegant flaring flowers rising from the soil before the leaves in a shade of "hair ribbon" pink. A clump is excessively pretty set in a sea of vibrant blue Siberian squills.

Bulbocodium is a classic for the rock garden and benefits from a thin mulch of pebbles. As might be expected, the bulb is rock hardy but may suffer in regions where summers are hot or dry, or both. Gardeners in cool mountainous areas who succeed with other alpines often grow this bulb to perfection.

# Squills

Few other plants can match the gorgeous shade of blue of Siberian squill (*Scilla siberica*). While it does not come from Siberia, it is quite hardy, being widely distributed in southern Russia, Crimea, the Caucasus, and northern Iran. Usually less than half a foot tall, the maroon stem holds a cluster of the six-petaled flowers, which generally face downward. The big attraction is the color, whether it occurs in a lawn, along walkways, or integrated into perennial borders. Siberian squill thrives like mad beneath deciduous shrubs, where it benefits from the cool summer shade. Early daffodils like 'February Gold' make the best of companions. The form 'Spring Beauty' has deeper blue flowers and is said to be scented. I'm not quite as enthralled with 'Alba', but it lights up my shade garden, poking through the emerging maroon leaves of *Sedum spurium* 'Red Carpet'.

Milk squill is even showier, with larger flowers of the palest blue—the color of a summer cloud or a glass of milk—with a darker stripe. The buds barely push through the soil when they begin to bloom. The stems finally top out at about six inches high as the shiny green leaves emerge. The species, formerly called *Scilla tubergeniana* and still often found under that name in catalogues and stores, is now correctly named *S. mischtschenkoana*. Nobody's too thrilled. Don't let this get in the way of keeping this species, native to stony hillsides in northern Iran and the Caucasus, from colonizing lightly shaded slopes, rock gardens, and borders.

*S. bifolia,* native to central and southern Europe into Turkey, is very much like *S. siberica* in height and cultural needs but has a distinct appearance, since its flowers face upward. The little squill usually has just two leaves, a brown-stained stem, and many flowers in various shades of blue, mauve, and pink. Catalogues may offer both blue and pink forms.

Meadow squill (*S. litardieri,* formerly called *S. pratensis*) comes from high moun-

*A*ggressive Siberian squills monopolize the ground beneath a thicket of leafless lilacs.

tain meadows of the former Yugoslavia. Its eight-inch flowering stem is thickly clus-tered with tiny flowers, almost in a bottlebrush arrangement. The color of the blos-soms is a pleasing amethyst purple. Established bulbs send up numerous flowering spikes, making a fine show in lightly shaded gardens, moist grassy areas, and borders.

*Puschkinia scilloides* (formerly known as *P. libanotica*) might as well be reviewed with the rest of the squills, even if it's classified in its own genus on a technicality of little interest to gardeners. Stems about eight inches tall can support a dozen flowers or more. When a drift of striped squill, as it is commonly known, bursts into bloom with its white, aqua-striped blossoms, the effect is unlike that of any other garden flower—it's like sea foam.

The flowers are a knockout planted with pink or apricot hyacinths or the early, mauve Kaufmanniana tulip 'Fritz Kreisler'. If conditions suit the bulb (indigenous

*Patches of blue glory-of-the-snow, white snowflakes, and yellow winter aconites carpet the Delaware woods at Winterthur.*

to high meadows near snowline in eastern Turkey, the Caucasus, and northern Iran to Lebanon), it won't stay put for long. Though the bulbs don't perform especially well in dry soil, mine simply love well-drained sandy loam and pop up in the lawn, in borders, and even in the vegetable garden. They never get in the way.

# Glory-of-the-snow

Despite its folk name, glory-of-the-snow rarely sees a snowstorm. The see-saw battle between winter and spring varies from year to year, but when it blooms, the tide has usually turned in the garden. The thick-petaled flowers stand up to cold or heat when necessary so they're an ideal flower for the unpredictable transition of seasons.

Glory-of-the-snow grows in mountainous Turkey near snowline. *Chionodoxa luciliae* sports a six-inch stem with six or eight flowers the color of blue denim, set off by a white eye. The variety 'Pink Giant' grows several inches taller and bears softly shaded pink flowers, also with the characteristic white eye. *C. sardensis* has become increasingly popular over the past few years because of its gentian-blue pendant flowers. The rich color is even more potent since this species, discovered near the ancient city of Sardis in western Turkey, lacks a white interior.

Glory-of-the-snow thrives under the same conditions as most of the squills, to which it is closely related. The bulbs seed and multiply freely in cool spots beneath deciduous trees and shrubs. Seedlings sometimes pop up with flowers of lavender blue, opal pink, or pale violet.

Within the genus *Chionodoxa* lies a case of mistaken identity. The common blue glory-of-the-snow has been grown, loved, and sold under the name *C. luciliae* for a very long time. It will probably continue to go by that name despite the fact that it's an impostor. The true *C. luciliae* from western Turkey is a smaller, less floriferous garden bulb, while the robust one we've been growing all these years is actually *C. siehei,* also from western Turkey.

The question must be asked: Who cares? The answer is, people who love a botanical mystery. I bring it up only because I think both species are in cultivation. I often see small glory-of-the-snow in old gardens. Since surrounding snowdrops and snowflakes stay full size, I've been puzzled by the apparent decline in vigor of the chionodoxas. My theory is that the smaller plants are long-term survivors, planted and shared by gardeners before *C. siehei* was introduced to western horticulture late in the nineteenth century. Nurseries apparently abandoned the smaller species in favor of the big one but continued to offer it under the same name. I may not have solved the mystery, but it's an explanation that satisfies my inquiring mind.

# 6

# SPRING

## *Bounty Across the Land*

Spring ripples across the country, painting a colorful trail from the South and West as the warmth moves inland. The retreat of winter leaves the land moist from melting snow and spring rain, and abundant sunshine encourages an explosion of plant growth. There's a bounty of bulbs from coast to coast. Gardeners see the fulfillment of their autumn labor and bask (time permitting) in the glories of the most colorful of seasons.

It's hard to wipe the grin off a gardener's face at this time of year, but the seasonal transformation sometimes comes with a price. Gentle as the face of spring can be, it can turn in an instant. Tumultuous masses of air collide, bringing torrents of rain, hail, and violent winds. Streams and rivers jump their banks, or if jet streams dictate, they receive no rain and slow to a trickle. A gardener attempts to take it in stride, savoring the triumphs and accepting the failures.

*Raised beds provide adequate drainage, ensuring the continued good health and multiplication of double 'Mt. Tacoma' tulips amid forget-me-nots.*

The tough gardeners I know have seen it all, and every disaster that strikes makes them stronger and smarter. I love these people. They're like a long-distance support group. Late Connecticut frost has nipped Mary Kay's emerging lilies. Daffodils wither under the rainless Virginia skies in Phillip's garden. Gophers have gotten into Ann's tulips. Torrential California rain has turned Ken's garden to mud. The unrelenting Wyoming wind has sucked Pat's garden dry. Lauren has been hailed out—again. Each of us knows what it takes to make a garden, and we feel the pain of another's bad fortune. Yet the tide always turns, and we get on with the activity that makes us who we are. It's spring, and all things are possible.

# Southern Hospitality

I'm always envious when I visit my southern friends in March and April. They're harvesting beets and spinach before I've managed to get my seeds in the ground. Their gardens are full and lush, and I hear myself exclaiming "cool" and "wow" and "wonderful," like a broken record. One of my visits must be a strain on my hosts' nerves.

I marvel at the wonders they coax from the soil, such as amaryllis. South American *Hippeastrum,* as the plants are properly called, remind me of the diversity of bulbs that southerners enjoy. The flaring trumpets of amaryllis look so formal in the pots on my sun porch that I'm startled how natural they appear in a real garden. The smaller-flowered hybrids such as 'Scarlet Baby', terra-cotta pink and white 'Spotty', or pale yellow 'Germa' are more resilient in rain and wind than the big-headed beauties. They nestle among columbines, pansies, and flowering tobacco, their straight stems adding structure rather than standing out like a sore thumb. The antique hybrid x *johnsonii,* known as St.

**A** *southern classic, St. Joseph's lily (Amaryllis x* johnsonii), *multiplies and blooms reliably.*

Joseph's lily, is a southern specialty noted for its dependable nature and outstanding long red trumpets with central white stripes on the petals. It can take some frost and damp winter soil and is the most durable amaryllis throughout the South. Ropes of purple heart (*Setcreasea pallida*) twined at its feet set it off dramatically.

Aztec lily, *Sprekelia formosissima,* is a relative of amaryllis from Mexico. The shape of the flowers is distinctly different, with a prominent space between the top three petals and the three on the bottom. This arrangement is said to resemble the hilt of a Jacobean sword, hence the rarely used folk name *Jacobean lily* (most of us are just not up on our medieval weaponry). Its crimson flowers, seemingly dusted with gold, appear on shorter stems than most amaryllis, growing to less than a foot tall. It dwells on rocky hills throughout much of Mexico and into Central and South America. Aztec lily's narrow green leaves grow through the summer months and it multiplies by offsets that can be detached to start new colonies. The selections 'Orient Red' and 'Peru' exhibit far more vigor than the common 'Superba', which grows best as a potted plant. A carpet of 'Iron Cross' oxalis looks fine shading its feet in a well-drained, afternoon-shaded spot.

Southern wildflowers dazzle every tourist. They flourish during spring and fizzle as heat takes hold. Some of them rely on their bulbous roots to carry them through the heat or drought, such as the spiderworts. Northern gardeners often grow *Tradescantia virginiana* and its many selections, but nothing beats the specimens grown in the South. They bloom early and profusely, opening their three-petaled purple, white, pink, or magenta flowers in the morning sun. The first rain lily of the year appears, the pretty Atamasco lily, *Zephyranthes atamasco,* native to swampy woods and fields from Alabama to Florida and north to Virginia. The common name comes from a Native American name, but because it blooms in April and May, it is sometimes called the Easter lily of the South. Moist, acidic soil enriched with humus, such as that found beneath azaleas or dogwoods, suits the bulbs. Their sweet scent highlights the white flowers with greenish yellow centers, held on slender six-to-twelve-inch stems above thin leaves that emerge in winter.

# Heirloom Iris

The wildflowers are joined by bulbs that have become a part of the natural landscape. Around old homesteads or even where no trace of them lingers, the white flags of *Iris albicans* bloom in midspring. A purple form is sometimes mixed in with the white. Native to Yemen on the Arabian Peninsula, this durable species flourishes on moist clay that bakes dry in summer. With their drooping falls, high standards, and moderate stature—about fifteen inches—the flowers possess a decidedly old-fashioned look with their bright yellow beards. Gardeners often call them the "cemetery white" iris, and they are indeed found flourishing amid ancient gravestones. This association dates back deeply in time, as *Iris albicans* was planted on the graves of fallen Muslim warriors as Islam spread across Africa and into Spain. The Spaniards brought the iris and the custom to Mexico and Texas.

*Iris florentina* blooms shortly before the "cemetery white" variety and could easily be confused with it since both are white. The falls of *I. florentina* are longer, the stems are better branched, and its flowers smell like violets. This is not a true species but a stable clone of *Iris germanica* that has long been grown around Florence for its pleasantly scented rhizomes that are sold as orris root. This old white iris may often be found in old farm gardens where it makes a dependable show. Whereas many bearded iris may rot, this one is very resistant.

Dutch iris (*Iris* x *hollandica*) performs admirably in the South and on the West Coast, and it's one of the few exotic bulbs that can tolerate life in the desert Southwest, as long as it is grown in an irrigated garden. The parentage of Dutch iris includes a number of species native to a limited area that includes southern France, Spain, Portugal, and North Africa. These parents are all found growing on dry, rocky, usually heavy soil. Dutch iris have an open, angular shape to their flowers.

Combined with their stiff carriage and limited foliage, this is an asset in borders among sprawling perennials like *Verbena* 'Homestead' and rounded mounds of dianthus. While the classic lavender blue varieties such as 'Wedgwood' or 'Sapphire Beauty' are understandably popular, there is something to be said for the white and custard-yellow forms like 'Cream Beauty' or 'Lemon Queen', which are especially effective planted with larkspur, Jerusalem sage (*Phlomis fruticosa*), and bronze fennel.

Due to its origin in Yemen, "cemetery white" iris (Iris albicans) *survives almost total neglect.*

A*lmost at home on the Texas range, Middle Eastern* Gladiolus byzantinus *contrasts boldly with bluebonnet, ox-eye daisy, pansy, ice plant, and buffalo rose* (Callirhoe involucrata).

*Gladiolus byzantinus* colonized southern states with the first pioneers. Native to Spain, Italy, and North Africa, it is found in the wild growing on stony clay soil. It bears up to fifteen wine red flowers on a graceful arching stem above fans of pleated leaves. Modern "baby" or "hardy" hybrids *(Gladiolus x colvillei)* have a look similar to these old "corn flags," but their parentage is from South African species rather than the Mediterranean. Consequently, they need more than the clay soil that satisfies *G. byzantinus* but will settle in for an extended period if planted in well-drained loam. They offer larger flowers in white, pink, and salmon, but none matches the vigor of the wine red gladiolus that has been handed down from generation to generation. It's as much a part of the spring as bluebonnets or ox-eye daisies and Texas sage *(Leucophyllum frutescens).*

The fascinating blossoms of Chinese ground orchid, *Bletilla striata,* may look exotic, but the plant is an "easy keeper." Native to subtropical forests of southern China and Japan, the tuberous rhizome sends up leaves that unfold like accordions,

Even though its pink flowers have closed for the day, an underpinning of Oxalis purpurata var. bowiei looks pleasing with sprays of Chinese ground orchid (Bletilla striata) in the Lockhart, Texas, garden of Tom and Diane Peace.

as well as foot-tall angular, curving stems with the flowers spaced well apart. The small carmine pink flowers have deeper pink nectary guides. Chinese ground orchid thrives in a humus-rich spot beneath trees, nestled between their roots with lamium, violas, and oxalis. A white-flowered form glows in the shade, and there's also one with a crisp white edge on the leaves to accentuate the white blossoms.

# South African Bulbs for the South

Very few South African bulbs naturalize in the South, since the summer heat, moisture, and heavy soils usually do them in. A few exceptions that demonstrate tolerance to the extremes of southern living include *Lapeirousia, Homeria, Rhodohypoxis, Zantedeschia, Tritonia,* and, of course, *Crinum.* They usually come from regions outside the Cape Province that have hotter, rainier summers.

Painted petals, *Lapeirousia laxa* (also called *Anomatheca laxa*), comes as a small surprise in old gardens. It seeds itself around, springing up beneath shrubs and stands of iris and columbines. The simple, flat flowers are about the size of a quarter and are coral red with a drop of deeper red "paint" at the base of the petals. They are held on one-sided spikes up to a foot tall. Painted petals is native to wet fields of the subtropical Transvaal Province. I remember seeing them in an old garden in San Antonio, where their bright blossoms edged a path leading to the garden shed. I was told by the elderly gardener that the volunteer corms were never a nuisance but had held their ground for a quarter of a century.

Gardeners often associate cape tulip, *Homeria collina,* with winter and spring on the West Coast. It's a feature of southern gardens as well, taking advantage of cool spring weather to display its salmon or honey-colored cups. Rose star, *Rhodohypoxis baurii,* is found growing in the Drakensberg Mountains. The corms produce short, pleated leaves that appear to be gray green because of the tiny hairs. The flowers are produced on single stems less than six inches high, but an established group puts on quite a show. The simple flowers, less than an inch across, look like ones a child would draw with a crayon. Selected forms flower in shades of pale pink, rose, and white, as well as bicolors. Good drainage and light shade suit them best.

The classic white calla lily, *Zantedeschia aethiopica,* is one of the most vigorous plants across South Africa, delving its rhizomes deeply into the mucky soil along streams and in boggy fields where winter rainfall collects. The white, vellum-textured spathes have become a symbol of high style and gracious living, but in its homeland it's often called the ditch lily or pig lily. During dry periods, it lives off its underground reservoirs. This trait makes it an adaptable plant that grows readily in divergent climates as long as frost doesn't penetrate the soil deeply. It thrives best in partial shade in most parts of the South and in moist spots on the West Coast.

Flame freesia, *Tritonia crocata,* comes from the southwestern side of the Cape Peninsula, so while it is a winter bloomer that dies down in late spring, the corms are accustomed to regular summer moisture. It grows equally well in parts of the South and on the West Coast. That's lucky, since the flowers are lovely, appearing on graceful, arching stems about a foot long above linear leaves. Selected forms bloom in sherbet shades of frosted peach, salmon, cream, and amber yellow. The similarity to freesia is obvious, but the flowers are quite distinct. The six petals are translucent on either side of their base. When they open wide, the little cellophane windows are very appealing.

Species of *Crinum* that thrive in the South come from several regions. One of the best is the Orange River lily, *Crinum bulbispermum,* a riverbank dweller from eastern parts of South Africa. What makes it so welcome is its long season of bloom and the fact that it is extremely difficult to kill. The bulbs pull themselves deeply into the soil (which makes it hardy as far north as Virginia), producing long succulent leaves in part shade or sun. Leafless stems appear sporadically throughout the year but most heavily in late winter and spring. The lily-like trumpets cluster at the top of the stem and make a fine show of four-inch-long white flowers with raspberry pink stripes. Some gardeners favor the pure white form. *Crinum bulbispermum*

V*intage clumps of Orange River lily* (Crinum bulbispermum) *are a spring feature in San Antonio and other points south.*

figures in the parentage of several hybrids known as milk and wine lilies with various degrees of the classic pink and white striped petals.

Like the cemetery white iris, *Crinum bulbispermum* can often be found blooming at the foot of headstones in old cemeteries throughout the South. Some might find it odd that horticulturists haunt old graveyards wherever they go, but these areas offer a unique view into the past. The flowers that survive there—iris, grape hyacinths, daffodils, roses, and such—tell about the gardening tastes of another era, and their survival suggests that these flowers still deserve a place in our contemporary gardens.

The white flowers of grand crinum, *Crinum asiaticum,* are quite different from most other crinums, with thin, wispy petals that impart a spidery appearance. Indigenous to the Asian tropics, it fares well along the Gulf and Atlantic Coasts where frost rarely threatens. There, the giant bulbs develop enormous clusters of evergreen spears that add to the landscape even when the plant is not in bloom. The thick flower spikes appear most often in fall and winter. Countless species and hybrids of *Crinum* are suitable for southern and West Coast gardens, although most bloom later in the year. It is easy to become fanatical about them, and those bit by the bug order by mail, grow them from seed, trade offsets with friends, and even visit old graveyards.

# On the Coast

Northern gardeners envy their West Coast counterparts for their frost-free soil and the exotic flowers that fill it. The envy factor goes the other way, too, with residents of California, Arizona, and Oregon missing tulips and peonies. What drives the horticultural world is the quest for adaptive plants that flower for everyone. My friend Panayoti has promised me seedlings of a South African protea collected high in the mountains. That should be enough for anybody, but it never is.

Bulb companies sometimes offer Cape bulbs like *Freesia, Babiana,* and *Sparaxis* to northern gardeners. The results are spotty, at best, since they are winter growers that bloom in spring. There's no way to reset their clocks and force them to flower in summer up north.

Freesias belong in a Mediterranean climate; that's why they're so adapted to the West Coast. Old colonies that have prospered for decades bloom in old neighborhoods, often springing up through a ground cover of ivy or vinca. The old strains of freesia are not especially showy—the flowers are milky white tinged with plum pink and splashed with gold in the throats—but the fragrance is wonderful. It's a replay of an oft-told story: that in breeding for bigger and brighter flowers, the scent has been forgotten. It's happened to sweet peas, flowering tobacco, and roses. I read a report that claims that nine out of ten people can't detect the smell of freesia at all, thereby justifying its disappearance in modern hybrids. I don't buy it. I remember a dinner party where freesias were the centerpiece and every one of the twelve people in the room could smell them quite clearly. May I suggest that the nine out of ten people in the report were given the wrong ones to sniff? Some of the modern hybrids do retain the classic vanilla-honey-lemon-gardenia fragrance, especially the lavender and yellow ones. The white ones smell like ground black pepper to me.

Freesias are pretty enough to grow with or without scent. I admire them clustered informally with calendulas or senecios. My friend Ken, who gardens northeast of the Bay Area, grows golden yellow freesias at the base of a trellis supporting *Tropaeolum tricolorum.* This tuberous-rooted nasturtium from Chile and Bolivia warrants close inspection for its spurred orange flowers tipped in black, highlighting the

Yellow *freesia cluster beneath a bamboo trellis supporting* Tropaeolum tricolorum *in Ken Monger's garden in Rodeo, California.*

yellow interior. *T. tuberosum* comes from the same region and is golden orange with red spurs, while *T. speciosum* is the scarlet flame nasturtium often admired in English gardens, draped across hedges and scampering along fences. The latter likes moist, peaty soil, but all three succeed in cool (but not freezing), humid conditions of parts of California and the Pacific Northwest that are similar to their native habitats in the low, coastal Andes.

Babianas are noted not for their scents but for the vibrancy of their cupped flowers. The purple-toned flowers are arranged along thin stems much like freesias, growing less than a foot high above pleated, olive green leaves. They close under clouds but sparkle after a shower. *Babiana stricta* is the most widely grown species, with many selections and hybrids in shades of lavender and violet. *B. pulchra* is another good purple bloomer, while the wine-cup babiana, *B. rubrocyanea*, bears deep blue flowers with an intense red purple center. *B. villosa* is magenta red with black

A *hillside planting in Berkeley designed by Sean Hogan features violet baboon root* (Babiana stricta) *and an opportunistic cape tulip* (Homeria ochroleuca *var.* aurantiaca) *with design ideas of its own.*

anthers. A hillside or bank with good drainage is a handsome sight when the babianas burst into bloom in late spring, perhaps punctuated by the rosettes of aloes, haworthias, sedums, and other succulents that hold the soil after the babianas go dormant.

*Sparaxis tricolor* is often called harlequin flower for the bands of color emanating from the center of the blossom. The middle is yellow surrounded by black stenciling, which dissolves into the red petals (which can also be cream, orange, or purple). The stems are thin, rigid, and about a foot tall, and the ribbed, olive gray leaves stay low. Harlequin flower is the most commonly grown of this Cape genus, but the species has never been very populous and is now a rarity in its homeland. *Sparaxis elegans* displays flowers colored like no other. Its six overlapping, rounded petals are peach with a bar of violet at the base encircling the grape purple center and curled anthers. Have I mentioned the word *exotic*?

*Scilla peruviana* makes northerners envious of the huge, domed flower heads of multiple, violet blue blossoms. It is not grown much in California anymore; a friend told me it's considered a "little old lady" plant. I'm amazed, since it's become a hot property in the rest of the country as a potted plant in winter for its very contemporary appearance. Rosettes of flat leaves send up strong, curving two-foot stems. Despite the name *Scilla peruviana* and the common name Cuba lily, the bulb is native to Spain and Portugal. *Scilla natalensis* is the grandest of the squills. As its name suggests, it is native to the Natal Province of South Africa. It would take a large pot to accommodate the giant bulbs, looking like they're made of brown papiér-mâché, that push themselves out of the soil. A rosette of spiked, broad foliage appears as the purple-tinted stems begin to open. The flowers are small and amethyst purple but are produced by the hundreds at the top of three-foot stems.

Many species of African gladiolus grace coastal gardens, but the outstanding

*O*ld-fashioned yet fabulous, Cuba lily (Scilla peruviana) *persists with little care in many parts of the West Coast.*

The night scent of Gladiolus tristis attracts nocturnal moths, but its graceful, pale flowers captivate visitors by day at the Botanical Gardens of the University of California at Berkeley.

spring-blooming one is *Gladiolus tristis,* from seasonally marshy areas of South Africa. *Tristis* means sad, but I don't associate sadness with this flower. The pale yellow blossoms are graceful and, best of all, sweetly scented. My friend Sean Hogan, who used to be curator of South African plants at the University of California Botanical Garden at Berkeley, told me he'd always doubted that this gladiolus was fragrant. One night, he stayed late at the gardens and suddenly began to notice the enticing sweetness, like honeysuckle and cloves, on the evening breeze. He had allowed *Gladiolus tristis* to seed itself in portions of the garden but was quick to uproot seedlings that sprouted in the middle of drifts of low-growing plants like *Babiana* and *Lachenalia* for fear of crowding them.

Ixias or corn lilies wave their thin wands in the breeze. Oval buds, alternately placed on the sides of each stem, open like tiny tulips under the sun but stay closed in cloudy weather. Most corn lily hybrids in gold, orange, white, or pink are related to yellow *Ixia maculata* or cream-flushed pink *Ixia paniculata,* the easiest species to grow on a sunny, well-drained slope. The beautiful turquoise green–flowered corn lily, *Ixia viridiflora,* is highly esteemed by collectors but tends to dwindle over time unless grown, like many Cape bulbs, where it dries out in summer.

*Moraea* fills the role of *Iris* in Africa. The family resemblance is strong, with the linear foliage and the flowers' standards and falls easily identifiable. What sets the plants apart is the richly colored "peacock eye" on the base of outer petals. *Moraea aristata* is white with a black-rimmed blue-and-yellow eye. The flowers of *M. tripetala* can be blue, yellow, or pink with a dark blue eye, while those of *M. villosa* may be violet, blue, mauve, peach, or white with dark-rimmed blue patch. There are many species and hybrids, all with lovely flowers, and gardeners who fall for peacock iris should buy every variety they come across.

Bugle lilies have long been a fixture in the Pacific states. The stiff, showy spikes of the tubular flowers of South African *Watsonia* can't be missed in spring and early summer. Dwarf species that stay under two feet tall include lilac rose *Watsonia laccata* (formerly *W. brevifolia*), white-tinged pink *W. humilis,* and pink *W. alectroides.* The showiest bugle lilies are the taller hybrids, bred from several species such as *W. borbonica* (also called *W. pyramidata*). They look grand growing at the back of the border in vivid shades of pink, coral, and red or claiming their territories in small strips between the sidewalk and street in older neighborhoods.

The western coast of South America has much in common with our own West Coast. Many plants from this region find a home in California, although South America is not nearly as rich in bulbs as South Africa. A spring bloomer that merits attention is *Libertia formosa* from Chile. Sprays of its saucer-shaped white flowers, small but abundantly produced, crown the top of the grassy leaves that look like Siberian iris. The foliage is an asset long after the flowers fade, gracing gardens in sun or partial shade. Orange seed pods appear in late summer and autumn. When in bloom, the plants look particularly good with silver plants such as dusty miller.

# Narcissus for Naturalizing

I can't imagine that I have anything to say about daffodils that hasn't been expressed—or felt—by others. What I can offer is some insight in selecting daffodils that live to a ripe old age. Only true species seed themselves and cover more territory with time. Hybrids "perennialize" by offsets, growing thicker through

*L*arge drifts of various daffodils stay showy over an extended period in Phillip Watson's garden in Fredericksburg, Virginia.

*Don't hate them because they're beautiful one moment and horrid the next—the expanding leaves of ferns and lady's mantle will disguise the daffodil leaves as they fade.*

duplicating themselves vegetatively. *Narcissus* are so numerous that they had to be sorted out into twelve categories, from the wild species to the big-cupped hybrids and everything in between. Wondrous new hybrids get cover-girl treatment in the fall catalogues each season. Today's sensation becomes yesterday's flash in the pan.

Good, plain yellow trumpet daffodils work for most of the country. These are the 'King Alfred' types (somewhere along the line, the pure 'King Alfred' was infiltrated with impostors) represented by trumpet types like 'Carlton', 'Unsurpassable', 'Dutch Master', or 'Golden Harvest', and in the deep South, 'Carlton' and 'St. Keverne'. They're dandy and are sold by the millions. What many gardeners forget is an under-planting for daffodils. Any shallow-rooted perennial (such as creeping veronicas) or self-sowing annual (such as forget-me-nots) planted above the bulbs shows the flowers to better advantage than bare earth and shades the soil during hot summers.

I'm suspicious of exotic types like double daffodils and split-cup varieties, even if some of them may be persistent growers. 'Rip van Winkle' (*N. pumilus* var. *plenus*) is a horrid little thing that looks like it's been pureed in the blender. Its cup has been replaced with a whirl of petals that looks like shredded crepe paper, but it's been around forever and is, unfortunately, difficult to kill. I don't grow any doubles, except for a cream-colored one with yellow streaks that looks like a half-beaten egg. It came labeled as 'Actaea', and I've been pulling it up whenever I spot it. The split-cup or split-corona types, where the normal trumpet has been replaced by pulled-back segments that fold back against the petals, can be rather pretty but never stick around for me. Like any other bulb, growing *Narcissus* becomes a trial-by-error process in each garden.

I'm no traditionalist when it comes to colors: The white ones or bicolors are just fine with me, and I'm becoming fonder of the varieties with pink cups, even if the shade should be more truthfully described as apricot or salmon pink (true pinks are now available, but I have not seen them). A planting of one of the older apricot pink ones, 'Salome', still stands out in my mind. At the Chicago Botanic Garden, in its famous walled garden, 'Salome' emerges beneath the new, salmon orange leaves of *Spirea* x *bumalda* 'Goldflame'. I've never much cared for this shrub. The spring foliage seems more appropriate for autumn, but I thought the tie-in with 'Salome' made sense of it. I also like 'Salome' or the great cream-white 'Ice Follies' in a woodland planting among bluebells and periwinkle, where the intrusion of bright yellow would spoil the tranquillity of the pastel flowers set against verdant foliage.

Hybrids with orange cups need a good jolt of contrasting color from companions. I'm thinking about yellow-petaled 'Ceylon' (from the large-cupped division), white-petaled 'Barrett-Browning' (from the small-cupped division), or white-petaled 'Geranium' (from the tazetta or paperwhite division, but remarkably hardy). The latter is one of my favorite daffodils, not only for its good looks and good smell, but because I can grow it in a pot indoors the first year, transplant it to the garden, and it will bloom the following spring. I first planted it with pale yellow cowslips. Dull. I added some grape hyacinths. Better. Some brilliant blue forget-me-nots moved in of their own accord. Perfection.

Many gardeners have a special affection for the old pheasant's-eye narcissus, *N. poeticus* var. *recurvus,* native to mountain pastures from France to Greece, and now sometimes found wild in the Northeast. It's also called the poet's daffodil, but I've never read an ode to these white-petaled flowers with the distinctive green eye of the red-rimmed yellow cup. The most famous of the poeticus hybrids is heirloom 'Actaea', although there are several variations on the same theme, including smaller-flowered 'Milan' and shorter 'Cantabile'.

There's nothing more disheartening in spring than a fresh batch of daffodils with their faces bowed over in the mud. This happens for me nearly every year, so I've increasingly relied on later-blooming varieties like 'Actaea' or miniatures and smaller-flowered varieties. Moisture doesn't weigh them down as much, and some right themselves even after a snowstorm, which regularly snaps the stems of the top-heavy trumpet types.

Cyclamineus daffodils are easily identified by the flared-back petals, reminding me of a horse whose pinned back ears show he does not intend to share his grain. They are principally derived from *N. cyclamineus,* native to damp mountain meadows and riverbanks in northwestern Portugal and Spain. They bloom early and have relatively small leaves. They include 'Peeping Tom', pure yellow with a very long trumpet; deep yellow 'February Gold'; 'Foundling', white with a pink cup; petite yellow 'Little Witch'; and golden yellow 'Jack Snipe'. 'Jenny' could almost be classified as the cult hit of this group. Her ivory flowers have earned an almost fanatical following.

Jonquilla daffodils bear several small, fragrant flowers and adapt to the hot summers of much of the South and Midwest. That's not much of a surprise, considering that the principal parent is *N. jonquilla* from Spain and Portugal. These clustered flowers are often what southerners have in mind when they speak of jonquils. 'Lintie' is yellow with a red-banded cup. 'Pipit' has pale yellow petals surrounding a deliciously scented white cup. 'Quail' is a heavy-blooming, deep bronzy yellow. 'Trevithian' is an heirloom variety that I especially like for its clusters of deep yellow, flat-cupped flowers with a knockout fragrance.

Miniature daffodils descend from divergent breeding lines but are grouped together because they generally stay under six inches tall. They don't necessarily need

a spot in the rock garden, but it's a good showcase for them. Miniatures look great clustered along paths, in rock walls, or in woodland gardens. 'Hawera' bears many little pale yellow bells. The canary yellow petals of 'Jumblie' are accented by its orange cup. One sibling of similar breeding is sulfur yellow 'Quince'; another is buttercup yellow, golden-cupped 'Tête-à-Tête'. White petals circle the yellow centers of 'Minnow'. 'Sundial' has short, flat-cupped yellow flowers with a green eye. All are superb.

A *can't-miss combination:* Narcissus *'Thalia'* is *massed beneath a crabapple.*

Angel's tears, *N. triandrus,* is found growing wild in hedgerows and rocky places in Spain, Portugal, and France. Ivory white 'Ice Wings' is tall and graceful, with the down-facing flowers characteristic of the Triandus division. 'Liberty Bells' is pure yellow, and 'Tuesday's Child' is white with a yellow cup. Perhaps the most famous and beloved offspring of *N. triandrus* is pure white 'Thalia'. Around since 1916, it lands near the top of a list of daffodils that perennialize. Could this be the most beautiful daffodil? It has a texture like kid gloves and is exquisite paired with white pieris or massed beneath pink crabapples. I stole both of these ideas from designer Phillip Watson from Virginia, whose fondness for—and extravagance with—'Thalia' is probably keeping several Dutch growers in business.

# The Trouble with Tulips

When I was a boy, my family lived in a little town on the eastern plains of Colorado. It had been founded by Russian immigrants who broke the sod to grow wheat. It's a harsh land of contrasting extremes, from cold winter to searing summer. And always, the wind blows. I have an early memory (I was only five) of my mom tying my brother and me to a telephone booth as we waited on the highway for the bus to Denver so we wouldn't blow away.

My mom struggled with her garden, as did the other gardeners in town, in the dry, inhospitable clay. There were many failures, but there were rewards, too, when the melting snow coaxed a multitude of tulips to bloom near our front porch. They simply came with the house, planted many years before we came to live there. It was then that I really began to take an interest in flowers, and I buried my nose in their multicolored cups. Gardeners rarely pay much attention to the faint, musty scent of tulips, but I treasure it to this day.

The tulips survived around our porch for the very good reason that the plains of Colorado differ little from the steppes and high plains of east-central Asia. Most tulips trace their ancestry to this region. Whether they naturalize or not depends on the hybrid itself and whether conditions are horrible enough for it. By that, I mean cold in winter, moist in spring, and hot and dry in summer.

Tulips are mysterious. The ones introduced into Europe in the sixteenth century were already hybrids, cultivated by the Turks. Nearly four hundred years of Dutch breeding has further obscured their genetic trail. Botanists theorize that the most significant parent of our garden tulips is *Tulipa armena,* native to Turkey, southern

Russia, Iran, and Iraq. No one is sure. For the most part, we must guess at the parentage of modern tulips. The tulips that have been handed down to us are direct descendants from those bred by the Turks. The offspring of the tulips that survived best in European gardens for several centuries are the ones available to us. What is a good "doer" in Amsterdam is not always a success here, but their complex genetic makeup often reasserts itself in their performance in our own gardens.

Many hybrids perform for only a short period of time wherever they are planted. They are bedding tulips, planted for one glorious spring display and that's often it. There are fifteen official classes of tulips, not including the true species. Pretty pictures in catalogues may be tempting, but experienced gardeners plant proven varieties and experiment with novelties on a limited basis.

By and large, hybrid tulips were not meant for the eastern half of the country, or the South, or the West Coast, or the Pacific Northwest. That doesn't mean that there aren't some tulips that do well in those regions, but they require careful selection and just as careful placement. Their roots are deep in eastern Asia. The region of our country with the most similar geographic and climatic features is the Rocky Mountain West, essentially the whole mountain time zone. That isn't meant to sound nearly as grim as it does for gardeners outside my own region, but I still feel like some demented football fan shouting, "We're number one!" I'm making an honest assessment. Tulips that transcend the regions of the country are rare, but there are a few.

The best tulips for naturalizing, apart from the true species, come from several groups. The Darwin hybrids grow like weeds in the Rocky Mountain West and have the best shot for survival elsewhere. Darwin hybrids, which debuted shortly after World War II, were derived by crossing the famous Fosteriana tulip 'Red Emperor' with a Darwin tulip. The Darwins were nineteenth-century selections of so-called cottage tulips (sometimes called single late tulips) salvaged from cottage gardens in England and France. What we have here then is the cross between a vigorous red species (*T. fosteriana*) from the mountainsides of Bukhara and long-term survivors from the earliest days of Tulipomania in Europe. No wonder they're tough.

Darwin hybrids exhibit excellent tolerance to cold, but a few, such as red 'Oxford', perform adequately even in southern California. Like most tulips, they tolerate drought during their dormant summer period, but more important, they can stand a wetter summer. This may be due to the hundreds of years of "field testing" in English and French cottage gardens, when the ancestors that couldn't take summer moisture died out.

*The world's most popular tulip, Darwin hybrid 'Apeldoorn,' puts up with poor soil, drought, and even a dusting of overnight snow.*

At about two feet high, Darwin hybrids come mainly in shades of yellow and red, including the world's most popular tulip, 'Apeldoorn'. When people think of a red tulip, this is the one. 'Golden Apeldoorn' is the classic canary yellow form. Dozens more—from cream yellow 'Jewel of Spring' to fragrant 'Orange Sun' and tangerine 'Daydream'—brighten the midspring garden. Pinks are represented as well, from reddish pink 'Big Chief' and lipstick rose 'Elizabeth Arden', named for the cosmetics magnate who was also an accomplished gardener (and must have had a great manicurist), to the fairly recent introductions 'Pink Impression' and mauve pink 'Ollioules', named for a French town that defies my attempts to pronounce it properly or even find it on a map. They appear to have the staying power of their illustrious cousins. A new line of "Darwin hybrid type" or "perennial" tulips has made a big splash in recent years and is offered by several retailers. Gardeners, who must often treat tulips as annuals, get at least five years of solid bloom from them. The selection is still limited to basic red, cream, rose, and scarlet with yellow edge.

Another class of dependable tulips that perhaps surpasses the Darwin hybrids in beauty is the lily form. These flowers display pointed petals that flare gracefully, although they don't look much like lilies to me. An interesting note is that this is the flower form that the Turks found the most desirable, while Europeans liked the cup or egg-shaped varieties best. Lily-flowered tulips trace their ancestry back to the venerable cottage tulips and an old line from Turkey called *T. retroflexa* (though it is not a true species), noted for its pointed, reflexed petals. Once again, this pedigree often confirms toughness and adaptability.

These lily-flowered tulips, borne on willowy, two-foot stems, are exceptionally graceful and lovely in a garden setting. They integrate well into perennial borders where they compete well and don't mind regular summer moisture as long as the soil drains freely. Outstanding track records have been established by lily-form tulips such as 'White Triumphator'; yellow 'West Point'; mauve, white-edged 'Ballade'; and

*Lily-form tulips, characterized by pointed petals, don't get any better than 'West Point', seemingly adrift in a sea of forget-me-nots.*

rose pink 'Mariette'. There are other worthy lily-flowering tulips, but 'Mariette' is my favorite. The garden would be completely overrun by it if I did not show the little restraint I can still muster.

Another pink tulip that deserves mention is 'Angelique'. It is not so doubled as to be unrecognizable as a tulip, and some gardeners are understandably fond of its clear pink petals, sometimes flecked with deeper pink. While it rarely can be said to multiply, this tulip does persist for a long time in some gardens. 'Angelique' comes from the class of double late tulips, none of which can match it in vigor, although white 'Mt. Tacoma' comes close.

Multiflowering tulips have not yet been elevated to the status of an official class, but their unique habit of producing three to five blossoms on each stem certainly sets them apart. They often last for an extended period, making them a good investment. 'Happy Family' is a deep rose; 'Toronto' is salmon red; and 'Praestens Fusilier' is scarlet.

The Kaufmanniana, Fosteriana, and Greigii tulips are descended from true Asian species, even if they have been extensively interbred with one another. All three are relatively short, relatively early to flower, and make good garden plants. The waterlily tulip, *T. kaufmanniana,* comes from Turkestan. Its flowers open flat in the sun. It is represented by such fine varieties as 'Stresa', yellow with wide scarlet bands on the exterior petals, and 'Johann Strauss' with rose red petals edged in yellow. There are many more. 'Ancilla', as I recounted earlier, gets my vote as the loveliest.

*T. fosteriana* is native to Bukhara and features huge vermilion flowers on stocky stems. Classic Fosteriana tulips include 'Red Emperor', 'White Emperor' (also called 'Purissima'), 'Pink Emperor', 'Orange Emperor', and, oddly enough, 'Yellow Empress'. Go figure. One that outdoes this entire royal clan is 'Zombie'. Its cream petals are flushed with dark raspberry red. Few gardeners would rush out to buy a flower called 'Zombie', but this is a fabulous tulip that my friend Jane planted in her garden around 1950. It is still going strong, and everybody who asks about it remembers the name.

*T. greigii* from Turkestan also bears large red cup-shaped flowers on short stems. Its distinctive foliage sets it apart and tags its descendants with maroon markings that look like rows of highway stripes repeated over and over. These handsome leaves complement Greigii tulips such as coral 'Sweet Lady', porcelain rose 'Corsage', and charming-as-a-folk-tale 'Red Riding Hood'. These, and the rest of the Greigii types, are great tulips.

# Species Tulips

Gardeners who ignore the species tulips are really missing out. Some are of more interest to collectors, but many are delightfully pretty. Best of all, they grow vigorously when given half a chance and are suitable for borders, rock gardens, lawns, and everywhere in between. They set seed—as opposed to hybrids, which are sterile or nearly so—and can expand their territories. The species, on the whole, thrive under a wide range of conditions. In the wild, most are found in clay soil, buried rather deeply despite the small size of the bulbs. They usually grow on sloping ground that dries out considerably in summer. In my experience, tulip bulbs tend to work themselves up and down in the soil to suit themselves. Get these bulbs about four inches deep—perhaps a bit more in sandy soil—and they'll make the best of the situation.

*Tulipa tarda* is one of the most versatile of the species. Native to Turkestan, it grows well for most gardeners who can provide good drainage, even in lightly shaded gardens planted with moisture-loving trilliums and hostas. The bulbs bulk up rapidly; in just a few years a single bulb may multiply to produce a dozen or more blossoms. The lemon yellow flowers fade to white at

*Each bulb of* Tulipa tarda *has multiplied in only three seasons to produce an entire bouquet of starry flowers, set off by* Phlox bifida *in my garden.*

their pointed tips. On sunny days they open into a star shape, although they are not very exciting during cloudy weather since the outside of the petals is reddish brown. During a rainy spring, their show is over before it's begun.

*Tulipa batalinii* grows on stony hillsides in central Asia. It, too, is dwarf at only four to six inches in height but in a short time makes big bunches that smother the leaves with flowers. The common form flowers in a pleasing shade of pale yellow, sometimes sold as 'Yellow Jewel'. 'Apricot Jewel' bears blossoms in a tantalizing (even appetizing) apricot tone. 'Bright Gem' is sulfur yellow, and 'Red Jewel' has red outside petals and a peach interior. 'Bronze Charm', said to be a hybrid between *T. batalinii* and *T. linifolia,* glows like a copper teakettle.

The little screaming red one that causes such excitement is *T. linifolia.* Its broad, pointed petals open to reveal a small dark interior base. The flowers rise on stems just six inches or so high above blue green leaves crimped like piecrust into wavy lines. *T. vvedenskyi,* also from central Asia, has a huskier appearance. Its brilliant flowers are quite enormous in relation to its short, ground-hugging leaves. It takes a stout stem to carry these flowers, which grow to about eight inches in height. Although these two species share a similar bright color, each displays a unique "personality" through its flower form. It would be pointless (and futile) to attempt to tone down the scarlet with pastel companions. An "in for a penny, in for a pound" attitude may prompt eye-popping pairings with purple rock cress, chartreuse *Euphorbia myrsinites,* or, for the truly bohemian, creeping phlox.

*Tulipa pulchella* is no longer determined to be a valid species by some authorities and has been lumped in with *T. humilis.* Gardeners and catalogues see it differently and continue to consider the species and its selections separately. These related bulbs grow wild from Iran through Asia Minor into the Caucasus, which may explain the variability in their looks, although they all grow about five inches high. *T. humilis,* as offered in the trade, is vivid pink with a yellow base.

*T. pulchella* tends to have rounder flowers and is represented by several distinct varieties. 'Violacea' is almost beet red with a black or yellow central blotch. 'Eastern Star' is magenta with an exotic olive center. 'Persian Pearl' is burgundy rose with a golden yellow base. All are stunning, but none affects me like the white form called 'Alba' or sometimes 'Albo coerulea oculata', which refers to its deep steel-blue eye. I'm not one of those gardeners who automatically thinks that the white form of any plant is superior, but I'm nuts for this one. I'll go out on a limb and call it the most beautiful tulip in my garden. The white petals have a silvery sheen, and the center is iridescent black fading to gunmetal blue. Since I've planted it all over the place, I can attest that it looks great with, among other things, the finely cut leaves of partridge feather *(Tanacetum densum* var. *amani)* in a dry, hot spot. Alas, it commands a price nearly triple the rest.

*Tulipa saxatilis* is native to Crete. No one can blame a gardener who falls under its spell, cast by lavender pink petals set off by a yellow center and glossy leaves. The only place I've ever seen decent specimens is on the West Coast, where the bulb thrives in sun or part shade as long as it dries out to bake under the summer sun. Pleasant partners for it include such pedestrian plants as variegated vinca or ice plants, as well as early annuals from the Mediterranean region, such as sweet alyssum and Virginia stock *(Malcomia maritima).*

Southerners take heart that lady tulip (*T. clusiana*) and *T. chrysantha* grow as well for them as for most of the rest of the country. The slender flowers of lady tulip grow above slender gray green leaves on stems up to ten inches tall. The blossoms are striped red and white, inspiring another folk name—peppermint stick tulip. The thin petals flare open to reveal an indigo central patch and purple anthers. *T. chrysantha* is similar except its stripes are yellow and red and it grows a few inches shorter. Some botanists consider them to be variants of the same species, distributed from Iran to the western Himalayas. Since *T. chrysantha* has never been found in the wild, it's possibly a "sport" of the lady tulip that occurred in a Turkish garden centuries ago, handed down from generation to generation.

# Offbeat Bulbs

More gardeners, I suspect, would plant more bulbs were it not for two big fears: First, they worry about the work involved in planting. It's a daunting task to dig holes for a couple hundred tulips or daffodils. It seems worth it when they bloom, but then there's the second big fear—the flowers fade and the foliage goes into an extended death scene more tragic than anything in grand opera.

I put out the effort for hybrid tulips and daffodils because I love them, but I'm increasingly enamored of many offbeat bulbs. They don't require deep planting, and their foliage disappears quickly and unobtrusively. They can also be worked in with existing perennials with little effort.

Grecian windflower, *Anemone blanda,* has a most unbulblike appearance. Its showy daisies in white, pink, or lavender blue bloom just inches off the ground, above leaves that resemble single parsley. Grecian windflowers bloom in sunny spots for many weeks in April and May unless smashed by a late snow. Catalogues offer varieties of selected

*Johnny-jump-ups infiltrate a colony of Grecian windflower* (Anemone blanda *'White Splendor'*).

color forms of which 'White Splendor', with large, white flowers, is the standout. I soak the brown, leathery tubers in lukewarm water overnight before I plant them three inches deep. It's difficult to tell which side is up (there's a depression with a round bump in it), so I usually insert them into the hole on their sides.

Sky blue lily, *Ixiolirion tataricum* (sometimes listed as *I. pallasii* or *I. montanum*), thrills me to pieces in late spring. I've added a hundred to my pastel perennial borders. Its foot-tall stems are topped by clusters of two-inch-long flaring trumpets of the clearest blue imaginable. It's best in full sun and well-drained soil because of its natural distribution in mountainous slopes and fields from Russia south to Turkey. Books often say this bulb is difficult to grow, and of course it is—in England—but in the western United States it flowers reliably and even seeds itself.

Among the most overlooked bulbs are alliums, the ornamental onions. Most bloom in very late spring and summer and so are covered in the following chapter, but Turkish onion, *Allium karataviense,* flowers in April or May depending on regional weather. It has three-inch balls of pale apricot pink, although it is a variable species and some flowers may be nearly white. Many alliums have insignificant foliage, but Turkish onion is an exception. Its leaves are broad, deep blue-green with a maroon edge, and make a pleasing counterpart to the flowers. I like to play up the foliage by contrasting it with the finely dissected leaves and white flowers of Mt. Atlas daisy (*Anacyclus depressus*). The undersides of these daisies, which close on cloudy days, are deep red. The foliage of silver-leaf plants like Scotch thistle (*Onopordum acanthium*) or rattlesnake master (*Eryngium yuccifolium*) add drama to the area. Like these partners, Turkish onion prefers dry, sunny spots similar to its homeland conditions in Turkestan and adjoining regions in central Asia.

I swore to myself when I began this project that I wouldn't make a big fuss over little-known bulbs of relative insignificance. I changed my mind. I probably would never have ordered Spanish hyacinth, *Brimeura amethystina,* of my own volition. I got it by mistake when I ordered white French-Roman hyacinths for my new garden several years ago. In the bustle of the first spring, I didn't even notice the mistake. It wasn't until the second season that the absence of hyacinth's sweet perfume made me take a closer look.

What I discovered was the white form of Spanish hyacinth, native to rocky slopes of the Pyrenees. It differs from French-Roman hyacinth in that its leaves are thin and grassy and its flowers are slender, even tubes. A small difference, but this little bulb has a special appeal when it sends up multiple graceful ten-inch spikes. It's a pretty addition to my all white and silver border, blooming through low, shallow-rooted perennials like Serbian yarrow and white-flowered thyme. I'm keen now to track down the original lilac blue form of the plant. Perhaps I'll just keep ordering French-Roman hyacinths.

*Charming but obscure, the white form of Spanish hyacinth* (Brimeura amethystina) *invites close inspection in my white border.*

*A planting that produces throughout the year includes grape hyacinths in spring, lady's mantle in summer, and fall-blooming colchicums that display their early glossy foliage.*

# Grape Hyacinth

Moving to a new home and starting a garden from scratch can be both exciting and scary. The first spring in my current home, when hundreds of grape hyacinths popped up beneath an old crabapple, pink petals raining down on the blue spikes, I was reassured that I was not the first gardener to live here. The most common species of grape hyacinth, named for the musky sweetness of the clusters of flowers, hardly need an introduction. Each region has its antique varieties, found in old neighborhoods, parks, and cemeteries. In most parts these are likely to be *Muscari armeniacum,* found in the wild from Turkey into the Balkans and Caucasus, or *M. botryoides* from France and Italy. In the South, starch hyacinth, *Muscari neglectum,* native to much of Europe and North Africa, decorates aged homestead gardens, neglected fields, and old lawns.

One-leaf grape hyacinth (*Muscari latifolium*) differs from common grape hyacinth in several respects. Each bulb usually produces one broad leaf, and its flowers, on spikes almost a foot tall, are black purple at the base of the spike and light blue on top. My plants confound what the books say by persistently producing two leaves, for which I have no explanation since I give them no special attention or feedings. Golden moneywort and bird's-eye veronica serve as ground covers, the better to accent the unique coloring of the deep-toned muscari flowers.

*M. azureum* has sky blue flowers that just barely open. It must be a difficult job for any insect to work its way inside the tiny hole at the bottom of the round blossoms. Only four to six inches tall, the flowers of *M. azureum* are perfect partners for species tulips like *T. batalinii* or *T. linifolia* in a hot, sunny spot. 'Blue Spike' is a large, double form of *M. armeniacum* with bright blue flowers jumbled on the spike. It is rather lumpy looking on close inspection but showy from a distance. The tassel hyacinth, *M. comosum* (now officially classified but ignored as *Leopoldia comosa*), is usually represented by the variety *plumosum,* which looks as if it's been tarred and feathered (in lavender feathers). A gardener either loves it or hates it. I've also experimented with a new grape hyacinth selection called 'Fantasy Creation'. Its fluffy spike of pale blue flowers changes to celery green and persists well into the summer. The transformation is interesting but not exactly front-page news.

# Fritillaries

Fritillaries are an acquired taste. The flowers, with the exception of brightly painted crown imperials, tend toward somber tones, often in combinations of plum, olive green, mauve, maroon, yellow, and brown. Some are downright bizarre. I'm reminded of what Harold Nicolson once said about his wife, Vita Sackville-West, one of the most famous gardeners of the century: "Vita only likes flowers which are brown and difficult to grow." Most fritillaries are not difficult to grow, but the colors have a strange appeal. I was curious what Vita had to say about the native guinea hen flower of England, *Fritillaria meleagris.* In 1939 she wrote, "It is a sinister little flower, sinister in its mournful colours of decay." She was quite fond of it.

Curiously patterned, sinister-toned guinea hen flower (Fritillaria meleagris) *possesses a strange appeal.*

I'm equally fond of guinea hen flower, but it's never struck me as sinister, unlike the British, who call it snakeshead, the sullen lady, or leper's bell. Its boxy, pendant flowers of dusky maroon or white bear unusual checkered markings—supposedly like the feathers of a guinea hen, which I have never seen. I have, however, seen sleazy lounge singers in maroon tuxedos with a similar checkerboard weave. I often have the inexplicable urge to break into a chorus of "My Way" when the flowers bloom in May.

Guinea hen flower performs best situated in moist, organically enriched soil in partial shade, similar to wet meadow conditions in its native Europe. *F. pyrenaica* comes from similar conditions in the Pyrenees. It's a good bet for moist borders or lightly shaded woodland beds, growing slightly less than two feet tall. Its reddish brown pendant bells also carry the tessellated checkered markings common to this genus, which contrast dramatically with their chartreuse interiors. *F. camschatcensis* also grows in moist woodland settings in its native habitat, which includes—remarkably—Oregon, Washington, Alaska, Japan, and northern China. It can grow up to a foot tall, usually less, and often presents a pair of nearly black flowers above whorls of glossy green leaves. It doesn't exactly light up the shade garden, but the mysterious flowers intrigue gardeners with a flair for the dramatic.

The most sensational of spring-blooming bulbs is crown imperial, *Fritillaria imperialis,* from the western Himalayas. This stately, Gothic-looking plant grows to four feet, and the stout stalk displays shiny green leaves. It is topped in midspring by a stunning "crown" of orange or yellow pendant flowers and a pineapplelike tuft of foliage.

Crown imperial bears an unusual scent. Some say it smells "foxy," but never having gotten close enough to a fox to sniff its cologne, I cannot attest to this. The smell is said to be a deterrent to rodents in the garden, but it's also a deterrent to most people. A botanical garden once planted hundreds of them in one area and found that rather than being overwhelmed by the spectacle, visitors were simply overcome. A half dozen seems to be sufficient to appreciate their beauty and for the breeze to dilute their smell.

Three points should be noted about growing crown imperial: First, the glossy green foliage is at the mercy of late frosts; sometimes I need to run out with bushel baskets or moon blankets to cover it. Second, the bulbs do not have much drought tolerance and actually grow best in a stiff loam that does not dry out. Third, yellow crown imperials produce larger bulbs than the orange kind. If they are grown together, and if the bulbs are invariably shared with friends, you must resist the temptation to keep all the biggest bulbs for yourself or you will run out of orange ones.

Persian bells, *Fritillaria persica,* from Turkey and Iran is another striking species that grows to several feet. The twisted blue green leaves spiral around the thick stems studded with flower bells of dusky plum color. 'Adiyaman', named for the town near which it was first discovered, is a vigorous, intensely colored form that grows up to four feet tall. The pale forms of this bulb are not widely grown, but I'm partial to the cream-colored bells flushed with pale green and lilac. No matter the color form, this fritillary is especially pretty planted with pink tulips or hyacinths, or with pansies the color of red wine. It is persistent where drainage is excellent. It does not have the scent of its cousin.

*F. pallidiflora* becomes increasingly popular as gardeners discover how easy it is to grow. Native to Siberia, it has no problems with its hardiness. Twisting petals of silvery turquoise accent its straw-yellow bells, strung at the top of the strong, ten-inch stems. The dangling flowers have slight traces of olive green, and the interior is spotted with reddish brown. Bulbs thrive in a wide range of soils and conditions as long as plentiful sun is available during its growing season.

Michail's flower, *F. michailovskyi,* was the "lost" fritillary for many decades. An expedition collected a specimen in 1914,

*The yellow form of crown imperial* (Fritillaria imperialis) *rises through winter's debris in the walled garden at Chicago Botanic Garden.*

but it was never introduced to western horticulture. In 1965 a British team redis-covered the flower growing near snowline in northeast Turkey and succeeded in in-troducing it to cultivation. A willing grower, the flashy flowers—maroon with acid yellow tips—now have become common in catalogues. Growing to about eight inches above thin, gray green leaves, Michail's flower thrives in freely draining soil that is moist at flowering time but drier during the rest of the summer. The ground-hugging, gray-leafed Spanish cinquefoil (*Potentilla nevadensis*) makes a good compan-ion. Its yellow flowers open in concert with Michail's flower, and there's no bare patch when the bulb fades.

Fritillaria fanciers can select from several other species that have become more available. *F. acmopetala* from Cyprus, Syria, and Lebanon has narrow gray green leaves and stems up to a foot high or more with wide yellow green bells stained brown. *F. assyriaca* from Iraq and Iran grows less than a foot tall, and its flowers are lime green and violet. *F. uva-vulpis* is not only fun to pronounce but is distinguished by the metallic sheen of its narrow maroon bells with golden bronze interiors above glaucous green leaves. A recent introduction from Iran and Turkey, it grows about a foot tall.

Species of *Fritillaria* native to the West Coast occupy somewhat specialized niches in the wild and may challenge gardeners except where conditions can be closely matched. *F. pudica* grows in light woodlands, often among rocks, from British Columbia south to California and east to Utah, Nevada, and Wyoming. Only about six inches tall, it is still graceful with several yellow flowers with a tint of purple. *E. purdyi* grows about as tall, and its flowers have cream or pale green petals heavily marbled with maroon or brown. The form 'Tinkerbell' has white petals with chocolate stripes and interior spots. Native to clay hillsides that dry out in summer, up into the mountains of California, *F. purdyi* is one of the easiest of the West Coast fritillaries to grow outside its native habitat. Mission bells, *F. biflora,* is native to Cali-fornia fields and has shiny green leaves and foot-tall stems topped by nodding pur-plish brown flowers with green markings.

# Beneath a Canopy

Shade plants evolved to catch as much light as possible beneath deciduous trees. They often emerge before the canopy above them grows increasingly dense, to soak up spring sunshine and spread their leaves wide to catch the filtered rays later.

Some bulbous plants complete their life cycles early and retreat, while others stick it out for the entire season. The foliage of woodland bulbs is often as beautiful as their flowers, and as mentioned before, the seed heads and berries they produce in autumn make many of these plants valuable over an extended season. In previous chapters, I've extolled the virtues of the great shade plants like *Dicentra, Trillium, Polygonatum,* and *Arisaema.* It's time to sing the praises of some that get over-looked.

I don't know why so few gardeners grow lily-of-the-valley, *Convallaria majalis,* these days. The fragrance of its tiny white bells is legendary, and few plants grow as readily in shade. It creeps by rhizomatous roots, called pips, that perhaps get too aggressive in small gardens, where colo-nizing must be kept to a minimum. Where there's room, lily-of-the-valley creates dense patches of broad, deep green, nearly indestructible leaves. A pale pink-flowered form behaves well, slowly increasing without thoughts of conquest. A variegated form must be coddled to keep it going at all. Orange berries sometimes decorate the stalks in autumn.

I inherited strong colonies of lily-of-the-valley, probably planted around the turn of the century. I've left them intact, growing thickly in dense summer shade at the foot of chokecherries and an old apple tree. The plant behaves as if it were home in European forests. A little patch grows by my front door on the north side of the house, squeezing itself into cracks in the aging steps. I don't suppose that anyone besides the postal carrier ever notices the pendant white

*After a Minnesota winter, crested iris* (Iris cristata) *and creeping phlox triumph in Frances Reid's garden.*

bells against the mossy concrete, but I'll regret losing it when the inevitable job of replacing the steps can't wait any longer.

Crested iris, *Iris cristata,* grows wild in forest clearings from Maryland and Georgia west to Missouri and Arkansas. It's easy to grow in moist, humus-rich soil in light shade or sun. The blue flowers bear the characteristic golden crests on short stems just a few inches high. Selected forms range from deep violet to pale blue and white, all of which combine nicely with creeping phlox.

Rue anemone, *Anemonella thalictroides* (formerly *Anemone thalictroides* or *Thalictrum anemonoides*), displays traits that suggest its inclusion in both *Anemone* and *Thalictrum*. It now has its very own genus, of which it is the only species. I'm going to muddy the waters further by suggesting that its finely cut leaves look like a cross between rue and maidenhair fern. That in itself is a good enough reason to grow this native of open woodland from New Hampshire to Florida and west to Kansas. The white flowers look like miniature white anemones perched atop the wiry stems, less than six inches tall, in April and May. Sometimes the flowers have a pink tinge, and there is a double pink form called 'Rosea Plena'.

About the middle of summer, I used to panic, thinking I'd killed my rue anemones. I'd find shriveled evidence of where they used to be and make a note to grow some more and take better care of them. The next season they'd be

*Wood hyacinth* (Hyacinthoides hispanicus) *underplanted with vinca bring an informal touch to boxwood parterres in a Williamsburg garden.*

back, as pretty as before with their tiny white flowers and delicate leaves. Bulbous roots give shade lovers an option: When the going gets tough, they can fold their tents and disappear.

If I had patience, I'd wait for wood hyacinths to colonize my shade gardens. Instead, I poke in a couple dozen or so every autumn around hostas, between ferns, and beneath daphnes. Their straight stems, laden with the beautiful blue bells, bloom with yellow trout lilies and the pink-flowered woodland cranesbill, *Geranium maculatum.* The sight pleases me immeasurably.

I call them wood hyacinths, but most gardeners know them as Spanish bluebells. Native to wooded areas of the Pyrenees, Spanish bluebell is difficult to tell from its close cousin, the English bluebell. The two are very similar, with the main difference being that the latter bears its bells on only one side of the stem, whereas in the Spanish bluebell they are evenly spaced on the spike. The English bluebell also is fragrant; the Spanish one is not. If planted side by side, they will cross naturally, resulting in interesting colors. Pink, white, and various shades of blue and lavender have been selected. They include dark blue 'Danube', pink 'Rose Queen', purple pink 'Dainty Maid', 'White Triumphator', and violet pink 'Rosabella'. Most grow about fifteen inches tall.

Because taxonomists have been batting names around like a cat with a ball of yarn, it's hard to tell under which name the wood hyacinths will be found in catalogues. They used to be members of *Scilla* but were reassigned to *Endymion* and then to *Hyacinthoides.* At the moment, the Spanish bluebell is officially *Hyacinthoides hispanica,* and the English bluebell is *H. non-scripta.*

These are bulbs that both seed themselves and form offsets. Colonies become thicker and farther-flung with time. People who like their plants to stay put should not plant them (nor should they be reading this book in the first place). They need space, not a tiny allocation of a spot where they're expected to remain. Even where wood hyacinths seed with abandon, they shouldn't get in the way much, since the foliage stays low and departs quickly as the hostas and other summer shade queens expand. I often read how messy the leaves of bluebells are, but this has never been my experience. They fade and crumble quickly before I can work up a good case of distress.

Species of *Erythronium* prove to be irresistible to shade gardeners. The six-petaled flowers look like tiny pendant lilies, and the foliage is thick, broad, and often beautifully marked. The leaves stay low, showcasing the delicate flowering stems that usually rise between six inches to a foot above it. Many species prove easy to grow in humus-rich soil, moist in spring but slightly less so in summer. Greedy tree

A *mossy outcrop makes a perfect home for* Erythronium revolutum.

roots can be a help rather than a curse—as they are in growing cyclamens—since they soak up excess moisture that can sometimes rot the dormant bulbs.

*Erythronium dens-canis* is called the dog-tooth violet because of the supposed resemblance of its bulb to a canine tooth. I've never had sufficient curiosity to dig up a plant and check for myself. Native to moist woodlands of Europe, across Asia to Japan, dog-tooth violet blooms in shades of pink and lavender rose above mottled mint green and chocolate leaves. Selected varieties include purple 'Frans Hals', pale pink 'Rose Queen', and 'Snowflake'. 'Charmer' is white with a brown eye.

Many of the American species go by the collective name of *trout lily* because the foliage is imagined by some to look like the markings on trout. The resemblance eludes me, but the glistening, brown-mottled leaves are extraordinarily handsome for a bulb or, for that matter, any plant. *E. americanum* is widely distributed across

much of the eastern part of the country, as far south as Florida, and as far west as Kansas. Its stoloniferous roots help it colonize and carpet woodland gardens with its good-looking leaves, but it is known as a shy bloomer. If *E. americanum* gets trapped between rocks, it concentrates more on producing its yellow flowers than on covering ground. *E. revolutum* is found in high woodlands from northern California to Vancouver. It bears charming pink blossoms with a pale yellow center. Its foliage is some of the best.

*E. tuolumnense,* from Tuolumne County in California—home of Yosemite National Park—is a vigorous species that bears yellow flowers but has plain green leaves. It has been supplanted to a degree by hybrids with the sought-after mottled leaves: The dangling bells of 'Pagoda' are sulfur yellow with a plum center, 'Jeannine' is pure yellow, the flowers of 'Kondo' are buttercup yellow with a brown center, while 'White Beauty' is cream highlighted by orange interior markings. The gorgeous white flowers of avalanche lily, *E. montanum,* make a breathtaking sight when they bloom by the thousands in lush mountain meadows of the Cascade and Olympic ranges just as the snow recedes. In Colorado, yellow masses of glacier lily, *E. grandiflorum*—so thick that it's impossible to avoid stepping on them—frame views of the Rockies from Rabbit Ears Pass. Avalanche and glacier lilies are difficult to please in cultivation but make wonderful vacation snapshots.

# 7

# SUMMER

*Let the Good Times Roll*

The transition from spring to summer sometimes happens nearly overnight, almost imperceptibly. We wake up one morning and it feels like summer. Some years this occurs on the first hot day that singes tulip petals, but other years it creeps up slowly. It's then that we wonder if summer will ever start. Later we wonder if it will ever end. Somewhere in the middle, the garden goes through a transformation. New and fresh in the beginning, it matures—more or less gracefully—through the season. Each day holds new promise and fascination as perennials, annuals, vines, shrubs, and bulbs come into full glory. Gardeners often think of spring as the traditional season for bulbs, but the ones that flower in summer are among the most spectacular.

The chores of the early summer garden are many. There are rows to hoe for corn and beans, seedlings to set out, patio pots to fill, and lawns to mow. The headliners of spring are yesterday's

A *sphere of star-of-Persia's* (Allium christophii) *flowers shines with a nearly metallic gleam.*

news, and we hardly give them another thought as new plants vie for our attention. As late tulips and daffodils fade, gardeners snap the seed pods off to prevent the bulbs from diverting their energies into seed production rather than renewing themselves belowground. The exceptions, of course, are the species that are allowed or encouraged to seed. The gardener performs the tasks impatiently, easily distracted by the arrival of the iris and alliums.

# Iris Season

A visit to an iris display garden or nursery field turns my mind to mush. It is too pretty. There's no way to take it all in and to focus on making selections. Gardeners in my area flock to a nursery where we can wander around the growing fields, dig our own plants, and load up our cars. We're like proverbial kids in a candy store. Our gardens gradually fill up with iris until there's nothing else to do but divide them and pass them on to friends with less iris than we have.

My garden isn't completely overrun by iris—yet. "Oh, I have a pink one that you'll really like," promises Carol. Mary Ellen drops by a grocery sack with divisions of an heirloom dwarf with violet petals that I admired. Paul and Susan bring pots of seedlings of *Iris typhifolia,* a Mongolian species with leaves like a cattail and exquisite violet blossoms. Eleanor digs me a clump of 'Ermine Robe' that she thinks will look great in my white-and-silver border. Ray brings me divisions of *Iris flavescens* that Lauren and Kelly found growing at an old homestead out on the plains. I find homes for them all, combined with pleasing companions like peonies, columbines, and dianthus.

I'm especially fond of the old varieties that pass from friend to friend. I'm unable to truly judge them on their merit. I move them around where they look their best, even if some of them seem dowdy by show bench standards. The old lavender *Iris pallida* pleases me more every year. Its relatively small flowers smell like grape bubble gum, and they fade unobtrusively, rather than hanging on in slimy wads. The variegated foliage forms—one with white stripes, the other with cream—are usually called zebra iris. They invite innovative plantings that make the most of their leaves throughout the year.

The straw-yellow flowers of *Iris flavesens* are small and quaint by modern standards, but I love them. It is not a true species but a stable selection of *Iris germanica* that's been cultivated for many centuries in Europe and came to this region with early settlers. I have far too much of it now but can't bring myself to thin it. *Iris flavescens, Iris germanica,* and *Iris florentina* are part of a mishmash of very ancient iris that eventually became the famous German bearded iris. We probably have the Turks to thank for these old hybrids (presumably descended mainly from *Iris pallida* and *Iris variegata*) that survived for millennia around old castles and monasteries throughout much of eastern and northern Europe and Asia Minor. They persisted not by seeding but through their tough rhizomes. That's naturalizing.

Most of the work with bearded iris hybrids has been accomplished in this century. They are divided into several classes including dwarf, intermediate, and tall. There are about sixty million hybrids, perhaps a few hundred fewer. It's tempting but fruitless to make recommendations, since people should grow the ones they like. Some love the frilly ones, or the bicolors, or the deep-toned ones, or even the brown ones. For practicality, the smaller ones stand up to wind and rain better than the tall ones, but a gardener simply crosses his fingers and hopes that storms are minimal in early summer. I refuse to grow iris that need staking. The old Turks would probably turn in their graves if they knew that these tough flowers now need such pampering.

Modern hybrids are a far cry from the original flowers that grew wild around crumbling medieval castles. The "ideal" form of the flower has changed, with breeders shooting for pert, horizontal falls rather than the drooping old ones. They perceive the older flowers as looking "forlorn." I'm not totally convinced, but I'm not a breeder. The destiny of a flower lies in the hands of its enthusiasts, and often it goes in strange directions. The people who breed iris, daylilies, or roses are similar to those who breed horses, dogs, or cats: They live in a strange world of shows and competition. Gardeners often benefit from their efforts when they result in new varieties with more vigor, more flowers, or more color choices. We grumble when the new fashions don't suit us. When confronted with new hybrids that no longer bear the traits that I valued in a flower to begin with, I sometimes think of Ogden Nash, who once said, "Progress may have been all right once, but it went on too long."

I don't mean to be so hard on the people who devote their lives to breeding their favorite flowers. Wonderful hybrids have resulted, sometimes from unexpected places. I'm grateful for the genius, Sir Michael Foster, who thought of crossing Japanese roof iris, *Iris tectorum* (traditionally grown on thatched roofs in Japan and China), with *Iris pallida*. The result was 'Paltec', sometimes called *Iris x pal-tec,* an iris that gives me goosebumps each year. The beautifully proportioned blossoms are a satiny shade of powder blue. I play it up with deep pink companions like *Geranium cinereum* 'Splendens' and *Centaurea hypoleuca* 'John Coutts', as well as deep blue

*A pink and blue medley in my garden includes Siberian iris 'Sky Wings', sky blue lily (Ixiolirion tataricum) at its feet, hot pink Centaurea hypoleuca 'John Coutts' with Iris 'Paltec' below it, and tall white native cow parsnip.*

*Ajuga genevensis.* 'Paltec' has been around since the turn of the century, but I have no idea how it came to my garden.

The iris season continues with the Siberians, noted for their perfectly structured flowers and bold, linear foliage. A big specimen has all the architectural interest of an ornamental grass. Not so long ago, Siberian iris were offered in just a few colors, but hybridists have expanded the range to include everything from velvety purple and royal blue to white and yellow. The long-dreamt-of pink hybrids are tantalizingly close to becoming a reality. The classics include deep purple 'Caesar's Brother', white and yellow 'Butter and Sugar', pale blue veined with navy 'Super Ego', and white 'Snow Queen'. The catalogue of a specialist will make your head swim. If I faced some theoretical catastrophe where I was allowed to choose only one for my garden, I'd take 'Sky Wings', which is not a bad description of its delightfully sky blue petals. I might also be tempted by 'Flight of Butterflies', deep purple-blue with dark veins etched on the white upper portion of the falls. It is close in appearance, by all accounts, to the original wild *Iris sibirica*.

More than the species *I. sibirica* (widely

*One of the parents of the spuria iris group, Iris orientalis does best with regular moisture until it blooms in early summer, after which it can withstand drought.*

distributed in central and eastern Europe but not actually in Siberia) is involved in the breeding of the Siberian group. Some of the parents have an intolerance for alkaline soil, resulting in yellowing of the leaves in some types where alkaline soil is the norm. Siberians, as a general rule, like sun and moist soil. The lighter the soil, the more water they need.

Spuria iris, among the last to bloom, are descended from a broad range of species native mainly to central and eastern Europe and western Asia. They have bold spears that grow up to five feet tall, but usually much less by about half. The flowers have tall standards that flare open widely from the center and rounded falls, usually in combinations of yellow, lavender, white, and sometimes bronze. The group of hybrids takes its name from lilac blue *Iris spuria,* native to Hungary and Russia. Another species that figures prominently is *Iris orientalis* from Greece, Turkey, and Syria. White with gold standards, it is beautiful in its own right. Spurias dot old neighborhoods since they tolerate clay soil and neglect. They take several years to really get up a full head of steam but are reliable thereafter. A moist spring is to their liking, but they may get parched in summer with no ill effect.

Some species of iris have so far escaped intervention by hybridists. An iris nut can easily be carried away. There are so many beautiful ones, like small, dark purple *Iris setosa,* native to Canada, Manchuria, and Siberia, or elegant lavender blue *Iris douglasiana* from the hills of northern California and southern Oregon. *Iris lactea* from the steppes of central Asia makes a fine perennial for borders or rock gardens. Its delicate flowers, with pale lavender standards and ivory white falls, are held within the safety of its thin leaves. I hope hybridists never set their sights on "improving" it.

Iris that sink their roots deep into the muddy ooze of streams and ponds include the yellow flag of Europe, *Iris pseudacorus,* and its American counterpart, blue flag, *Iris missouriensis. Iris versicolor* from the northeast part of the country looks wonderful on a bank of a pond, its violet flowers crowning the leaves bending

The delicate flowers of Iris lactea *belie its tough nature, forged on the steppes of Central Asia.*

Growing in a moist spot, Iris laevigata 'Rose Queen' complements astilbes.

into arches above still water. An Oriental species, *Iris japonica*, has never been extensively hybridized. It appears today much as the wild populations along creeks and bogs in Japan. It's a casual-looking plant that forms extensive colonies in partial shade. The azure blue or white flowers, graceful as orchids, are heavily produced in late spring and early summer on banks above water features where winter temperatures (that could otherwise damage its evergreen leaves) stay above freezing.

Japanese iris, generally known as *Iris kaempferi* but correctly named *I. ensata*, have been cultivated in Japan for many centuries. They are the Oriental counterparts of the bearded iris of the western world. They are huge and sumptuous with their exaggerated falls, sometimes heavily veined or streaked, in shades of purple, white, maroon, and pink. Japanese iris are the last to flower, usually in late June and July, and need acid soil. They are not true marsh plants but have become accustomed to the traditional Japanese practice of flooding the gardens in spring. *Iris laevigata* grows in boggy ground in Japan, China, and Korea. It has a more classic iris flower than its highly bred cousin and is noted for its broad, drooping falls and short, narrow standards. The species type is a strong blue, but a selection called 'Rose Queen' is about as pink as an iris can get. Candelabra primroses and astilbes that also require constant moisture are traditional companions.

# Ornamental Onions

Only a handful of the world's onions are cultivated. Of the estimated five hundred to six hundred species of the genus *Allium*, almost all native to the northern hemisphere, only a dozen or so of the ornamental species are widely available to most gardeners. Often characterized by round, puff-ball heads of flowers, they range in size from tiny plants suitable for the rock garden to strapping giants.

One onion rises above them all—*Allium giganteum*. It's a mainstay of Dutch bulb catalogues, with the obligatory photo of a child (the bulb company president's daughter or grandchild, I suspect) holding on to the four-foot stem of this purple lollipop of a flower. I'm almost certain that with large orders, they actually include a blond child with your order.

I'm immune to the dubious charms of *Allium giganteum*. Its image almost put me off ornamental onions altogether. "I only like the ones I can eat, and they belong in the vegetable garden," I used to tell myself. I've learned, little by little, to eat my own words. Ornamental onions vary considerably in color, size, and form. Undemanding in their cultural requirements, they make rewarding additions to beds and borders. I begrudgingly admitted a few to my perennial plantings, and they gradually won me over with their good looks and usually gracious manners.

As my interest in ornamental onions increased, I discovered how easy they are to grow. No back-breaking labor is required to get them into the ground—plant most of them just a few inches deep in a partly sunny spot. They can take clay or sandy soil, although most alliums thrive best in well-drained sandy loam. Most are quite hardy throughout the country and are best planted in autumn. All demonstrate at least moderate drought resistance and, in most cases, will rot if overwatered. They are rarely bothered by diseases or pests. I'm hard pressed to remember so much as an aphid on any allium in my garden. Some, however, attract butterflies and bees. Most alliums are long-lived and rarely if ever need dividing. Most alliums will self-sow in moderation; only a few are intent on world domination.

The foliage is insignificant or even negligible on most ornamental types, so there's no giant death scene, such as that put on by prima donna bulbs like tulips and daffodils. The leaves of many species have all but disappeared by the time the flowers bloom, so a companion plant becomes an aesthetic necessity to cloak the base of the naked stems. It's possible to exploit this trait to advantage. An ideal way to showcase smaller alliums is by planting them beneath front-of-the-border shallow-rooted perennials, such as creeping veronicas or phlox, or in the spaces between larger clump-forming perennials, such as cranesbills, catmint, or lavender. With their thin stems, even the tallest species can be given a spot among lower-growing companions. The effect is airy and often whimsical.

Several low-growing alliums perform admirably throughout most of the country in a wide range of conditions. Perhaps the lily leek, *Allium moly,* is the best known. Native to eastern Spain and southwest France, its canary yellow umbels of flowers appear on stems eight inches tall in early summer. It can be a lovely asset in loosely structured, partially shaded gardens. The selected form 'Jeannine' is bigger and taller.

Lily leek will tolerate more shade (the leaves burn easily in full sun) and moisture than most other alliums. Contrary to oft-repeated warnings, it is not usually inclined to rampant self-seeding.

I like common chives, especially the taste of the flowers, but it usually looks like an outcast, stuffed in the corner by the garage. I saw a delightful planting where it had been allowed to seed itself (which it will do) among lady's mantle and magenta *Geranium sanguineum*. I never thought of chives in the same way again. *Allium przwalskianum* isn't widely known yet, but it looks much like chives except for its deep violet flowers. Imagine that with chartreuse and magenta.

*A. oreophilum* (formerly *A. ostrowskianum*) grows wild in eastern Turkey, the Caucasus, and central Asia. Its rose pink flowers on seven- to ten-inch stems are a late-spring delight. It seeds, but not—in my experience—to a fault. Its pretty color goes with almost everything, so I'd never quarrel if it appeared somewhere I hadn't intended. One bulb company has promoted this plant as "alpine rosy bells." I admit it could use a common name, having been tagged with two difficult scientific names in a row, but this moniker makes me cringe.

*A. flavum* looks like a golden sparkler in midsummer. This is a variable species, perhaps because of its wide geographic distribution in southern and central Europe.

Its flower color varies from straw to bright yellow on stems from four to thirty inches in height (most cultivated forms average about a foot tall). *A. flavum* forms clumps, much like chives, with many flower heads. It also takes partial shade.

*A. cernuum,* widely distributed between both coasts from Canada to Mexico, is arguably the most beautiful of American onions. The flowers of nodding onion range vary from deep to pale pink, depending on its region. The stalks, a foot or two tall, bend near the top, letting the flowers dangle in a charming manner. A drift of them is a gorgeous sight with pinks and columbines.

O*nly one of a handful of the truly blue flowers, blue garlic (Allium caeruleum) echoes the midsummer sky with yellow gaillardia and larkspur.*

*The seed heads of star-of-Persia* (Allium christophii) *fade to amber gold, enhancing midsummer companions pink veronica, blue* Clematis integrifolia, *lavender, and* Campanula punctata.

The thin leaves of blue garlic, *A. caeruleum,* have all but disappeared by the time it comes into bloom in early summer. The pretty true-blue spheres, slightly smaller than a Ping-Pong ball, are perched atop thin, wiry stems about two feet tall. They can be paired with golden *Coreopsis verticillata* 'Zagreb' or 'Golden Showers' or planted behind a low-growing artemisia such as 'Silver Mound'. Native to the Russian steppes, blue garlic tolerates drought.

Many gardeners—I among them—consider star of Persia, *A. christophii* (formerly *A. albopilosum*), as the best of the ornamental onions. I would ordinarily never even consider a flower head the size of a cantaloupe as anything I'd plant. Seeing is believing. Extraordinarily beautiful, each round head is composed of hundreds of loosely spaced lavender stars. The petals have a metallic sheen.

Star of Persia, native to northern Iran and central Asia, looks magical coming up and blooming through other perennials. Stems are relatively short, just a foot or so, and the thin foliage is hardly noticeable. The dried flower heads are highly prized for dried arrangements. I leave them to dry to an amber color in the garden, since they look lovely even in their skeletal form. When the border looks susceptible to a brush fire in midsummer, I reluctantly pick them. The bulbs are adaptable and drought tolerant but perform especially well in a rather moist, partially shaded area.

*A. aflatunense* (so named for its origin in Aflatun in central Asia) grows in many gardens—or does it? As many as six look-alike species are often sold as *A. aflatunense*. With stems about three feet tall, the baseball-size flower heads bloom in pleasing shades of lavender (depending which impostor inhabits your garden) in early summer. It takes an expert to identify the true species, and most of us couldn't care less. Expect variations when ordering this bulb. Several selections have been introduced, including darker 'Purple Sensation', pale 'Mother of Pearl', and one in white.

'Lucy Ball', a hybrid between *A. aflatunense* and *A. macleanii,* blooms dark lilac purple, although I half-expected a flower named for the comedienne to have fiery orange flowers the shade of her famous hair. 'Gladiator' is a product of the same breeding with a rose purple flower head on two- to three-foot-tall stems. *A. macleanii* (a close relative and look-alike of *A. giganteum*) also figures in the parentage, along with *A. karataviense,* of the much-heralded new hybrid 'Globemaster'.

'Globemaster' is unique in several ways. It is expensive because it takes years to build up stocks of a bulb to sell at reasonable price. (I spent a small fortune on three bulbs and can only claim temporary insanity.) The flowers of 'Globemaster' are sterile, supposedly resulting in a longer show in the garden, since they don't concentrate on seed production after pollination. It does make an impressive round umbel the size of a head of iceberg lettuce, studded thickly with rosy purple flowers. The ball balances on a thick stem about two feet high. The bulbs often split after flowering, resulting in smaller flower heads the next season. *Allium jesdianum (A. rosenbachianum)* from northern Afghanistan makes multiple two-foot stems of deep violet flowers. It's ideal for a dry situation, perhaps with orange and yellow gaillardias as shocking companions.

Southern European drumstick allium, *A. sphaerocephalon,* is more subtle. I enjoy the maroon red flower heads, tightly packed into ovals the size of a kiwi fruit, blooming in midsummer. They wave in the breeze on stems three feet long. They are charming contrasted by gray foliage. I planted them to poke through the arching foliage of the handsome shrub rose *Rosa glauca,* which is gray with a maroon underside to each leaf. The maroon flower heads also show to advantage with silvery artemisias.

One of the most intriguing tall alliums is Sicilian onion, *A. siculum* (reclassified as *Nectaroscordum siculum*). It grows in the wild from France to Turkey and blooms in May or June. At about three feet tall, it has relatively large pendant bells tinged with pale green, ivory, and adobe pink. A few bulbs will eventually seed themselves to form large colonies over time. The bulbs take part shade and the flower heads dry to a golden ivory tone.

*The heads of drumstick allium* (Allium sphaero-cephalon) *inject strong notes of maroon to an otherwise pastel arrangement of* Artemisia x 'Powis Castle', Verbena patagonica, *white* Osteospermum 'Dazzler', *and* Salvia pratensis.

The national appetite for ornamental onions continues to grow, but few other species are available commercially. Specialty plant societies often offer unusual species through seed sales and exchanges. It is worth scouting for seed, since most species germinate easily and flower within a few years. Worth the search are two stunning blues: *A. beesianum* from western China, with drooping royal blue flowers on eight-inch stems in late summer, and *A. cyaneum,* also from China, featuring cobalt blue or blue purple flowers on six-inch stems in late summer.

*A. narcissiflorum* is an exciting species from the Alps. Blooming in summer, it bears pink nodding, flared bells like satin skirts. The name is an unfortunate choice since the flowers bear no resemblance to narcissus in form or color. They are very pretty nonetheless, and with its ten-inch stems, it's a natural for the rock garden. So is tiny *A. acuminatum,* the pink wild onion of the American West. Only about four inches tall, its deep hot magenta flowers appear in late spring or early summer.

Naples garlic, *A. neapolitanum,* is native to the Mediterranean region. Its umbels of fragrant, star-shaped white flowers open on stems about fifteen inches tall. A tender bulb performing best in sun and well-drained soil, it's a good bet for West Coast and southern gardeners. Another good choice for that region is a native of the coastal mountains, *A. unifolium,* the one-leaf onion. Despite its common and scientific names, it usually produces two or three thin leaves. It resembles Naples garlic in its culture, height, and flower shape but bears charming pure pink blossoms in early summer. Both go dormant or rest in midsummer.

It's difficult to avoid comparing the flower heads of *A. schubertii* with fireworks.

A *backdrop of blue suits a Rocky Mountain garden whimsically planted with lavender, poppies, and a smattering of giant onion* (Allium giganteum).

The pedicels of each flower in an umbel are of a different length—some long, some short—with the resulting explosive look: Each umbel can measure as much as ten inches across. The flowers are usually violet, sometimes pink, and appear on stems one to two feet high. Native to the eastern Mediterranean and North Africa, this exotic-looking allium needs excellent drainage. Its hardiness is still being tested, but once again, West Coast gardeners may have the best results.

It takes time to become accustomed to designing with ornamental onions. The clump formers, such as nodding onion, are the easiest to work into a border. Since they hold their leaves, they're as easy as daylilies to position with companion plants.

The drumstick types take some thought to position. They look forlorn and out of place against a backdrop of bare soil. Those naked stems need covering. They look silly otherwise. Perhaps that was my original complaint with *Allium giganteum*. I had been bombarded by those images of a freaky-looking purple lollipop with those omnipresent Dutch toddlers clutching its stem. A prejudice had been implanted in my mind, and it takes something dramatic to change it.

My turning point came at my friend Laurie's garden, high in the Colorado

Rockies. Against a backdrop of blue mountains, her garden knits seamlessly with the pastures beyond the fenced enclosure. A scarecrow with a camel's face guards the garden, brightly splashed with poppies, annual baby's breath, lavender, and ox-eye daisies. The purple balls of my despised giant onion poke up here and there. Who would have guessed it would look so wonderful? My hat is off to Laurie for her creative planting. I'll never have her light touch, but now I'm open to new possibilities using the giant onion. I planted a few bulbs last fall. If worse comes to worst, I'll eat them.

# Summer Spikes

A garden needs variety. One area where American gardens need help is with vertical accents. Many of us figure if we've got delphiniums, that's plenty. It's not. Wind takes their toll on them in my garden. I used to end up with more of them in vases than in the border. Because I'm adverse to staking, I employ plants with summer spikes in varying heights that don't need help from me to stay upright.

St. Bernard's lily, *Anthericum liliago,* blooms in the alpine meadows of Europe. Its white flowers don't show until well after the snow has melted. The flowers are like tiny lilies—only an inch across when they open flat—but are produced generously on willowy, two-foot stems. St. Bernard's lily grows best in alkaline soil, well-drained but moist.

King's spear, *Asphodeline lutea,* from the Mediterranean region, is the most widely grown species of its genus, but that's not saying much. What intrigues gardeners is its ramrod stiff stems up to four feet tall, studded with bright golden stars produced in early summer. They rise from a grassy tuft of narrow, blue

*St. Bernard's lily* (Anthericum liliago) *thrives in the rock alpine garden at Denver Botanic Gardens, where conditions mimic its home in European alpine meadows.*

green leaves, and in sandy soil, the rhizomes spread slowly to form new plants. After the flowers fade, round green pods replace them for continued interest. It is reputed not to be hardy in my zone, but that's odd since I've grown it for more than a decade. Good drainage is the key to its survival. The plants add important linear accents to borders or rock gardens. *Asphodeline liburnica* is shorter by half, and its yellow blossoms have green stripes down the center of the petals. It grows wild in Greece, Austria, Italy, and the Balkans. *A. taurica* from Greece and the Caucasus grows as tall but its flowers are white with buff pink veins. Related *Asphodelus albus* comes from southern Europe and makes handsome stems to four feet tall above yuccalike foliage. Its white flowers have a pink midvein. *A. ramosus* from southern Europe and North Africa is also white with a rusty streak on the flowers.

Camassias, sometimes called Indian hyacinths, look like distant cousins of asphodels and St. Bernard's lily and, in fact, they all belong to the *Liliaceae*. They bloom in great colonies in mountain meadows flooded by the melting spring runoff. They integrate easily into moist borders, although the bulbs may be allowed to dry out somewhat later in summer. *Camassia cusickii* comes from Oregon and bears two-foot spikes of wispy, starry flowers, usually pale violet-blue. Its foliage is long and two inches wide (somewhat like an amaryllis), and the stems are rarely held completely upright (it tends to flop, but with dignity). *Camassia leichtlinii* is widely distributed in northern California and British Columbia and also has blue flowers, but they are bigger and better placed on the strong stems up to three feet tall. It makes a lovely spike border plant. There is also a white form and a double one that looks, for better or worse, like a double blue tuberose. *Camassia quamash* has a widespread habitat across much of the Rocky Mountains and the coastal ranges from California to British Columbia. Its slender, flower-packed spikes rise above thin, glossy leaves. Flower colors and stem heights (usually one to two feet) vary by location, but nurseries offer the deep blue-violet selections 'Orion' and 'San Juan'.

*Liatris* is the pride of the American plains. The border, meadow, or rock garden gets an enormous, long-lasting lift out of the midsummer doldrums when the lavender-pink or white flowers bristle along the straight stems. Kansas gayfeather, *Liatris pycnostachya,* shoots up to four feet tall. *Liatris aspera* has shaggy, long-rayed flowers that give it a softer look. *Liatris punctata* grows in dry areas of the Great Plains and stays about a foot tall, while *L. spicata* can triple that. Most gardeners recognize its selections 'Kobold', only two feet tall, and slightly taller 'Floristan White'. The trick to growing gayfeathers or blazing stars, as they are sometimes called, is to plant the corms an inch or less below the soil surface. *L. spicata* and *L. punctata* are drought tolerant and bloom through the hot days of July and August.

Anne Weckbaugh's summer border relies on gayfeather
(Liatris spicata) *for color and vertical emphasis with
yellow nasturtiums and white acidanthera.*

I'll never forget a slide at a lecture given by
the English plantsman Christopher Grey-
Wilson. In one slide, the golden spires of "desert
candles" rose by the hundreds from the barren,
desolate hills of Afghanistan. The land has been
overgrazed for many centuries, but goats and
sheep leave the unpalatable species of *Eremurus*
alone. The stark contrast made the tall plants
even more riveting, but they're pretty spectacular in the garden as well. Most grow at least
three feet tall, but some tower much higher.

Their grandeur comes not from the small individual flowers but from their enormous quanti-
ties bristling along the strong stems, suggesting
the common name foxtail lily. Golden orange
*Eremurus stenophyllus* (often sold as *E. bungei*) is
the most familiar species, native to Iran and
Turkestan as well as Afghanistan. It stays relatively
short and blooms in early summer. The Shelford
hybrids are derived from it and pink-flowered *E.
olgae* from Iran, and they range in color from
pink, peach, and tangerine to lemon, moonlight
yellow, and white. *Eremurus himalaicus* comes
from Kashmir and its pure white spikes—up to
six feet tall—steal the summer show. *Eremurus ro-
bustus* tops them all with spires of pink buds that
fade to white, at a whopping eight feet tall.

There are two precarious times for foxtail
lilies. Their cream-colored bulbs are wrapped in

The amazing spikes of Himalayan foxtail lily
(Eremurus himalaicus) *rocket through the frothy sprays
of giant sea kale* (Crambe cordifolia).

*R*ed-hot poker (Kniphofia uvaria) *adds a spark to a textural combination dominated by a variegated New Zealand flax.*

roots like the membrane of an orange (images from *Star Trek* come to mind) and are brittle and easily damaged during shipping and planting. They're carefree after that and self-sow in some of my friends' gardens, but I've not yet been that fortunate. The bulbs don't grow very deeply in the wild, especially in clay soil, and need only three or so inches of cover on top of them. Foxtail lilies revel in sun and dry heat. They laugh at deer.

It's taken me years to work up any enthusiasm for red-hot pokers (*Kniphofia*), since my most vivid impression of them was in clichéd combinations with wagon wheels and souvenir rocks. The pale yellow varieties made me take a second look at the kniphofias of South Africa (and my memories of the Death Valley Days scenarios instilled in me the rhizomatous plant's need for excellent drainage). If they stay high and dry in winter, pokers are much hardier than most gardeners might expect. They grow beautifully on the West Coast—there are a number of interesting species, such as orange *K. galpinii* and pale orange *K. thomsonii* var. *sondenii*—but many hybrids survive winters in my garden with no extra protection. 'Little Maid' is the yellow selection introduced by premier plantswoman Beth Chatto, who gardens in the eastern part of England, where summer drought is commonplace. The buds on the two-foot spikes of 'Little Maid' emerge green and change to straw yellow as they open. I can't resist. Other varieties have since caught my eye, in shades of deeper yellow, white, and orange. Most bloom in the heat of summer and into autumn.

# Lilies

The best way to kill a lily is to plant the bulb in clay soil in a shady spot under a downspout. I should know—I've been killing off lilies for years. At the same time, I've had great success when I've been able to fulfill their requirements for sun and well-drained soil. Most parts of my old garden were simply too shady to accommodate all the lilies I wanted to grow. It's not true that I moved to a new house just to grow more lilies, but I knew as soon as I turned over the first spadeful of sandy loam in my new garden that I had found lily heaven.

There's a big distinction between true lilies (*Lilium*) and daylilies (*Hemerocallis*). As much as I like the grassy clumps of the latter, producing scapes of flowers that shine for only a single day, it's the true lilies that have captivated me. They grow from large, artichoke-like bulbs composed of scales (daylilies grow from tuberous roots) and produce straight stems topped by splendid, often scented, flowers that last for a week or more.

The easiest lilies are the tough and adaptable Asiatic hybrids. They need well-drained soil and at least six hours of sun each day. Asiatics bloom in June and July in a vast array of colors from white and pastel pink or peach to yellow, plum, orange, and velvety red. They are classified in catalogues by the direction the flowers face: As face upward, Bs face out, and Cs are pendant.

I especially favor the Cs, since their graceful down-facing blossoms remind me of the wild Turk's cap lilies of the eastern or far western parts of the country. Some can grow as tall as six feet, so they look grand planted between and behind drifts of perennials such as baby's breath, coneflower, cranesbills, and mallows. They are at their best paired with old-fashioned shrub roses.

My favorite Asiatic hybrids include 'Citronella', an old hybrid with nodding golden-yellow blossoms dotted with brown spots; 'Red Velvet', another old-timer with a huge inflorescence of out-facing, burgundy red flowers; 'Doeskin', with many Turk's cap flowers the color of pink champagne; 'Tiger Babies', with out-facing pale peach blossoms charmingly sprinkled with brown spots; and 'Viva', a graceful six-footer with pendant vermilion flowers that look as if they've been

*The classic Asiatic lily 'Citronella' holds its own in my overstuffed garden with pink mallow, primrose yellow* Cephalaria alpina, *and blue cupid's dart.*

sculpted from wax. This list could go on for many pages. Most books recommend old hybrids like 'Enchantment' or 'Connecticut King'. I don't. 'Enchantment' was never an attractive lily. Its orange flowers, while bright, were muddy and bunched too closely together. Yellow 'Connecticut King' is better, but the commercial stocks of both became contaminated with virus. If you consider buying these strong old clones, insist that they come from virus-free stock.

Where drainage is adequate, most modern Asiatics will persist and multiply. In autumn, I probe carefully in the soil around the base of the frosted stems, where most lilies form "daughter" bulbs. They're about the size of a hazelnut and can easily be teased away from the main stem. They can be replanted eight or ten inches away from the mother bulb or lined up like onions in the vegetable garden to increase in size, usually reaching the blooming stage in two years.

Trumpet lilies bloom mainly in July. They never fail to knock my socks off with their enormous flowers (preceded by buds nearly as big as bananas) and heady fragrance. Their scent is almost too potent to recommend them for bouquets indoors, but it's wonderful on a soft breeze in the early evening in the garden. Trumpets need full sun to hit their stride, growing up to six feet tall with as many as twenty blossoms. Bulbs often plump up to the size of small cantaloupes. My favorites? The classic 'Black Dragon' displays maroon buds that open to reveal a white interior, while 'Pink Perfection', 'Moonlight', and 'Golden Splendor' describe themselves perfectly and have proved themselves over several decades. 'Lady Anne' is hard to come by because every gardener seems to want the apricot sunset displayed in the throat of the flowers. Starburst forms open their petals wider, such as the striking white 'Bright Star' with a golden throat.

Although lily species are often much more difficult to please in cultivation than hybrids, one exception is the regal lily, *Lilium regale,* from China. Some gardeners consider it the best trumpet lily of all with its pure white flowers accented by yellow throats and heavenly fragrance. It is a good choice for beginning lily growers but one

*Headily fragrant and remarkably tenacious,* Lilium regale *accents yellow* Alcea rugosa *in Lauren Springer's garden in northeast Colorado.*

*T*owering *Chinese* Lilium brownii *takes to this California hillside the way a pig takes to mud.*

of which an experienced gardener never tires. *Lilium brownii* comes from subtropical China, so it grows well for most of the West Coast and—I'm guessing—might fare well in some parts of the South, though I'm unaware of any gardeners who have tried it. The specimens I've seen in California tower well over my head (I'm six feet tall) in midsummer with thick stems that don't need staking and huge, yellow-throated white trumpets.

My theory is that there are far more daylilies in America than ever grew wild in China. The tawny daylily (*Hemerocallis fulva*) has long been cultivated in the Orient as a food source. (I've tried it myself, with the almost-open buds battered and fried.) Tawny daylily seems to fit in wilder parts of the gar-den—along a ditch or lane—since its volcanic-colored flowers of gold and reddish brown make it difficult to place in the rest of the garden.

During the course of my lifetime, this has become a nation of daylily addicts. I used to see a smattering of tawny daylilies in old gardens, or perhaps fine old vari-eties like pure yellow 'Hyperion'—still one of the best—or the lemon-scented species *H. flava,* also from China, that opens its pure yellow petals in the evening. Now daylilies are everywhere, from median strips to strip malls. They grow almost too well, and it takes restraint and planning to showcase them in the garden. The question must be asked: How much daylily foliage can one garden stand? I can only answer for myself, saying, Not much.

Not every daylily hybrid—of which there are legions—grows well in every part of the country. The evergreen varieties do best, of course, where winters don't freeze their leaves. For the others, it's a question of testing them to see how they perform in an individual garden and fit an individual's taste.

I'm ruthless. If daylilies don't appeal to me or fail to live up to their hype, I dig them up. 'Stella de Oro' got the hook last summer after too many exasperating sea-sons where the promised repeat blooming never materialized. I wrote about the purge in my newspaper column and was flooded with letters. Many people were relieved to find out that they weren't the only ones who couldn't get Stella to perform, but others thought it was just the best daylily in the universe and how dare I say terrible things about Stella. You'd have thought I'd vilified Mother Teresa.

I'm not antidaylily. I'm picky. I like the clear lemon yellows, some of the apricots, the near whites, and the deep, smoldering reds. The latter look especially dramatic with goldenrods since they both have such an intensity of color. And I like the tall "altissima" types, which send their scapes six or eight feet into the air, near the back of a border. I'm stingy with my space, even if I have a lot of it by some standards. I give a plant three years to prove itself. The good ones get a prominent spot and are divided with a quick thrust of a flat shovel to make a better show. The rest are history.

# Summer Bulbs on the Coast

The West Coast dries out each summer. Bulbs from the Cape Province of South Africa ripen their leaves and go dormant. Those from summer-rainfall areas of the country burst into bloom. A garden needs two separate areas to be able to grow them all. The one with the Cape bulbs should go without supplemental moisture, while the one with the summer bloomers needs to be kept at least slightly damper. While most South African bulbs naturalize best in well-drained soil, moisture at the wrong time of the year can cause trouble.

Summer gardens wouldn't be the same without old favorites like crocosmias and montbretia. It's hard to find a spot that the latter, officially titled *Crocosmia* x *crocosmiiflora,* doesn't find hospitable. Orange montbretias are a common sight in parks, where they make themselves at home in sun or shade. In nearly every neighborhood, it's easy to spot long-standing colonies of cannas, ginger lilies, and pineapple lilies. Other favorites include crinums, especially *Crinum moorei* and *C.* x *powelii.* (All of these plants also grow in southern gardens and are discussed in more detail a little further along.)

It's hard to find a Californian that doesn't recognize an *Agapanthus.* The stately blue ones are the favorites, but there are white-flowered forms, as well as dwarf varieties like 'Peter Pan' and 'Queen Anne'. The deep violet-blue flowers of 'Thundercloud' make it a standout. I've finally tracked down a small division and am waiting impatiently for it to reach flowering size, even if my specimen will be displayed in a pot on my patio.

Coastal gardens often feature *Dierama,* which goes by the whimsical name

*S*elf-sowing montbretia (Crocosmia x crocosmiiflora) *glow brilliantly among summer's hazy, muted shades of silver, blue, and green in a Vancouver garden.*

Venus' fishing rod. The thin stems and fine filaments that hold the pendulous pink "bait" couldn't be better described. *Dierama* grow from corms and make evergreen leaves, so should be kept moist year-round. In colder climates the leaves may be cut down by frost, but the plants recover if the freeze doesn't penetrate the earth deeply. Two species, *D. pendulum* and *D. pulcherrimum,* are quite similar with their long, narrow leaves and plum pink flowers, but *D. pendulum* can be distinguished by open, bell-shaped flowers, whereas the other species has narrow flowers that don't open very wide. Some hybrids and forms are white or pale pink.

The flowers waver in the breeze and bring a touch of whimsy to the garden (fairies and angels are said to fish with the rods), whether seen as a single accent plant or massed for bigger impact. One of the prettiest combinations I've seen is in

*Swaying in the slightest breeze off the San Francisco Bay, Venus' fishing rod* (Dierama pendulum) *arches above pastel-tinted agapanthus.*

the gardens of the Strybing Arboretum in Golden Gate Park, where Venus' fishing rods dangle with rigid blue agapanthus.

Summer hyacinth, *Galtonia candicans,* makes attractive four-foot spikes with flowers that are shaped somewhat like those of hyacinth. The resemblance ends there, for the flowers aren't fragrant. I've sniffed every one I could find for six or eight years, searching for the elusive scent promised in books and catalogues. My nose might not be able to detect it, but it's also possible that other species of the South African genus that are fragrant have been confused with the tall white *Galtonia candicans.* Unfortunately, they are rarely cultivated. Summer hyacinth is an easy border plant and is also grown successfully along the mid-Atlantic and southern states.

*Amaryllis belladonna* is the one and only naked lady. She's been starring in California gardens since the era of silent movies. Nowhere does naked lady grow better, sending up maroon-tinted stalks crowned by pink trumpets throughout the summer and into autumn. The long foliage that could have cloaked the bare stems emerges in winter. The bulbs grow up into the mountains of the Cape Province and thrive in poor soil dry in

*A garden flourished here once, with a row of naked ladies* (Amaryllis belladonna) *separating two neighbors' yards. The bulbs have outlived the neighbors and hold their own with weeds in Humboldt County, California.*

A *salmon pink* Alstroemeria *hybrid enlivens a mixed border of steely sea holly* (Eryngium giganteum), *pink gas plant, lavender milky bellflower* (Campanula lactiflora), *and variegated aralia.*

summer. Drought-tolerant plants like salvias, succulents, and rosemary make suitable companions. I stopped by a pretty front garden in Berkeley several years ago and asked to take a picture of the glorious pink trumpets set against the fuzzy purple flowers of Mexican bush sage (*Salvia leucantha*), and toadflax (*Linaria purpurea*). I especially like the idea of employing dwarf agapanthus like 'Peter Pan' to provide a green skirt for the infamous naked lady.

A big stand of Peruvian lily, *Alstroemeria*, makes a lovely sight in summer gardens in the Pacific Northwest and California, and some species and hybrids perform well in the South and even into colder winter states. The golden orange flowers of *Alstroemeria aurantiaca* are the most brilliant, especially fronted by purple cranesbills and the purple-leaf form of culinary sage, *Salvia officinalis* 'Purpurea'. The flowers of *Alstroemeria psittacina* are decked for the December holidays with red and green markings on a white base, but they're six months too early. This unusual coloration is enhanced by a backdrop of red barberries or bronze-leaf cannas. Southerners grow this Brazilian species with the help of squirrels, who dig up and rebury the peanut-shaped rhizomes. Plants can sprout in the oddest places. No wonder the folk name is peanut lily.

Hybrids make up the bulk of most Peruvian lilies in the garden. They come in shades of pink, salmon, yellow, white, and red, intriguingly marked with fine "pencil-line" patterns on the petals leading to the centers. Long-flowering and drought-resistant qualities make these hybrids desirable, but make sure you really want them where you plant them. They form thick rhizomatous roots that burrow deeply into the earth. Friends of mine in California claim that it takes a backhoe to remove them, and they're just barely joking.

# Steam Heat

Summer steams the starch out of southern gardens. It's a time for the gardener to retreat to the porch and rely on the plants that revel in torrid weather. These include bulbous plants from subtropical and tropical climes that thrive on the conditions that reduce most of us to puddles.

*Crocosmia masonorum* and related montbretia (*Crocosmia* x *crocosmiiflora*) glow brilliantly beneath the relentless sun. Swords of green fans are topped by zigzag stems with small tubular flowers. Those of crocosmia are dull red, but the selection 'Lucifer' is fiery red. Montbretias fall into the fiery range as well, from golden orange 'Emily McKenzie' to smoky red 'James Coey', and the much-coveted 'Solfatare', yellow with bronze leaves. They are heavy feeders, benefiting from an annual top-dressing of compost. Spider mites multiply when rainfall ceases but can be kept at bay with strong squirts from a cold hose.

Nowhere do cannas flourish in this country as they do in the South, also growing like gangbusters into the Midwest and Northeast. The miniatures like 'Tropic

*Steamy summer heat suits bold cannas, including red-flowering 'Red Ribbons' and yellow-striped 'Pretoria', as well as purple barberry, chartreuse coleus, and showy scarlet* Clerodendrum speciosissimum *at Chanticleer in Pennsylvania.*

*Sweetly scented butterfly ginger* (Hedychium coronarium) *evokes an image of the island tropics at Montrose, Nancy Goodwin's North Carolina garden.*

Rose' or 'Pfitzer's Primrose' stay compact at three feet tall, but the giant beauties, with glossy green or bronze leaves, are the signature plants of the deep South, sinking their roots into wet, sticky clay. Many heirloom varieties abound throughout the region, and gardeners in old neighborhoods can sometimes be persuaded to part with a small rhizome. Mass public plantings don't do these handsome plants justice, since they invite great combinations with castor beans, bananas, tall verbena, dahlias, and hibiscus.

Ginger lilies, natives of tropical Asia, also boast fabulous foliage—similar to but thinner than that of cannas—while their flowers are quite different from the tussles of bright but sloppy cannas. Butterfly ginger, *Hedychium coronarium,* bears huge spikes of ivory flowers, deliciously scented like vanilla. Its red cousin, *H. coccineum,* bears ten-inch spikes of coral red with long, showy stamens projecting from the flowers. *H. flavescens* from India is pale yellow with long orange stamens. Each grows five feet tall in sun or part-shade in moist spots.

The all-time foliage champion title belongs to elephant ears, *Colocasia antiquorum* var. *esculenta,* grown widely in tropical lands around the world for its edible tubers that, after serious cooking to soften the crystalline particles that can cut the throat like glass, turn into poi. I'm in no hurry to try it on my next jaunt to Hawaii. Mainland Americans stick to growing the plant for its massive, white-veined leaves that I suppose might do justice to an elephant, several feet long and produced in jungle splendor. Selected varieties have dramatic purple veins or bronze leaves. Like elephants, the plants drink enormous amounts of water and so are at home along streams and lakes. The tubers sometimes break off and float downstream to start new colonies. The banks of the San Marcos River in Texas are covered with elephant ears as far as the eye can see.

Summer is also a time for sensational tropical blossoms. *Hymenocallis* are sometimes called Peruvian daffodils or spider lilies, and both common names have merit. Several species native to Mexico and South America bloom in early summer with elegant, ethereal flowers in white or yellow. The leaves are like the amaryllis prototype—long and green—and it must seem monotonous to read it over and over. How many fresh ways can I think of describing them? I've just run out. Watch for this same monotony of foliage in the garden. Think of ways to combat it by pairing crinums, amaryllis, and the like with companion plants with rounded leaves and postures, or fine-cut leaves and sprawling habits.

The summer callas come in many shades now, the result of breeding with South African species such as yellow *Zantedeschia elliottiana* and pink to plum *Z. rehmannii,*

*Elephant ears* (Colocasia antiquorum *var.* esculenta) *colonize miles of the San Marcos River in Texas.*

*The springlike delicacy of x* Amarcinum memoria-corsii *withstands the summer heat.*

both from summer-rainfall areas. Pink, mauve, red, orange, and yellow callas present a startling contrast as the white winter calla takes a rest. Gloriosa lilies (*Gloriosa rothschildsiana*) scamper up trellises and through shrubs, clinging by tendrils at the tips of their leaves. They then proceed to explode into scarlet-and-yellow blossoms of such beauty that only the word *exotic* applies. Gloriosas grow from long, thin tubers that look like cigars. They are planted horizontally—rather than like a carrot—just a few inches deep. They grow beautifully for some gardeners, returning faithfully year after year, but are a miserable failure for others. I suspect upscale slugs or snails to be the culprits, since Rothschild lilies appeal to slugs the way Beluga caviar does to people.

Pineapple lilies are often associated with a West Coast summer, but *Eucomis* comes from the summer-rainfall areas of South Africa and can withstand hot, humid air. It produces spikes of flowers from its rosette of broad leaves. The arrangement of the small flowers on the stem, capped by a topknot of leaves, does indeed resemble a pineapple. *E. bicolor* bears pale green flowers outlined in purple, while those of *E. comosa* are white or plum pink. They give quite a show, blooming for a month or more, and the flowers are replaced with pods that never interrupt the pineapple illusion. The South is crinum country, and summer species include pink *Crinum moorei,* evening-blooming *C. latifolium,* white or pink *C. x powelii*—all fragrant—and many more. When it really gets hot, x *Amarcrinum memoria-corsii* is there. The *x* indicates that humans created this genus by crossing *Amaryllis belladonna* with *Crinum moorei*. The sweet-scented, satin pink flowers look like those of the famous naked lady, but the stems of x *Amarcrinum* are accompanied by leaves at flowering time.

# 8

# BULBS FOR NATURALIZING

**NOTES**

**Regions:**

SOUTH (S): Texas, Louisiana, Alabama, Mississippi, Georgia, South Carolina, Florida

MID-ATLANTIC (MA): Pennsylvania, Virginia, North Carolina, Maryland, Delaware, New Jersey, Connecticut, Rhode Island

NORTHEAST (NE): Vermont, Maine, New Hampshire, Massachusetts, New York

BORDER STATES (BS): Kentucky, Tennessee, West Virginia, Arkansas, Oklahoma

MIDWEST (MW): Ohio, Illinois, Iowa, Nebraska, Indiana, Kansas, Missouri

UPPER MIDWEST (UM): Wisconsin, Michigan, North Dakota, South Dakota, Minnesota

ROCKY MOUNTAIN (RM): Colorado, New Mexico, Wyoming, Utah, Montana, Idaho, Nevada, northern Arizona, mountainous regions of California, Oregon, Washington

WEST COAST (WC): California, Arizona

PACIFIC NORTHWEST (PN): Oregon, Washington

**Height**

Short <10 inches; Medium >10 inches and <24 inches; Tall >24 inches

| Species | Geo. Reg. | Ht. | Color | Bloom Time | Garden Uses | Moist. Req. | Sun Req. | Soil Req. | Native Habitat |
|---|---|---|---|---|---|---|---|---|---|

## *Agapanthus* (Lily of the Nile)

| Species | Geo. Reg. | Ht. | Color | Bloom Time | Garden Uses | Moist. Req. | Sun Req. | Soil Req. | Native Habitat |
|---|---|---|---|---|---|---|---|---|---|
| *africanus* | S, WC | T | blue | summer | border, rock and cottage garden | medium to dry | full sun | adaptable | South Africa |
| *campanulatus* (Bell agapanthus) | S, WC | M | blue | summer | border, rock and cottage garden | moist to dry | full sun | adaptable | E. Cape Province, South Africa |
| *praecox* ssp. *orientalis* | S, WC | T | blue, white | summer | border, rock and cottage garden | medium to dry | full sun | adaptable | S. and E. South Africa |

## *Allium* (Ornamental Onion)

| Species | Geo. Reg. | Ht. | Color | Bloom Time | Garden Uses | Moist. Req. | Sun Req. | Soil Req. | Native Habitat |
|---|---|---|---|---|---|---|---|---|---|
| *aflatunense* | MA, NE, BS, MW, UM, RM, WC, PN | T | lavender | early summer | border, meadow, wild garden | medium | full sun to part shade | adaptable | Asia Minor and central Asia |
| *amabile* (Lovely onion) | S, MA, NE, BS, MW, RM, WC, PN | S | magenta | mid-summer | rock garden, edging | wet | full sun | adaptable | S.W. China: stony alpine meadows |
| *caeruleum* (Blue garlic) | MA, NE, BS, MW, UM, RM, WC, PN | M | blue | early summer | border, dryland | medium to dry | full sun | well drained | Russia: steppe |
| *cepa* var. *aggregatum* (Egyptian onion) | MA, NE, BS, MW, UM, RM, WC, PN | T | white | summer | border, vegetable and herb garden | medium | full sun | adaptable | central Asia, long cultivated |
| *cernuum* (Nodding onion) | S, MA, NE, BS, MW, UM, RM, WC, PN | M | pink | summer | border, rock garden, meadow | medium to wet | full sun | adaptable | North America |
| *christophii* (Star of Persia) | MA, NE, BS, MW, RM, WC, PN | M | lilac | early summer | border, herb garden | medium | full sun | well drained | central Asia to Iran: rocky slopes |

| Species | Geo. Reg. | Ht. | Color | Bloom Time | Garden Uses | Moist. Req. | Sun Req. | Soil Req. | Native Habitat |
|---|---|---|---|---|---|---|---|---|---|

**_Allium_ (Ornamental Onion)**, continued

| Species | Geo. Reg. | Ht. | Color | Bloom Time | Garden Uses | Moist. Req. | Sun Req. | Soil Req. | Native Habitat |
|---|---|---|---|---|---|---|---|---|---|
| _drummondii_ (Drummond's onion) | S, BS, MW | S | pink or white | spring | meadow, cottage garden | moist to dry | full sun | adaptable | Texas, Great Plains: thin, rocky ground |
| _flavum_ (Golden onion) | S, MA, NE, BS, MW, UM, RM, WC, PN | M | yellow | summer | border, shade garden, herb garden | medium | full sun to part shade | adaptable | S. and central Europe: dry slopes |
| _fraseri_ | S, MA, BS, MW, RM | M | white | spring | meadow, border | medium to dry | full sun | adaptable | Great Plains from South Dakota to Texas |
| _giganteum_ (Giant onion) | MA, NE, BS, MW, UM, RM, WC, PN | T | purple | early summer | border | medium | full sun | adaptable | Iran, Afghanistan, central Asia: lower mountain slopes |
| _hyacinthoides_ | S, BS, MW | S | pink | spring | meadow, cottage and shade garden, border | medium to dry | full sun to part shade | adaptable | N. Texas and Oklahoma |
| _jesdianum_ (syn. _rosenbachianum_) | MA, NE, MW, RM, PN | T | purple | late spring to early summer | border | medium to dry | full sun | adaptable | Iran and Iraq, Afghanistan |
| _karataviense_ (Turkish onion) | MA, NE, BS, MW, RM, WC, PN | S | pinkish white | late spring | border (front), dry land, rock, and herb garden | medium to dry | full sun | adaptable | central Asia: loose limestone scree |
| _moly_ (Lily leek, golden garlic) | S, MA, NE, BS, MW, UM, RM, WC, PN | S | yellow | early summer | border, shade and herb garden | medium to moist | sun to part shade | adaptable | S. Europe: shady, rocky mountainous |

| Species | Geo. Reg. | Ht. | Color | Bloom Time | Garden Uses | Moist. Req. | Sun Req. | Soil Req. | Native Habitat |
|---|---|---|---|---|---|---|---|---|---|
| *Allium* (Ornamental Onion), continued | | | | | | | | | |
| *neapolitanum* (daffodil garlic, Naples garlic) | S, MA, BS, WC, PN | M | white | spring | border, meadow, cottage garden | medium to dry | full sun | adaptable | N. Italy |
| *oreophilum* (Rosy onion) | S, MA, NE, BS, MW, RM, WC, PN | S | carmine | early summer | border (front), rock and cottage garden | medium | full sun | adaptable | Caucasus, Pakistan, Afghanistan, Iran, Turkey: rocky scree |
| *przwalskianum* (Tibetan chives) | NE, MW, RM, MW, PN | M | violet | summer | border, herb and cottage garden | medium | full sun | adaptable | Tibet |
| *pulchellum* (syn. *carinatum*) (Pretty onion) | MA, NE, BS, MW, RM, WC, PN | T | red-violet, white | summer | border, rock garden | medium | full sun | adaptable | S. Europe, Asia Minor: heaths, rocky ground |
| *ramosum* (Siberian garlic) | MA, NE, BS, MW, UM, RM, PN | M | white, purple | autumn | border, rock and herb garden | medium | full sun | adaptable | Siberia |
| *schoenoprasum* (Chives) | S, MA, NE, BS, MW, UM, RM, WC, PN | M | lavender | early summer | border, herb and cottage garden | medium | full sun to part shade | adaptable | Northern Hemisphere, long cultivated |
| *senescens* (Mountain or German garlic) | MA, NE, BS, MW, UM, RM, WC, PN | S | pink | autumn | edging, herb and rock garden | medium to dry | full sun | adaptable | Europe and central Asia as far as Siberia: dry rocky places |
| *sphaerocephalon* (Drumstick allium) | S, MA, NE, BS, MW, RM, WC, PN | T | maroon | summer | border, herb and cottage garden | medium | full sun | well drained | Europe, North Africa to W. Asia: limestone ledges and bluffs |

| Species | Geo. Reg. | Ht. | Color | Bloom Time | Garden Uses | Moist. Req. | Sun Req. | Soil Req. | Native Habitat |
|---|---|---|---|---|---|---|---|---|---|

## *Allium* **(Ornamental Onion)**, continued

| Species | Geo. Reg. | Ht. | Color | Bloom Time | Garden Uses | Moist. Req. | Sun Req. | Soil Req. | Native Habitat |
|---|---|---|---|---|---|---|---|---|---|
| *stellatum* (Prairie onion) | S, MA, NE, BS, MW, UM, RM | M | pink | autumn | border, meadow, cottage garden | medium | full sun | adaptable | Texas to Minnesota |
| *texanum* (White King) | S, MW | M | white | late spring | border, meadow | medium | full sun | adaptable | Texas and Oklahoma: upland |
| *thunbergii* 'Ozawa' | MA, NE, BS, MW, UM, RM, PN | M | violet | autumn | border, cottage garden | medium | full sun | adaptable | Japan |
| *triquetrum* (Three-cornered leek) | S, MA, BS, WC | M | white | late spring | cottage garden, meadow | medium to dry | sun to part shade | adaptable | Mediterranean region |
| *tuberosum* (Chinese or garlic chives) | S, MA, NE, BS, MW, UM, RM, WC, PN | M | white | late summer, early autumn | border, herb garden | dry to medium | full sun | adaptable | China, long cultivated |

## *Alstroemeria* **(Peruvian lily)**

| Species | Geo. Reg. | Ht. | Color | Bloom Time | Garden Uses | Moist. Req. | Sun Req. | Soil Req. | Native Habitat |
|---|---|---|---|---|---|---|---|---|---|
| *braziliensis* | S, MA, BS, WC, NW | T | reddish | summer | border, hillside, cottage garden | medium | full sun to part shade | well drained | central Brazil: forest edge |
| *aurantiaca* | WC, PN | T | golden orange | summer | border, hillside, cottage garden | medium | full sun to part shade | well drained | Chile: forest edge |
| *ligtu* and hybrids | MA, RM, WC, PN | T | variable | summer | border, hillside, cottage garden | medium | full sun to part shade | well drained | Chile: forest edge |
| *pelegrina* (Lily of the Incas) | WC, PN | M | variable | summer | border, hillside, cottage garden | medium | full sun to part shade | well drained | Chile: open thickets |
| *psittacina* (syn. *pulchella*) | S, MA, BS, WC, PN | T | reddish | summer | border, hillside, cottage garden | medium | full sun to part shade | well drained | N. Brazil: forest edge |

| Species | Geo. Reg. | Ht. | Color | Bloom Time | Garden Uses | Moist. Req. | Sun Req. | Soil Req. | Native Habitat |
|---------|-----------|-----|-------|-----------|-------------|-------------|----------|-----------|----------------|

## x *Amarcrinum* (Crinodonna lily)

| Species | Geo. Reg. | Ht. | Color | Bloom Time | Garden Uses | Moist. Req. | Sun Req. | Soil Req. | Native Habitat |
|---------|-----------|-----|-------|-----------|-------------|-------------|----------|-----------|----------------|
| *memoria-corsii* | S, WC, PN | T | pink | summer | border | medium | full sun to part shade | adaptable | man-made |

## *Amaryllis* (Naked lady)

| Species | Geo. Reg. | Ht. | Color | Bloom Time | Garden Uses | Moist. Req. | Sun Req. | Soil Req. | Native Habitat |
|---------|-----------|-----|-------|-----------|-------------|-------------|----------|-----------|----------------|
| *belladonna* | S, WC, PN | T | pink, white | summer | border, cottage garden, hillside | winter moisture, dry summer | full sun to part shade | adaptable | South Africa, S.W. Cape |

## *Amorphophallus* (Devil's tongue)

| Species | Geo. Reg. | Ht. | Color | Bloom Time | Garden Uses | Moist. Req. | Sun Req. | Soil Req. | Native Habitat |
|---------|-----------|-----|-------|-----------|-------------|-------------|----------|-----------|----------------|
| *bulbifera* | S | T | greenish | summer | shade garden | moist | shade | humus-rich | N.E. India to Burma: forest |
| *riveri* var. 'Konjac' | S, MA | T | purple | summer | shade garden, stream side | moist, drier in winter | shade | humus-rich | Indonesia to Japan: forest |
| *titanum* (Titanarum) | S, WC | T | greenish, red | summer | shade garden | moist | shade | humus-rich | Sumatra: forest |

## *Anemone*

| Species | Geo. Reg. | Ht. | Color | Bloom Time | Garden Uses | Moist. Req. | Sun Req. | Soil Req. | Native Habitat |
|---------|-----------|-----|-------|-----------|-------------|-------------|----------|-----------|----------------|
| *apennina* | S, MA, NE, BS, MW, UM, RM, WC, PN | S | white, blue | spring | shade garden, meadow | moist | part shade | humus-rich | S. Europe: open woodlands |
| *biflora* | S, BS, MA, WC, PN | S | reddish | spring | meadow, shade garden | medium | full sun to part shade | adaptable | Iran to India |
| *blanda* (Grecian windflower) | S, MA, NE, BS, MW, UM, RM, WC, PN | S | blue, white, pink | spring | border, edging, rock garden | medium to dry | full sun | well drained | Greece, Turkey: scrub, rocks, or meadows |
| *canadensis* | MA, NE, BS, MW, UM, RM, PN | S | white | spring | shade garden | medium to moist | part shade | adaptable | Northeast woodlands |

| Species | Geo. Reg. | Ht. | Color | Bloom Time | Garden Uses | Moist. Req. | Sun Req. | Soil Req. | Native Habitat |
|---|---|---|---|---|---|---|---|---|---|

**Anemone**, continued

| Species | Geo. Reg. | Ht. | Color | Bloom Time | Garden Uses | Moist. Req. | Sun Req. | Soil Req. | Native Habitat |
|---|---|---|---|---|---|---|---|---|---|
| *caroliniana* (Carolina anemone) | S, MA, BS, MW | S | purple, white, pink | winter, spring | meadow, woodland | medium | part shade | sandy | South, Midwest (U.S.): woodlands |
| *coronaria* (Poppy anemone) | S, WC | M | variable | spring | border, cottage garden | medium | full sun | well drained | Mediterranean region, W. Asia: meadow |
| x *fulgens* (Peacock eye) | S, WC | M | red | late spring | border, cottage garden | medium | full sun | well drained | S. France |
| *nemorosa* (Wood anemone) | S, MA, NE, BS, MW, UM, RM, WC, PN | S | white | spring | shade and rock garden, meadow | moist | shade | humus-rich | Europe: woodlands |
| *heterophylla* | S, MA, BS | S | white, pink, blue | winter, spring | lawn | medium to moist | sun to part shade | adaptable | Texas to Alabama: fields |

**Anemonella**

| Species | Geo. Reg. | Ht. | Color | Bloom Time | Garden Uses | Moist. Req. | Sun Req. | Soil Req. | Native Habitat |
|---|---|---|---|---|---|---|---|---|---|
| *thalictrioides* (Rue anemone) | S, MA, NE, BS, MW, RM, WC, PN | S | white | spring | shade garden | moist | part shade | humus-rich | Maine to Florida, west to Oklahoma: open woodland |

**Anthericum**

| Species | Geo. Reg. | Ht. | Color | Bloom Time | Garden Uses | Moist. Req. | Sun Req. | Soil Req. | Native Habitat |
|---|---|---|---|---|---|---|---|---|---|
| *liliago* (St. Bernard's lily) | NE, MA, BS, MW, RM, PN | M | white | early summer | border, rock garden | medium | full sun | well drained, alkaline | Europe: alpine meadows |

**Arisaema**

| Species | Geo. Reg. | Ht. | Color | Bloom Time | Garden Uses | Moist. Req. | Sun Req. | Soil Req. | Native Habitat |
|---|---|---|---|---|---|---|---|---|---|
| *candidissimum* | S, MA, NE, BS, MW, WC, PN | M | white | early summer | shade garden, streamside | moist | part sun to full shade | humus-rich | W. China: woodlands |

| Species | Geo. Reg. | Ht. | Color | Bloom Time | Garden Uses | Moist. Req. | Sun Req. | Soil Req. | Native Habitat |
|---|---|---|---|---|---|---|---|---|---|
| *Arisaema*, continued | | | | | | | | | |
| *dracontium* (Green dragon) | S, MA, NE, BS, MW, UM, RM, WC, PN | M | greenish | spring | shade garden, streamside | moist | shade | humus-rich | North America: eastern woodlands |
| *flavum* | S, MA, BS, WC, PN | M | yellow-green | spring | shade garden | moist | shade | humus-rich | Afghanistan, Himalayas: woodlands |
| *ringens* | S, MA, BS, PN | M | white, purple-brown | spring | shade garden | moist | part shade | humus-rich | Japan: woodlands |
| *sikokianum* | S, MA, NE, BS, MW, UM, RM, WC, PN | M | purple and white | early summer | shade garden | moist | shade | humus-rich | Japan: woodlands |
| *triphyllum* (Jack-in-the-pulpit) | S, MA, NE, BS, MW, UM, RM, WC, PN | M | purple and white | spring | spring shade garden | moist | shade | humus-rich | North America: eastern woodlands |

## *Arum*

| Species | Geo. Reg. | Ht. | Color | Bloom Time | Garden Uses | Moist. Req. | Sun Req. | Soil Req. | Native Habitat |
|---|---|---|---|---|---|---|---|---|---|
| *creticum* | S, MA, BS, WC, PN | M | yellow | spring | full sun | medium to dry | full sun | adaptable | Crete: rocky hillsides |
| *italicum* 'Pictum' (Lords and Ladies) | S, MA, NE, BS, MW, UM, RM, WC, PN | M | white flowers, red berries | autumn (berries) | shade garden, border | medium | full sun to shade | adaptable | S. and W. Europe: hedges, rocky places, woodlands |
| *maculatum* (Cuckoopint, Adam and Eve) | S, MA, NE, BS, MW, UM, RM, WC, PN | M | white, red berries | autumn (berries) | shade garden, border | medium | full sun to shade | adaptable | central and S. Europe: hedgerows |
| *palestinum* (Black calla) | S, WC | M | green, purple | spring | shade garden, border | medium | full sun to part shade | adaptable | Syria, Lebanon: Israel |

| Species | Geo. Reg. | Ht. | Color | Bloom Time | Garden Uses | Moist. Req. | Sun Req. | Soil Req. | Native Habitat |
|---|---|---|---|---|---|---|---|---|---|

## *Asphodeline* (Jacob's rod)

| Species | Geo. Reg. | Ht. | Color | Bloom Time | Garden Uses | Moist. Req. | Sun Req. | Soil Req. | Native Habitat |
|---|---|---|---|---|---|---|---|---|---|
| *tuarica* | MA, BS, WC, PN | M | white with pink | spring, summer | border, rock garden | medium to dry | full sun | well drained | Greece, Caucasus: hillside |
| *liburnica* | MA, NE, BS, MW, RM, WC, PN | M | yellow | spring, summer | border, rock garden | medium | full sun | well drained | Balkans, S. Europe |
| *lutea* (King's spear) | MA, BS, MW, RM, WC, PN | T | golden yellow | summer | border | medium in spring, dryer later | full sun | well drained | Mediterranean region: rocky hills |

## *Asphodelus*

| Species | Geo. Reg. | Ht. | Color | Bloom Time | Garden Uses | Moist. Req. | Sun Req. | Soil Req. | Native Habitat |
|---|---|---|---|---|---|---|---|---|---|
| *albus* | WC, PN | T | white with pink | late spring, summer | border, hillside | medium in spring, dryer later | full sun | well drained | S. Europe |
| *ramosus* | WC, PN | T | white with rust | late spring, summer | border, rock garden | medium in spring, dryer later | full sun | well drained | S. Europe, North Africa |

## *Babiana* (Baboon root)

| Species | Geo. Reg. | Ht. | Color | Bloom Time | Garden Uses | Moist. Req. | Sun Req. | Soil Req. | Native Habitat |
|---|---|---|---|---|---|---|---|---|---|
| *pulchra* | S, WC | S | purple | early spring | border, rock garden | wet winter, dry summer | full sun | well drained | South Africa: meadows |
| *stricta* | S, WC | S to M | variable | spring | border, rock garden | wet winter, dry summer | full sun | well drained | South Africa: S.W. Cape |
| *rubrocyanea* (Wine cup babiana) | S, WC | S | dark red | spring | border, rock garden | wet winter, dry summer | full sun | well drained | South Africa: W. Cape |
| *villosa* | S, WC | S | magenta | spring | border, slope | wet winter, dry summer | full sun | well drained | South Africa |

| Species | Geo. Reg. | Ht. | Color | Bloom Time | Garden Uses | Moist. Req. | Sun Req. | Soil Req. | Native Habitat |
|---|---|---|---|---|---|---|---|---|---|

## *Begonia*

| Species | Geo. Reg. | Ht. | Color | Bloom Time | Garden Uses | Moist. Req. | Sun Req. | Soil Req. | Native Habitat |
|---|---|---|---|---|---|---|---|---|---|
| *grandis* (Hardy begonia) | S, MA, BS, WC, PN | M | pink | late summer | border, shade and cottage garden | moist | shade to part sun | adaptable | China and Japan: woodlands |
| *heracleifolia* (Star begonia) | S | M | pink | summer | shade garden | moist | shade | humus-rich | Mexico |

## *Belamcanda*

| Species | Geo. Reg. | Ht. | Color | Bloom Time | Garden Uses | Moist. Req. | Sun Req. | Soil Req. | Native Habitat |
|---|---|---|---|---|---|---|---|---|---|
| *chinensis* (Blackberry lily) | S, MA, NE, BS, MW, RM, WC, PN | T | yellow, orange; black berries | summer (flowers); autumn (berries) | border | medium | full sun | well drained | E. Asia |

## *Bletilla* (Ground orchid)

| Species | Geo. Reg. | Ht. | Color | Bloom Time | Garden Uses | Moist. Req. | Sun Req. | Soil Req. | Native Habitat |
|---|---|---|---|---|---|---|---|---|---|
| *striata* | S, MA, BS, WC, PN | M | pink, white | spring | shade garden | medium to moist | shade to part sun | humus-rich | China, Japan: light woodlands |

## *Bulbocodium*

| Species | Geo. Reg. | Ht. | Color | Bloom Time | Garden Uses | Moist. Req. | Sun Req. | Soil Req. | Native Habitat |
|---|---|---|---|---|---|---|---|---|---|
| *vernum* (Mountain saffron) | MA, NE, RM, PN | S | pink | spring | rock garden | medium | full sun to part shade | well drained | Spain, Alps: alpine meadows and slopes |

## *Canna*

| Species | Geo. Reg. | Ht. | Color | Bloom Time | Garden Uses | Moist. Req. | Sun Req. | Soil Req. | Native Habitat |
|---|---|---|---|---|---|---|---|---|---|
| *childsii* 'Cleopatra' (Harlequin or tiger canna) | S, WC | T | yellow, red | summer | border, streamside | moist | full sun | adaptable | Asia |
| *edulis* | S, WC | T | red, yellow | summer | border, streamside, cottage garden | moist | full sun | adaptable | West Indies and South America |
| *flaccida* | S, BS, WC | T | yellow | summer | border, streamside, cottage garden | moist | full sun | adaptable | Florida: moist places |

| Species | Geo. Reg. | Ht. | Color | Bloom Time | Garden Uses | Moist. Req. | Sun Req. | Soil Req. | Native Habitat |
|---|---|---|---|---|---|---|---|---|---|
| **Canna**, continued | | | | | | | | | |
| *glauca* | S, WC | T | pale yellow; blue green leaves | summer | border, streamside, cottage garden | moist | full sun | adaptable | West Indies |
| *indica* (Indian shot) | S, BS, WC | T | red, pink | summer | border, streamside, cottage garden | moist | full sun | adaptable | West Indies, Central and South America |
| *iridiflora* (Iris-flowered canna) | S, WC | T | pink | summer | border, streamside | moist | full sun | adaptable | Peru |
| *warscewiczii* 'Robusta' | S, WC | T | scarlet; bronze foliage | summer | border, streamside, cottage garden | moist | full sun | adaptable | Costa Rica, Brazil |
| **Calochortus** | | | | | | | | | |
| *albus* (Cat's ears) | RM, WC, PN | M | white to pink | spring | meadow, rock garden | moist winter, dry summer | full sun | well drained | California: coastal ranges |
| *uniflorus* (Cat's ears) | RM, WC, PN | M | pink | early summer | meadow, rock garden | medium | full sun | well drained | S. Oregon |
| *venustus* (Mariposa lily) | RM, WC | M | variable | spring | meadow, rock garden | moist winter, dry summer | full sun | well drained | California: Sierra Nevada |

| Species | Geo. Reg. | Ht. | Color | Bloom Time | Garden Uses | Moist. Req. | Sun Req. | Soil Req. | Native Habitat |
|---|---|---|---|---|---|---|---|---|---|

## *Camassia* (Indian hyacinth)

| Species | Geo. Reg. | Ht. | Color | Bloom Time | Garden Uses | Moist. Req. | Sun Req. | Soil Req. | Native Habitat |
|---|---|---|---|---|---|---|---|---|---|
| *cusickii* | NE, RM, WC, PN | T | pale blue | summer | meadow, border, streamside | moist | full sun | humus-rich | Oregon: moist meadows |
| *leichtlinii* | NE, RM, WC, PN | T | blue, white | early summer | meadow, border, streamside | moist | full sun | humus-rich | California to British Columbia: mountain meadows |
| *quamash* (Wild hyacinth) | NE, RM, WC, PN | M | blue, white | late spring | meadow, streamside | moist | full sun to part shade | humus-rich, moisture retentive | W. North America: mountain meadows, light woodlands |

## *Chasmanthe* (Flame flower)

| Species | Geo. Reg. | Ht. | Color | Bloom Time | Garden Uses | Moist. Req. | Sun Req. | Soil Req. | Native Habitat |
|---|---|---|---|---|---|---|---|---|---|
| *aethiopica* | WC | T | orange red | winter, spring | slope, cottage garden, border | moist in winter, dry in summer | full sun to part shade | well drained | South Africa, Cape Province coast |
| *floribunda* var. *duckittii* | WC | T | yellow | winter, spring | border, slope | moist in winter, dry in summer | full sun | well drained | S.W. Cape Province: wet fields |

## *Chionodoxa*

| Species | Geo. Reg. | Ht. | Color | Bloom Time | Garden Uses | Moist. Req. | Sun Req. | Soil Req. | Native Habitat |
|---|---|---|---|---|---|---|---|---|---|
| *luciliae* (Glory-of-the-snow) | MA, NE, BS, MW, UM, RM, WC, PN | S | blue, white, pink | early spring | border, rock, cottage and woodland gardens | medium | full sun to part shade | adaptable | central Turkey: mountains |
| *sardensis* | MA, NE, BS, MW, UM, RM, WC, PN | S | deep blue | spring | border, rock, cottage and woodland gardens | medium | sun to part shade | adaptable | W. Turkey: mountains |

| Species | Geo. Reg. | Ht. | Color | Bloom Time | Garden Uses | Moist. Req. | Sun Req. | Soil Req. | Native Habitat |
|---|---|---|---|---|---|---|---|---|---|

*Clivia*

| Species | Geo. Reg. | Ht. | Color | Bloom Time | Garden Uses | Moist. Req. | Sun Req. | Soil Req. | Native Habitat |
|---|---|---|---|---|---|---|---|---|---|
| *miniata* | S, WC | M | orange, yellow | winter, spring | shade garden, border | medium | part shade | adaptable | South Africa, Natal: evergreen forests |
| *nobilis* | WC | M | red, yellow, green tip | winter, spring | shade garden | medium | part shade | adaptable | South Africa |

*Colchicum* **(Meadow saffron, Naked boys)**

| Species | Geo. Reg. | Ht. | Color | Bloom Time | Garden Uses | Moist. Req. | Sun Req. | Soil Req. | Native Habitat |
|---|---|---|---|---|---|---|---|---|---|
| *autumnale* | S, MA, NE, BS, MW, UM, RM, WC, PN | S | lavender pink | autumn | shade, dryland and cottage gardens, border, meadow | medium to dry | full sun to part shade | adaptable | Europe: meadows |
| *bivonae* | MA, NE, BS, MW, RM, WC, PN | S | lavender purple | autumn | border, meadow, shade garden | medium | sun to part shade | adaptable | Europe, Asia: fields |
| *cilicicum* | WC | S | lilac pink | autumn, winter | border, meadow, rock garden | medium to dry | sun to part shade | adaptable | S. Turkey |
| *giganteum* | MA, NE, BS, MW, RM, WC, PN | M | pink | autumn | shade, dryland, cottage gardens, border, meadow | medium to dry | full sun to part shade | adaptable | Turkey: meadows |
| *speciosum* | MA, NE, BS, MW, RM, WC, PN | S | rose purple | autumn | shade, dryland, cottage gardens, border, meadow | medium to dry | full sun to part shade | adaptable | Turkey, Caucasus, Aegean islands: meadows, light woodland |
| *variegatum* | WC | S | deep lilac | autumn | rock garden | medium to dry | sun to part shade | well drained | Turkey |

| Species | Geo. Reg. | Ht. | Color | Bloom Time | Garden Uses | Moist. Req. | Sun Req. | Soil Req. | Native Habitat |
|---------|-----------|-----|-------|------------|-------------|-------------|----------|-----------|----------------|

## *Colocasia* (Elephant ear)

| Species | Geo. Reg. | Ht. | Color | Bloom Time | Garden Uses | Moist. Req. | Sun Req. | Soil Req. | Native Habitat |
|---------|-----------|-----|-------|------------|-------------|-------------|----------|-----------|----------------|
| *antiquorum* var. *esculenta* | S | T | foliage | summer | streamside | moist | full sun to part shade | adaptable | tropical Asia |

## *Convallaria* (Lily-of-the-valley)

| Species | Geo. Reg. | Ht. | Color | Bloom Time | Garden Uses | Moist. Req. | Sun Req. | Soil Req. | Native Habitat |
|---------|-----------|-----|-------|------------|-------------|-------------|----------|-----------|----------------|
| *majalis* | MA, NE, BS, MW, UM, RM, WC, PN | S | white, pink | spring | shade and cottage gardens | moist to medium | part shade | adaptable, humus-rich | N. temperate zones: woodland, high meadows |

## *Crinum*

| Species | Geo. Reg. | Ht. | Color | Bloom Time | Garden Uses | Moist. Req. | Sun Req. | Soil Req. | Native Habitat |
|---------|-----------|-----|-------|------------|-------------|-------------|----------|-----------|----------------|
| *americanum* (Swamp lily) | S, MA, BS | T | white | spring, summer | shade garden, streamside | moist | shade | humus-rich | Georgia, Florida: swamplands |
| *asiaticum* (St. John's lily) | S | T | white | winter | cottage garden, border | moist | full sun | humus-rich | Japan to Australia |
| *bulbispermum* (Orange River lily) | S, MA, WC | T | white, pink | winter | cottage garden, border | moist | full sun | adaptable | South Africa, river banks |
| *macowanii* | S, WC, PN | Tall | white, pink striped | summer | cottage garden, border | medium | full sun | adaptable | South Africa |
| *moorei* (Cape coast lily) | S, WC, PN | T | white, pink | summer | cottage garden, border | moist to medium; summer moisture, dry winter | part shade | humus-rich | South Africa, Natal Province: forest |
| x *powellii* | S, WC, PN | T | pink to white | summer | cottage garden, border | medium | full sun | adaptable | hybrid |

| Species | Geo. Reg. | Ht. | Color | Bloom Time | Garden Uses | Moist. Req. | Sun Req. | Soil Req. | Native Habitat |
|---|---|---|---|---|---|---|---|---|---|

## *Crocosmia*

| Species | Geo. Reg. | Ht. | Color | Bloom Time | Garden Uses | Moist. Req. | Sun Req. | Soil Req. | Native Habitat |
|---|---|---|---|---|---|---|---|---|---|
| *aurea* | S, MA, BS, WC, PN | T | yellow, orange | summer | border, cottage garden | medium to moist | full sun | well drained, moisture retentive | South Africa: moist grassland |
| x *crocosmiiflora* | S, MA, BS, WC, PN | M | yellow, orange | summer | border, meadow, cottage garden | medium | full sun | adaptable | South Africa |
| x *curtonus paniculatus* 'Lucifer' | S, MA, NE, BS, MW, RM, WC, PN | T | flame red | summer | border, cottage garden | medium | full sun | adaptable | South African man-made hybrid |
| *masoniorum* (*masonorum*) | S, MA, NE, BS, MW, RM, WC, PN | T | red | summer | border, cottage garden | medium | full sun | adaptable | S.E. South African coast |
| *pottsii* | S, BS, WC | T | orange | summer | woodland, streamside | moist | part shade | well drained, moisture retentive | South African woodland |

## *Crocus*: Spring

| Species | Geo. Reg. | Ht. | Color | Bloom Time | Garden Uses | Moist. Req. | Sun Req. | Soil Req. | Native Habitat |
|---|---|---|---|---|---|---|---|---|---|
| *ancyrensis* (Golden bunch) | S, MA, NE, BS, MW, RM, WC, PN | S | golden yellow | late winter, early spring | lawn, border, rock garden | medium to dry | full sun | well drained | Turkey |
| *angustifolius* (Cloth of gold) | S, MA, NE, BS, MW, RM, WC, PN | S | yellow with maroon | late winter, early spring | lawn, border, rock garden | medium | full sun | adaptable | Russia, Ukraine, Armenia |
| *biflorus* | S, MA, BS, MW, RM, WC, PN | S | white, lilac, blue | late winter, early spring | lawn, border, rock garden | medium to dry | full sun | well drained | Turkey: hillsides |
| *chrysanthus* (Snow crocus) | MA, NE, BS, MW, UM, RM, PN | S | white, blue, yellow, purple | spring | lawn, border, rock garden | medium to dry | full sun | well drained | Turkey, Balkans (widely distributed) |

| Species | Geo. Reg. | Ht. | Color | Bloom Time | Garden Uses | Moist. Req. | Sun Req. | Soil Req. | Native Habitat |
|---|---|---|---|---|---|---|---|---|---|

*Crocus*: **Spring**, continued

| Species | Geo. Reg. | Ht. | Color | Bloom Time | Garden Uses | Moist. Req. | Sun Req. | Soil Req. | Native Habitat |
|---|---|---|---|---|---|---|---|---|---|
| *corsicus* | S, MA, BS, WC | S | lavender | spring | lawn, border, rock garden | medium to dry | full sun | well drained | Corsica |
| *etruscus* (Italian crocus) | WC, PN | S | lavender | late winter, early spring | lawn, hillside, rock garden | medium | sun to part shade | well drained | Italy: light woodlands |
| *flavus* 'Dutch Yellow' | S, MA, NE, BS, MW, UM, RM, WC, PN | S | yellow | spring | lawn, border, rock garden | medium to dry | full sun | well drained | Turkey to Balkans |
| *seiberi* | S | S | white with purple and yellow | spring | lawn, border, rock garden | medium to dry | full sun | well drained | Crete, Greece |
| *tommasinianus* (Tommies) | S, MA, NE, BS, WC, PN | S | lavender blue | spring | lawn, border, rock garden | medium to dry | full sun | well drained | Balkans, Hungary, Bulgaria |
| *vernus* (Dutch crocus) | S, MA, NE, BS, MW, UM, RM, WC, PN | S | white, violet, blue | late winter, spring | lawn, border, rock garden | medium to dry | full sun | well drained | Italy, Austria, E. Europe |

*Crocus*: **Autumn**

| Species | Geo. Reg. | Ht. | Color | Bloom Time | Garden Uses | Moist. Req. | Sun Req. | Soil Req. | Native Habitat |
|---|---|---|---|---|---|---|---|---|---|
| *banaticus* | WC | S | purple | autumn | rock garden, hillside | medium to dry | full sun | well drained | Romania: hills |
| *cancellatus* | WC | S | white, lavender | autumn | rock garden, hillside | medium to dry | full sun | well drained | Greece: rocky hills |
| *caspius* | WC | S | white, pink | autumn | rock garden, seaside | medium to dry | full sun | well drained | shore of Caspian Sea |

| Species | Geo. Reg. | Ht. | Color | Bloom Time | Garden Uses | Moist. Req. | Sun Req. | Soil Req. | Native Habitat |
|---|---|---|---|---|---|---|---|---|---|

**Crocus: Autumn**, continued

| Species | Geo. Reg. | Ht. | Color | Bloom Time | Garden Uses | Moist. Req. | Sun Req. | Soil Req. | Native Habitat |
|---|---|---|---|---|---|---|---|---|---|
| *goulimyi* | S, MA, BS, RM, WC, PN | S | lavender | autumn | border, meadow, cottage and rock garden | medium | full sun | well drained | Greece: olive groves |
| *kotschyanus* (syn. *C. zonatus*) | S, MA, NE, BS, MW, RM, WC, PN | S | lilac | autumn | border, meadow, cottage and rock garden | medium | full sun | well drained | Turkey, Syria, Lebanon |
| *laevigatus* | S, BS, WC | S | white, mauve, bronze, yellow | autumn | border, meadow, cottage and rock garden | medium | full sun | well drained | Greece, Crete |
| *longiflorus* | WC | S | pale violet, bronze | autumn | dryland, rock garden | medium to dry | full sun | well drained | S. Italy |
| *medius* | S, MA, BS, RM, WC | S | red violet | autumn | border, meadow, cottage and rock garden | medium | full sun | well drained | N.W. Italy, S.W. France |
| *niveus* | WC | S | white | autumn | rock garden, hillside | medium to dry | full sun | well drained | Turkey |
| *ochroleucus* | S, WC | S | cream | autumn | border, meadow, cottage and rock garden | medium | full sun | well drained | Lebanon |
| *pulchellus* | MA, BS, MW, RM, WC, PN | S | pink | autumn | border, rock and cottage garden | medium | full sun | well drained | Turkey |
| *sativus* (Saffron crocus) | MA, BS, MW, RM, WC | S | purple | autumn | border, meadow, cottage, rock and herb gardens | dry | full sun | well drained | Italy to Turkey |

| Species | Geo. Reg. | Ht. | Color | Bloom Time | Garden Uses | Moist. Req. | Sun Req. | Soil Req. | Native Habitat |
|---------|-----------|-----|-------|------------|-------------|-------------|----------|-----------|----------------|

*Crocus*: **Autumn**, continued

| Species | Geo. Reg. | Ht. | Color | Bloom Time | Garden Uses | Moist. Req. | Sun Req. | Soil Req. | Native Habitat |
|---------|-----------|-----|-------|------------|-------------|-------------|----------|-----------|----------------|
| *serotinus* | WC | S | lilac | autumn | shade garden | medium to dry | part shade | well drained | Spain, North Africa: stony hills |
| *speciosus* | MA, NE, BS, MW, RM, WC, PN | S | lavender | autumn | border, meadow, cottage and rock garden | medium | full sun | well drained | Caucasus, Turkey, Iran |

*Cyclamen*

| Species | Geo. Reg. | Ht. | Color | Bloom Time | Garden Uses | Moist. Req. | Sun Req. | Soil Req. | Native Habitat |
|---------|-----------|-----|-------|------------|-------------|-------------|----------|-----------|----------------|
| *coum* | MA, NE, BS, MW, RM, WC, PN | S | pink, white | winter and early spring | shade garden, woodland, meadow, rock garden | medium | full sun to part shade | adaptable | Bulgaria, Turkey, Lebanon, mountains |
| *hederifolium* | S, MA, NE, BS, MW, RM, WC, PN | S | pink, carmine, white | early to mid autumn | shade garden, rock garden | medium | part shade | adaptable | Italy to Turkey: mountains (beneath trees) |
| *persicum* | S, WC | S | pink, red, white | winter | shade garden | medium | sun to shade | adaptable | S. Mediterranean region |
| *repandum* | WC, PN | S | pink, rose, white | spring | shade garden, rock garden | medium | shade | adaptable | Mediterranean region |

*Dicentra*

| Species | Geo. Reg. | Ht. | Color | Bloom Time | Garden Uses | Moist. Req. | Sun Req. | Soil Req. | Native Habitat |
|---------|-----------|-----|-------|------------|-------------|-------------|----------|-----------|----------------|
| *canadensis* (Squirrel corn) | MA, NE, BS, MW, UM, RM, PN | S | white | spring | shade garden | moist | shade | humus-rich | E. North America |
| *cucullaria* (Dutchman's breeches) | MA, NE, BS, MW, UM, RM, WC, NW | S | white | spring | shade garden | moist | shade | humus-rich | E. North America |

| Species | Geo. Reg. | Ht. | Color | Bloom Time | Garden Uses | Moist. Req. | Sun Req. | Soil Req. | Native Habitat |
|---------|-----------|-----|-------|------------|-------------|-------------|----------|-----------|----------------|

**Dicentra**, continued

| Species | Geo. Reg. | Ht. | Color | Bloom Time | Garden Uses | Moist. Req. | Sun Req. | Soil Req. | Native Habitat |
|---------|-----------|-----|-------|------------|-------------|-------------|----------|-----------|----------------|
| *eximia* (Ever-blooming bleeding heart) | MA, NE, BS, MW, UM, RM, WC, PN | M | pink, white | spring | shade garden | moist to medium | shade to part sun | humus-rich | New York to Georgia |
| *formosa* | NE, MW, RM, WC, PN | M | pink to white | spring | shade garden | medium to moist | shade | humus-rich | W. U.S. to British Columbia: woodlands |
| *spectabilis* (Bleeding heart) | MA, NE, BS, MW, UM, RM, WC, PN | M to T | pink or white | spring | shade and woodland gardens | moist | shade | humus-rich | Siberia, Japan: woodlands |

**Dierama (Venus' fishing rod)**

| Species | Geo. Reg. | Ht. | Color | Bloom Time | Garden Uses | Moist. Req. | Sun Req. | Soil Req. | Native Habitat |
|---------|-----------|-----|-------|------------|-------------|-------------|----------|-----------|----------------|
| *pulcherrimum* | WC, PN | M | plum pink, white | summer | border, streamside | medium to moist | sun to part shade | well drained, humus-rich | South Africa: near water |
| *pendulum* | WC, PN | M | plum pink, pink, white | summer | border | medium | sun to part shade | well drained, humus-rich | South Africa: high grasslands |

**Dietes (Fortnight lily)**

| Species | Geo. Reg. | Ht. | Color | Bloom Time | Garden Uses | Moist. Req. | Sun Req. | Soil Req. | Native Habitat |
|---------|-----------|-----|-------|------------|-------------|-------------|----------|-----------|----------------|
| *bicolor* | S, WC | T | cream | summer, autumn, early winter | border, cottage garden, streamside | medium to moist, reduce in summer | full sun | adaptable | Cape Province, South Africa |
| *iridoides* | S, WC | M | white with purple | late winter | border, cottage garden, streamside | medium | full sun to part shade | adaptable | Cape Province, South Africa |

| Species | Geo. Reg. | Ht. | Color | Bloom Time | Garden Uses | Moist. Req. | Sun Req. | Soil Req. | Native Habitat |
|---|---|---|---|---|---|---|---|---|---|

## *Eranthis* (Winter aconite)

| Species | Geo. Reg. | Ht. | Color | Bloom Time | Garden Uses | Moist. Req. | Sun Req. | Soil Req. | Native Habitat |
|---|---|---|---|---|---|---|---|---|---|
| *cilicica* | MA, NE, BS, MW, UM, RM, WC, PN | S | yellow | winter, early spring | shade, cottage and rock garden, border, lawn | medium | shade to part sun | adaptable | S. Turkey |
| *hyemalis* | MA, NE, BS, MW, UM, RM, WC, PN | S | yellow | late winter to early spring | shade, cottage and rock garden, border, lawn | medium to moist | shade to part sun | adaptable | W. Europe |

## *Eremurus* (Foxtail lily)

| Species | Geo. Reg. | Ht. | Color | Bloom Time | Garden Uses | Moist. Req. | Sun Req. | Soil Req. | Native Habitat |
|---|---|---|---|---|---|---|---|---|---|
| *himalaicus* | MA, NE, MW, RM, PN | T | white | summer | border, meadow, cottage garden | medium to dry | full sun | adaptable | Kashmir: high slopes and meadows |
| *robustus* | NE, MW, UM, RM, PN | T | pink | summer | border, meadow, cottage garden | medium to dry | full sun | adaptable | Russia, Afghanistan |
| x *shelford* | MA, NE, BS, MW, RM, PN | T | variable | summer | border, meadow, cottage garden | medium to dry | full sun | adaptable | man-made hybrid |
| *stenophyllus* (syn. *bungei*) | MA, NE, BS, MW, RM, WC, NW | T | golden orange | summer | border, meadow, cottage garden | medium to dry | full sun | adaptable | Iran, Turkestan, Afghanistan: dry hills |

| Species | Geo. Reg. | Ht. | Color | Bloom Time | Garden Uses | Moist. Req. | Sun Req. | Soil Req. | Native Habitat |
|---|---|---|---|---|---|---|---|---|---|

## *Erythronium*

| Species | Geo. Reg. | Ht. | Color | Bloom Time | Garden Uses | Moist. Req. | Sun Req. | Soil Req. | Native Habitat |
|---|---|---|---|---|---|---|---|---|---|
| *albidum* (White dog-tooth violet) | S, MA, NE, BS, MW, UM, RM, WC, PN | S | white | spring | shade, rock garden | moist | shade | well drained | Canada to Texas: woodland |
| *americanum* (Trout lily) | S, MA, NE, BS, MW, UM, RM, WC, PN | S | yellow | spring | shade, rock garden | moist | shade | well drained | E. North America: woodland |
| *dens-canis* (Dog-tooth lily) | MA, NE, BS, MW, UM, RM, WC, PN | S | pink to purple | spring | shade, rock garden | moist | shade | well drained | Europe and Asia: woodland |
| *grandiflorum* (Glacier lily) | NE, RM, PN | S | yellow | spring | shade, rock garden | moist | shade | well drained | West U.S.: mountains |
| *revolutum* (Trout lily) | WC, PN | S | pink | spring | shade, rock garden | moist | shade | well drained | N. California to Vancouver |
| *tuolumnense* (Fawn lily) | WC, PN | S | pink | spring | shade, rock garden | moist | shade | well drained | central California |

## *Eucomis* (Pineapple lily)

| Species | Geo. Reg. | Ht. | Color | Bloom Time | Garden Uses | Moist. Req. | Sun Req. | Soil Req. | Native Habitat |
|---|---|---|---|---|---|---|---|---|---|
| *bicolor* | S, MA, WC | M | chartreuse and purple | summer | hillside, border, cottage and rock garden | medium in summer, dry in winter | full sun | well drained | Natal, South Africa |
| *punctata* | S, MA, WC | M | chartreuse and pink | summer | hillside, border, cottage and rock garden | medium | full sun | adaptable | Natal and E. Cape, South Africa |

| Species | Geo. Reg. | Ht. | Color | Bloom Time | Garden Uses | Moist. Req. | Sun Req. | Soil Req. | Native Habitat |
|---|---|---|---|---|---|---|---|---|---|

### *Freesia*

| Species | Geo. Reg. | Ht. | Color | Bloom Time | Garden Uses | Moist. Req. | Sun Req. | Soil Req. | Native Habitat |
|---|---|---|---|---|---|---|---|---|---|
| *alba* | WC | M | white | winter to spring | cottage and rock garden | moist in spring, dry in summer | full sun to part shade | well drained | Cape Province, South Africa |
| *corymbosa* | WC | M | ivory, yellow, pink | winter to spring | cottage and rock garden | moist in spring, dry in summer | full sun to part shade | well drained | Cape Province, South Africa |
| *x hybrida* | WC | M | various | winter to spring | cottage and rock garden, cutting garden | moist in summer, dry in spring | full sun to part shade | well drained | Cape Province, South Africa |
| *refracta* | WC | M | yellow with orange and purple | winter to spring | cottage and rock garden | moist in spring, dry in summer | full sun to part shade | well drained | Cape Province, South Africa |

### *Fritillaria*

| Species | Geo. Reg. | Ht. | Color | Bloom Time | Garden Uses | Moist. Req. | Sun Req. | Soil Req. | Native Habitat |
|---|---|---|---|---|---|---|---|---|---|
| *acmopetala* | RM, WC, PN | S to M | yellow green with brown | spring | border, rock garden, meadow | medium | full sun to part shade | well drained | Cyprus, Syria, Lebanon: hillsides |
| *assyriaca* | MA, NE, BS, MW, RM, WC, PN | S | green and violet | spring | border, rock garden | medium | full sun | adaptable | Iraq, Iran, Turkey: dry rocky scrub |
| *biflora* (Mission bells) | WC | S to M | purple with green | spring | meadow, rock garden | moist in spring, dry in summer | full sun | adaptable | California: fields |
| *camschatcensis* | MA, NE, BS, MW, UM, RM, WC, PN | M | blackish | spring | woodland | moist | part shade | humus-rich | Pacific Northwest, Alaska, Japan: woodlands |

| Species | Geo. Reg. | Ht. | Color | Bloom Time | Garden Uses | Moist. Req. | Sun Req. | Soil Req. | Native Habitat |
|---|---|---|---|---|---|---|---|---|---|

*Fritillaria*, continued

| Species | Geo. Reg. | Ht. | Color | Bloom Time | Garden Uses | Moist. Req. | Sun Req. | Soil Req. | Native Habitat |
|---|---|---|---|---|---|---|---|---|---|
| *imperialis* (Crown imperial) | MA, NE, BS, MW, UM, RM, WC, PN | T | yellow, orange | spring | border, woodland, streamside | moist | full sun to part shade | adaptable | W. Himalayas, Turkey to Kashmir: along streams |
| *meleagris* (Guinea hen flower) | MA, NE, BS, MW, UM, RM, WC, PN | S to M | white, maroon | spring | border, meadow, woodland, cottage, and rock garden | moist | full sun to shade | adaptable | Europe: grasslands and woodlands |
| *michailovskyi* (Michail's flower) | MA, NE, BS, MW, RM, PN | S | maroon with yellow | spring | rock, dryland garden, border edge | moist in spring, dry in summer | full sun | well drained | Turkey: on rocky slopes near snowline |
| *pallidiflora* | MA, NE, BS, MW, UM, RM, PN | S | pale yellow | spring | rock garden, border | medium | full sun | well drained | Siberia and N.W. China |
| *persica* | NE, MW, RM, PN | T | dark plum | spring | border, rock garden, hillside, meadow | medium to dry | full sun to part shade | adaptable | Turkey, Iran: meadows |
| *pontica* | MA, NE, BS, MW, RM, PN | S to M | green and brown | spring | border, woodland | medium | full sun to part shade | adaptable | Balkans |
| *pudica* | RM, WC, PN | S | yellow with purple | spring | shade and rock garden | medium | part shade | humus-rich | Pacific Northwest to Utah and Wyoming |
| *purdyi* | RM, WC, PN | S | cream with brown | spring | rock garden, hillside | moist in spring, dry in summer | full sun | heavy | N. California: clay hillsides |

| Species | Geo. Reg. | Ht. | Color | Bloom Time | Garden Uses | Moist. Req. | Sun Req. | Soil Req. | Native Habitat |
|---------|-----------|-----|-------|------------|-------------|-------------|----------|-----------|----------------|

*Fritillaria*, continued

| Species | Geo. Reg. | Ht. | Color | Bloom Time | Garden Uses | Moist. Req. | Sun Req. | Soil Req. | Native Habitat |
|---------|-----------|-----|-------|------------|-------------|-------------|----------|-----------|----------------|
| *pyrenaica* | MA, NE, BS, MW, RM, WC, PN | M | reddish brown with chartreuse | spring | border, woodland, meadow | medium to moist | full sun to part shade | humus-rich | France, Spain: mountain slopes and meadow |
| *uva-vulpis* | MA, NE, BS, MW, RM, WC, PN | M | maroon with bronze | spring | rock garden, border | medium | full sun | well drained | Turkey |

## *Galanthus* (Snowdrop)

| Species | Geo. Reg. | Ht. | Color | Bloom Time | Garden Uses | Moist. Req. | Sun Req. | Soil Req. | Native Habitat |
|---------|-----------|-----|-------|------------|-------------|-------------|----------|-----------|----------------|
| *byzantinus* | S, MA, NE, BS, MW, UM, RM, WC, PN | S | white | winter to spring | woodland, rock garden | moist | full sun to part shade | heavy | W. Turkey: woodlands |
| *elwesii* | S, MA, NE, BS, MW, RM, WC, PN | S | white | winter to spring | woodland, rock garden | moist | full sun to part shade | adaptable | S.E. Europe and Turkey |
| *nivalis* | S, MA, NE, BS, MW, UM, RM, WC, PN | S | white | winter to spring | woodland, rock garden | moist | full sun to part shade | adaptable | Europe: woodlands |

## *Galtonia* (Summer hyacinth)

| Species | Geo. Reg. | Ht. | Color | Bloom Time | Garden Uses | Moist. Req. | Sun Req. | Soil Req. | Native Habitat |
|---------|-----------|-----|-------|------------|-------------|-------------|----------|-----------|----------------|
| *candicans* | S, MA, BS, WC, PN | T | white | summer | border, cottage and cutting garden | medium | full sun | well drained | Cape Province, South Africa |

## *Gladiolus*

| Species | Geo. Reg. | Ht. | Color | Bloom Time | Garden Uses | Moist. Req. | Sun Req. | Soil Req. | Native Habitat |
|---------|-----------|-----|-------|------------|-------------|-------------|----------|-----------|----------------|
| *byzantinus* | S, MA, BS | M | magenta | spring | border, cutting and cottage garden, meadow | medium | full sun | heavy | Spain, Italy, North Africa: stony clay |

| Species | Geo. Reg. | Ht. | Color | Bloom Time | Garden Uses | Moist. Req. | Sun Req. | Soil Req. | Native Habitat |
|---|---|---|---|---|---|---|---|---|---|
| **Gladiolus**, continued | | | | | | | | | |
| *callianthus* (*Acidanthera bicolor*) var. 'Murielae' | S, WC | T | white with maroon | summer autumn | border, cutting garden | medium | full sun | adaptable | tropical Africa |
| *cardinalis* (Waterfall gladiolus) | S, WC | M | red | summer | rock garden, streamside, light woodland | moist | full sun to part shade | adaptable | S.W. Cape, South Africa: along stream |
| x *colvillei* | S, WC | M | red, pink, white | summer | border, cutting garden | medium | full sun | well drained loam | man–made hybrid of South African sp. |
| *tristus* | S, WC | M | pale yellow | winter to spring | rock garden, hillside, border | medium, moist in winter | full sun | adaptable | Cape Province, South Africa |

## Gloriosa

| Species | Geo. Reg. | Ht. | Color | Bloom Time | Garden Uses | Moist. Req. | Sun Req. | Soil Req. | Native Habitat |
|---|---|---|---|---|---|---|---|---|---|
| *rothschildiana* | S, WC | T | red, yellow | summer | train into shrubs | moist | full sun to part shade | adaptable | India, Africa: among shrubs |

## *Hedychium* (Ginger lily)

| Species | Geo. Reg. | Ht. | Color | Bloom Time | Garden Uses | Moist. Req. | Sun Req. | Soil Req. | Native Habitat |
|---|---|---|---|---|---|---|---|---|---|
| *coccineum* (Red ginger lily) | S, WC | T | coral red, yellow | summer | streamside, shade garden | moist, drier in winter | part shade | humus–rich | Himalayas: along streams |
| *coronarium* (Butterfly ginger) | S, WC | T | ivory white | summer | streamside, shade garden | moist, drier in winter | part shade | humus–rich | India: near water |
| *flavescens* (Yellow ginger) | S, WC | T | pale yellow | summer | shade garden, streamside | moist, drier in winter | part shade | humus–rich | India: forest edge |
| *gardnerianum* (Kahili ginger) | S, WC | T | yellow with red | summer, autumn | border, shade garden | moist, drier in winter | full sun to part shade | humus–rich | N. India, Himalayas |

| Species | Geo. Reg. | Ht. | Color | Bloom Time | Garden Uses | Moist. Req. | Sun Req. | Soil Req. | Native Habitat |
|---|---|---|---|---|---|---|---|---|---|

## *Hemerocallis* (Daylily)

| Species | Geo. Reg. | Ht. | Color | Bloom Time | Garden Uses | Moist. Req. | Sun Req. | Soil Req. | Native Habitat |
|---|---|---|---|---|---|---|---|---|---|
| *fulva* (Tawny daylily) | S, MA, NE, BS, MW, UM, RM, WC, PN | T | orange | summer | border, hillside | medium to dry | sun to part shade | adaptable | China, long cultivated |
| *flava* (Lemon lily) | S, MA, NE, BS, MW, UM, RM, WC, PN | T | yellow | summer | border, cottage garden, | medium | sun to part shade | adaptable | China |
| x *hybrida* | S, MA, NE, BS, MW, UM, RM, WC, PN | M to T | various | summer, autumn | border, cottage garden, hillside | medium | sun to part shade | adaptable | hybrids of Oriental species |

## *Hippeastrum* (Amaryllis)

| Species | Geo. Reg. | Ht. | Color | Bloom Time | Garden Uses | Moist. Req. | Sun Req. | Soil Req. | Native Habitat |
|---|---|---|---|---|---|---|---|---|---|
| x *hybrida* | S, WC | M | various | spring | border, cottage garden | medium | sun to part shade | adaptable | South America |
| x *johnsonii* (St. Joseph's lily) | S | M | red, white | spring | border, cottage garden | medium | sun to part shade | adaptable | South America |

## *Homeria* (Cape tulip)

| Species | Geo. Reg. | Ht. | Color | Bloom Time | Garden Uses | Moist. Req. | Sun Req. | Soil Req. | Native Habitat |
|---|---|---|---|---|---|---|---|---|---|
| *collina* (syn. *breyniana*) | S, WC | M | salmon, yellow | winter, spring | rock garden, border, hillside | moist in winter, dry in summer | full sun | well drained | Cape Province: banks, hillsides |
| *ochroleuca* var. *aurantiaca* | S, WC | M | golden yellow | winter, spring | rock garden, hillside, border | moist in winter, dry in summer | full sun | well drained | Cape Province |

| Species | Geo. Reg. | Ht. | Color | Bloom Time | Garden Uses | Moist. Req. | Sun Req. | Soil Req. | Native Habitat |
|---|---|---|---|---|---|---|---|---|---|

### *Hyacinthoides* (Wood hyacinth, bluebell)

| Species | Geo. Reg. | Ht. | Color | Bloom Time | Garden Uses | Moist. Req. | Sun Req. | Soil Req. | Native Habitat |
|---|---|---|---|---|---|---|---|---|---|
| *hispanica* (syn. *Scilla campanulata, Endymion hispanica*) | S, MA, NE, BS, MW, UM, RM, WC, PN | M | blue, white, pink | spring | shade garden | moist to medium | part shade | adaptable | S.W. Europe: meadows, woods |
| *non-scripta* (English bluebell) | S, MA, NE, BS, MW, UM, RM, WC, PN | M | blue | spring | shade garden, woodland | moist to medium | part shade to shade | adaptable | England, W. Europe: woodlands, fields |

### *Hyacinthus* (Hyacinth)

| Species | Geo. Reg. | Ht. | Color | Bloom Time | Garden Uses | Moist. Req. | Sun Req. | Soil Req. | Native Habitat |
|---|---|---|---|---|---|---|---|---|---|
| *orientalis* | MA, NE, BS, MW, UM, RM, WC, PN | S | various | spring | border | medium | sun to part shade | adaptable | hybrid origin |
| *o.* var. *albulus* | S, MA, NE, BS, MW, RM, WC, PN | S | white, pink, blue | spring | border, rock garden, hillside | medium | sun to part shade | well drained | Spain and France: rocky hillsides |

### *Hymenocallis* (Peruvian daffodil, Spider lily)

| Species | Geo. Reg. | Ht. | Color | Bloom Time | Garden Uses | Moist. Req. | Sun Req. | Soil Req. | Native Habitat |
|---|---|---|---|---|---|---|---|---|---|
| x *festalis* | S, WC | M | white | summer | border, rock garden | medium | full sun | well drained | hybrid of Bolivian and Peruvian species |
| *littoralis* | S, WC | M | white | summer | border, shade garden | medium, drier in winter | sun to part shade | humus-rich, well drained | Colombia, Mexico |
| *narcissiflora* | S, WC, PN | M | white, yellow | summer | border | medium | sun to part shade | well drained | Bolivian Andes |

### *Ipheion* (Star flower)

| Species | Geo. Reg. | Ht. | Color | Bloom Time | Garden Uses | Moist. Req. | Sun Req. | Soil Req. | Native Habitat |
|---|---|---|---|---|---|---|---|---|---|
| *uniflorum* | S, MA, NE, BS, MW, RM, WC, PN | S | blue | spring | border, lawn, shade and rock garden | medium | sun to part shade | adaptable | Argentina, Uruguay: moist fields and light shade |

## Iris

| Species | Geo. Reg. | Ht. | Color | Bloom Time | Garden Uses | Moist. Req. | Sun Req. | Soil Req. | Native Habitat |
|---|---|---|---|---|---|---|---|---|---|
| *albicans* (Cemetery white) | S, MA, BS, WC | M | white | spring | border, cottage garden | moist in spring, dry in summer | full sun | clay | Yemen |
| *bucharica* | MA, NE, MW, RM, PN | S to M | yellow and white | spring | border, hillside | moist in spring, dryer in summer | full sun to part shade | well drained | Russia, Afghanistan |
| *cristata* (Crested iris) | MA, NE, BS, MW, UM, RM, PN | S | blue | spring | rock and shade garden | moist | sun to part shade | humus-rich | Maryland, Georgia to Arkansas: forest clearings |
| *danfordiae* | S, MA, NE, BS, MW, UM, RM, PN | S | yellow | late winter, early spring | rock garden, edging | medium in spring, drier in summer | sun to part shade | adaptable | Turkey: high meadows |
| *douglasiana* | WC, PN | M to T | purple | spring | rock garden, border | medium | full sun | well drained | N. California, Oregon: hillsides |
| *ensata* (syn. *kaempferi*) | S, MA, NE, BS, MW, UM, RM, WC, PN | T | various | summer | streamside, pond, moist border | moist early, drier later | sun to part shade | humus-rich, acidic | Japan, long cultivated |
| *flavescens* | MA, NE, BS, MW, UM, RM, NW | M to T | pale yellow | spring | border, cottage garden, hillside | medium to dry | full sun | adaptable | Europe, long cultivated |
| *florentina* | S, MA, BS | M | white | spring | border, cottage garden | medium | full sun | adaptable | Middle East, long cultivated |
| *histroides* | MA, NE, BS, MW, UM, RM, NW | S | blue | late winter, early spring | rock garden, lawn | medium in spring, drier in summer | sun to part shade | well drained | N. Turkey |
| x *hollandica* (Dutch iris) | S, MA, BS, WC | M | various | spring | border, cottage garden | moist in winter and spring, drier in summer | sun to part shade | adaptable | hybrids of S. European species |

| Species | Geo. Reg. | Ht. | Color | Bloom Time | Garden Uses | Moist. Req. | Sun Req. | Soil Req. | Native Habitat |
|---|---|---|---|---|---|---|---|---|---|
| | | | | | | | | | |

**Iris**, continued

| Species | Geo. Reg. | Ht. | Color | Bloom Time | Garden Uses | Moist. Req. | Sun Req. | Soil Req. | Native Habitat |
|---|---|---|---|---|---|---|---|---|---|
| *japonica* | S, WC, PN | M | blue, white | spring, summer | streamside | moist | full sun to part shade | adaptable, humus-rich | Japan: bogs and streams |
| *lactea* | NE, MW, UM, RM, PN | M | lavender and ivory | late spring | border, rock garden | medium | full sun | well drained | central Asia: steppes |
| *laevigata* | MA, NE, BS, MW, UM, RM, PN | M to T | blue, pink | spring, summer | streamside | moist | full sun | humus-rich | Japan, Korea, China: marshes |
| *missouriensis* (Blue flag) | MA, NE, BS, MW, RM, PN | M | blue, white | spring | moist border, streamside | moist to medium | full sun | humus-rich | U.S.: widely distributed |
| *orientalis* | MA, NE, BS, MW, RM, PN | T | yellow and white | summer | border, cottage garden | moist in spring, drier later | sun to part shade | adaptable, heavy | Greece, Turkey, Syria |
| *pallida* | S, MA, NE, BS, MW, RM, PN | M | lavender purple | spring | border, dryland | medium to dry | full sun | adaptable | Middle East, long cultivated |
| *pseudacorus* (Yellow flag) | S, MA, NE, BS, MW, RM, WC, PN | T | yellow | spring, summer | streamside, border | moist to medium | sun to part shade | adaptable | Europe: pond and river banks |
| *reticulata* (Snow iris) | MA, NE, BS, MW, UM, RM, PN | S | blue, purple, white | late winter, early spring | rock garden, lawn, shade garden, dryland | medium in spring, drier in summer | sun to part shade | adaptable | Turkey to Iran: rocky hillsides, meadows |
| *setosa* | NE, MW, UM, RM, PN | S to M | purple | late spring, early summer | border | moist to medium | sun to part shade | humus-rich | Canada, Manchuria, Siberia: moist meadows |
| *sibirica* | MA, NE, BS, MW, UM, RM, PN | M to T | various | spring, early summer | border, streamside, cottage garden | medium to moist | sun to part shade | adaptable | central and E. Europe |

| Species | Geo. Reg. | Ht. | Color | Bloom Time | Garden Uses | Moist. Req. | Sun Req. | Soil Req. | Native Habitat |
|---|---|---|---|---|---|---|---|---|---|

***Iris***, continued

| Species | Geo. Reg. | Ht. | Color | Bloom Time | Garden Uses | Moist. Req. | Sun Req. | Soil Req. | Native Habitat |
|---|---|---|---|---|---|---|---|---|---|
| *spuria* | MA, NE, BS, MW, UM, RM, PN | T | lilac blue | summer | border | moist in spring, drier later | sun to part shade | adaptable | Hungary, Russia: meadows |
| *tectorum* (Japanese roof iris) | S, MA, BS, WC, PN | M | blue, white | spring | border, streamside | medium to moist | full sun to part shade | adaptable | Japan |
| *typholia* | MA, NE, BS, MW, RM, PN | M | violet | summer | border, streamside | medium to moist | full sun to part shade | adaptable | Mongolia |
| *versicolor* | MA, NE, BS, MW, UM, RM, PN | M | violet | spring, summer | streamside, moist border | moist to medium | full sun | adaptable | Northeast U.S.: wetlands |

## *Ixia* (Corn lily)

| Species | Geo. Reg. | Ht. | Color | Bloom Time | Garden Uses | Moist. Req. | Sun Req. | Soil Req. | Native Habitat |
|---|---|---|---|---|---|---|---|---|---|
| *maculata* | S, WC | M | yellow | spring | border, cottage garden | medium in winter, dry in summer | full sun | well drained | South Africa, Cape Province |
| *paniculata* | WC | M | cream with pink | spring | border, cutting and cottage garden | medium in winter and spring, dry in summer | full sun | well drained | South Africa, Cape Province |
| *viridiflora* | WC | M | turquoise | spring | rock garden, hillside | medium in winter, dry in summer | full sun | well drained | South Africa, Cape Province |

## *Ixiolirion* (Sky blue lily)

| Species | Geo. Reg. | Ht. | Color | Bloom Time | Garden Uses | Moist. Req. | Sun Req. | Soil Req. | Native Habitat |
|---|---|---|---|---|---|---|---|---|---|
| *tataricum* (syn. *pallasii, montanum*) | RM | M | blue | spring | border, rock garden | medium | full sun | well drained | Russia to Turkey: mountain slopes |

| Species | Geo. Reg. | Ht. | Color | Bloom Time | Garden Uses | Moist. Req. | Sun Req. | Soil Req. | Native Habitat |
|---|---|---|---|---|---|---|---|---|---|

## *Kniphofia* (Red–hot poker)

| Species | Geo. Reg. | Ht. | Color | Bloom Time | Garden Uses | Moist. Req. | Sun Req. | Soil Req. | Native Habitat |
|---|---|---|---|---|---|---|---|---|---|
| *galpinii* | WC, PN | T | orange | summer | border, hillside, rock garden | medium in summer, dry in winter | full sun | well drained | South Africa |
| x *praecox* | WC, PN | M to T | various | summer | border | medium | full sun | well drained | hybrid origin |
| *thomsonii* var. *sondenii* | WC | T | pale orange | summer | rock garden, slope | medium in summer, dry in winter | full sun | well drained | South Africa |
| *uvaria* | MA, NE, BS, MW, RM, WC, PN | T | red and yellow | summer | border, hillside | medium in summer, dry in winter | full sun | well drained | South Africa |

## *Lachenalia* (Leopard lily)

| Species | Geo. Reg. | Ht. | Color | Bloom Time | Garden Uses | Moist. Req. | Sun Req. | Soil Req. | Native Habitat |
|---|---|---|---|---|---|---|---|---|---|
| *aloides* var. *quadricolor* | WC | S to M | yellow, red, olive | winter, spring | rock garden, hillside, border | moist in winter, dry in summer | full sun | well drained | South Africa, Cape Province |
| *bulbifera* | WC | S | red | winter, spring | rock garden, border | moist in winter, dry in summer | full sun | well drained | Cape Province |
| *glaucina* | WC | S to M | amethyst | winter, spring | rock garden, edging | moist in winter, dry in summer | full sun | well drained | Cape Province |
| *viridiflora* | WC | S to M | turquoise | winter, spring | rock garden, hillside | moist in winter, dry in summer | full sun | well drained | Cape Province |

## *Lapeirousa* (Painted petals)

| Species | Geo. Reg. | Ht. | Color | Bloom Time | Garden Uses | Moist. Req. | Sun Req. | Soil Req. | Native Habitat |
|---|---|---|---|---|---|---|---|---|---|
| laxa (*Anomatheca laxa*) | S, WC | M | coral red | spring | meadow, cottage garden | moist in spring, drier in summer | full sun to part shade | adaptable | South Africa, Transvaal: wet fields |

| Species | Geo. Reg. | Ht. | Color | Bloom Time | Garden Uses | Moist. Req. | Sun Req. | Soil Req. | Native Habitat |
|---|---|---|---|---|---|---|---|---|---|

## *Leucojum* (Snowflake)

| Species | Geo. Reg. | Ht. | Color | Bloom Time | Garden Uses | Moist. Req. | Sun Req. | Soil Req. | Native Habitat |
|---|---|---|---|---|---|---|---|---|---|
| *autumnale* (Autumn snowflake) | S, MA, BS, WC, PN | S | white | autumn | rock garden, hillside | medium | sun to part shade | well drained | Portugal, Spain: light woodland, dry grass |
| *aestivum* (Summer snowflake) | S, MA, NE, BS, MW, UM, RM, WC, PN | M | white | summer | streamside, border | moist to medium | sun to part shade | heavy | Europe: wet fields, swamps |
| *vernum* (Spring snowflake) | S, MA, NE, BS, MW, RM, WC, PN | S | white | late winter, early spring | shade garden, lawn, rock garden | medium to moist | sun to part shade | adaptable | S. and E. Europe: woodlands |

## *Liatris* (Gayfeather, blazing star)

| Species | Geo. Reg. | Ht. | Color | Bloom Time | Garden Uses | Moist. Req. | Sun Req. | Soil Req. | Native Habitat |
|---|---|---|---|---|---|---|---|---|---|
| *aspera* | MA, NE, BS, MW, RM | T | lavender | summer | border, meadow | medium | full sun | | southeastern U.S.: fields |
| *punctata* | MW, RM | S to M | lavender | summer | meadow, rock garden | dry to medium | full sun | adaptable, heavy | Great Plains |
| *pycnostachya* (Kansas gayfeather) | MA, NE, BS, MW, UM, RM | T | lavender | summer | border, meadow | medium | full sun | adaptable | U.S. Midwest |
| *spicata* | MA, NE, BS, MW, UM, RM, PN | M to T | lavender, white | summer | meadow, border | medium to dry | full sun | adaptable, heavy | eastern U.S.: meadows |

## *Lilium* (Lily)

| Species | Geo. Reg. | Ht. | Color | Bloom Time | Garden Uses | Moist. Req. | Sun Req. | Soil Req. | Native Habitat |
|---|---|---|---|---|---|---|---|---|---|
| Asiatic hybrids | MA, NE, BS, MW, UM, RM, WC, RM | M to T | various | summer | borders, cottage and cutting garden | medium | sun to part shade | well drained | hybrids of species native to Asia |
| *brownii* | S, WC, PN | T | white | summer | border | medium | full sun | well drained | China subtropics |

| Species | Geo. Reg. | Ht. | Color | Bloom Time | Garden Uses | Moist. Req. | Sun Req. | Soil Req. | Native Habitat |
|---|---|---|---|---|---|---|---|---|---|

***Lilium* (Lily)**, continued

| Species | Geo. Reg. | Ht. | Color | Bloom Time | Garden Uses | Moist. Req. | Sun Req. | Soil Req. | Native Habitat |
|---|---|---|---|---|---|---|---|---|---|
| *canadense* | MA, NE, BS, MW, UM, RM, PN | T | yellow or red | summer | meadow, border, streamside | moist | sun | humus-rich | Canada to the Appalachians |
| *candidum* | S, MA, NE, MW, WC, PN | T | white | summer | border, cottage garden | medium | full sun | well drained | Middle East, Europe, long cultivated |
| *henryi* | S, MA, NE, BS, MW, UM, RM, WC, PN | T | orange | summer | border | medium | sun to part shade | well drained | China: woodland edge with shrubs |
| *lancifolium* (*tigrinum*) | S, MA, NE, BS, MW, UM, RM, WC, PN | T | orange | summer | cottage garden, border | medium | sun to part shade | adaptable | China, Japan, long cultivated |
| *martagon* | MA, NE, BS, MW, UM, RM, WC, PN | T | plum, white | late spring, summer | cottage garden, meadow, woodland | medium to moist | sun to part shade | humus-rich | Europe: light woodlands, meadows |
| Oriental hybrids | MA, NE, BS, MW, RM, WC, PN | T | various | summer, autumn | border, shade garden | medium | sun to part shade | well drained | hybrids of species native to Asia |
| *regale* | S, MA, NE, BS, MW, RM, PN | T | white | summer | border, cutting garden | medium | sun to part shade | well drained | China: amid shrubs |
| *speciosum* | S, MA, NE, BS, MW, RM, WC, PN | T | white, red spots | late summer, autumn | shade garden, border | medium | sun to part shade | humus-rich, well drained | China: light woods |
| *superbum* | S, MA, NE, BS, MW, UM, RM, PN | T | orange | summer | meadow, border | moist | sun to part shade | humus-rich | eastern U.S.: moist meadows |

| Species | Geo. Reg. | Ht. | Color | Bloom Time | Garden Uses | Moist. Req. | Sun Req. | Soil Req. | Native Habitat |
|---------|-----------|-----|-------|------------|-------------|-------------|----------|-----------|----------------|

## *Lilium* (Lily), continued

| Species | Geo. Reg. | Ht. | Color | Bloom Time | Garden Uses | Moist. Req. | Sun Req. | Soil Req. | Native Habitat |
|---------|-----------|-----|-------|------------|-------------|-------------|----------|-----------|----------------|
| Trumpet hybrids | MA, NE, BS, MW, RM, WC, PN | T | various | summer | border, cottage garden | medium | sun | well drained | hybrids of species native to Asia |

## *Lycoris*

| Species | Geo. Reg. | Ht. | Color | Bloom Time | Garden Uses | Moist. Req. | Sun Req. | Soil Req. | Native Habitat |
|---------|-----------|-----|-------|------------|-------------|-------------|----------|-----------|----------------|
| *aurea* (Hurricane lily) | S | M to T | citrus orange | autumn | border, shade garden | medium to moist | sun to part shade | humus-rich | China, Japan |
| *incarnata* | S, WC | M | flesh pink | autumn | border | medium, drier in summer | sun to part shade | humus-rich | China |
| *sanguinea* | S, WC | M | red | late summer, autumn | border | medium, drier in summer | sun to part shade | humus-rich | China, Japan: mountain slopes |
| *squamigera* (Surprise lily) | S, MA, NE, BS, MW, RM, WC, PN | M | pink | late summer, autumn | border, cottage garden | medium, drier in summer | sun to part shade | adaptable, well drained | Japan: slopes, fields |
| *radiata* (Red spider lily) | S, WC | T | red | autumn | border | medium, dry in summer | sun to part shade | humus-rich | Chinese subtropics |

## *Lysichiton* (Skunk cabbage)

| Species | Geo. Reg. | Ht. | Color | Bloom Time | Garden Uses | Moist. Req. | Sun Req. | Soil Req. | Native Habitat |
|---------|-----------|-----|-------|------------|-------------|-------------|----------|-----------|----------------|
| *americanum* | MA, NE, BS, MW, UM, RM, PN | T | greenish yellow | summer | shade garden, streamside | moist | part shade | humus-rich | U.S.: woodlands along streams |

## *Moraea* (Peacock flower)

| Species | Geo. Reg. | Ht. | Color | Bloom Time | Garden Uses | Moist. Req. | Sun Req. | Soil Req. | Native Habitat |
|---------|-----------|-----|-------|------------|-------------|-------------|----------|-----------|----------------|
| *aristata* | WC | M | white with eye | spring | border, cottage garden, slope | medium | full sun | adaptable | South Africa |
| *polystachya* | WC | M | blue | autumn, winter | border | medium to moist | full sun | adaptable | South Africa |

| Species | Geo. Reg. | Ht. | Color | Bloom Time | Garden Uses | Moist. Req. | Sun Req. | Soil Req. | Native Habitat |
|---|---|---|---|---|---|---|---|---|---|

### *Moraea* (Peacock flower), continued

| Species | Geo. Reg. | Ht. | Color | Bloom Time | Garden Uses | Moist. Req. | Sun Req. | Soil Req. | Native Habitat |
|---|---|---|---|---|---|---|---|---|---|
| *tripetala* | WC | M | blue, yellow, pink with eye | spring | border, slope | medium | full sun | adaptable | South Africa, Cape Province |
| *villosa* | WC | M | various | spring | border, cottage garden | medium | full sun | adaptable | South Africa |

### *Muscari* (Grape hyacinth)

| Species | Geo. Reg. | Ht. | Color | Bloom Time | Garden Uses | Moist. Req. | Sun Req. | Soil Req. | Native Habitat |
|---|---|---|---|---|---|---|---|---|---|
| *armeniacum* | S, MA, NE, BS, MW, UM, RM, PN | S | blue | spring | lawn, shade garden | medium | sun to part shade | adaptable | Turkey to the Balkans |
| *azureum* | MA, NE, BS, MW, RM, PN | S | sky blue | spring | edging | medium to dry | sun to part shade | well drained | E. Turkey |
| *botryoides* | S, MA, NE, BS, MW, RM, WC, PN | S | blue | spring | lawn, cottage garden | medium | sun to part shade | adaptable | France, Italy |
| *comosum* (Tassel hyacinth) | MA, NE, BS, MW, RM, WC, PN | S to M | lavender | spring | border, cottage garden | medium | sun to part shade | adaptable | S. and central Europe |
| *latifolium* (One-leaf grape hyacinth) | MA, NE, BS, MW, RM, PN | S to M | blue, black purple | spring | border, cottage garden, edging | medium | sun to part shade | well drained | S. and W. Asia |
| *neglectum* (Starch hyacinth) | S, MA, BS, MW | S | blue | spring | lawn, edging | medium | sun to part shade | adaptable | Europe, North Africa |

### *Narcissus* (Daffodil)

| Species | Geo. Reg. | Ht. | Color | Bloom Time | Garden Uses | Moist. Req. | Sun Req. | Soil Req. | Native Habitat |
|---|---|---|---|---|---|---|---|---|---|
| *bulbocodium* (Hoop petticoat) | S, MA, BS, MW, PN | S | yellow, white, cream | winter, spring | meadow, hillside, rock garden | medium | sun to part shade | well drained | Spain, France: hillsides |

| Species | Geo. Reg. | Ht. | Color | Bloom Time | Garden Uses | Moist. Req. | Sun Req. | Soil Req. | Native Habitat |
|---|---|---|---|---|---|---|---|---|---|

***Narcissus* (Daffodil)**, continued

| Species | Geo. Reg. | Ht. | Color | Bloom Time | Garden Uses | Moist. Req. | Sun Req. | Soil Req. | Native Habitat |
|---|---|---|---|---|---|---|---|---|---|
| *cyclamineus* | MA, NE, BS, MW, UM, RM, PN | M | yellow | late winter, spring | meadow, rock garden, shade garden | medium to moist | sun to part shade | adaptable | Portugal, Spain: mountain meadows, riverbanks |
| *jonquilla* (Jonquil) | S, MA, BS, MW, WC, PN | M | yellow | late winter, spring | rock garden, cottage and rock garden | medium to moist | sun to part shade | adaptable | Spain, Portugal: high slopes |
| *poeticus* var. *recurvus* (Pheasant-eye narcissus) | MA, NE, BS, MW, UM, RM, PN | M | white with eye | spring | meadow, border, cottage garden, woodland | medium | sun to part shade | adaptable | France to Greece: mountain pastures |
| *pseudonarcissus* (Lent lily) | S, MA, NE, BS, MW, RM, WC, NW | S | yellow | winter, spring | meadow, lawn, rock garden | medium | sun to part shade | adaptable | W. Europe: meadows, light woodland |
| *tazetta* (Paperwhites) | S, WC, PN | M | white, yellow | winter, early spring | shade, cottage garden, border | medium | sun to part shade | adaptable | S. Europe: long cultivated |
| *triandrus* | S, MA, NE, BS, MW, UM, RM, WC, PN | S to M | white, yellow | late winter, spring | border, meadow, shade garden | medium to moist | sun to part shade | adaptable | Spain, Portugal, France: hedgerows, rocky hills |

***Nectaroscordum***

| Species | Geo. Reg. | Ht. | Color | Bloom Time | Garden Uses | Moist. Req. | Sun Req. | Soil Req. | Native Habitat |
|---|---|---|---|---|---|---|---|---|---|
| *siculum* (syn. *Allium siculum*) | MA, NE, BS, MW, RM, WC, PN | T | pink and green | spring, early summer | border | medium | sun to part shade | well drained | France, Italy: fields |

| Species | Geo. Reg. | Ht. | Color | Bloom Time | Garden Uses | Moist. Req. | Sun Req. | Soil Req. | Native Habitat |
|---|---|---|---|---|---|---|---|---|---|

**Nerine**

| Species | Geo. Reg. | Ht. | Color | Bloom Time | Garden Uses | Moist. Req. | Sun Req. | Soil Req. | Native Habitat |
|---|---|---|---|---|---|---|---|---|---|
| *bowdenii* | WC | M | pink | autumn | border hillside | moist in winter, dry in summer | full sun | well drained | South Africa, Natal: fields |
| *crispa* | WC | M | pink | autumn | border, hillside | moist in winter, dry in summer | full sun | well drained | South Africa |
| *duparquetiana* | WC | M | white with pink | autumn | border | moist in winter, dry in summer | full sun | well drained | South Africa |
| *filamentosa* | WC | M | pink | autumn | border | moist in winter, dry in summer | full sun | well drained | South Africa |
| *sarniensis* (Guernsey lily) | WC | M | red | late summer, autumn | border | dry in winter, moist in summer | full sun | well drained | South Africa, Table Mountain |
| *undulata* | WC | M | pale pink | late summer, autumn | border | moist in winter, dry in summer | full sun | well drained | South Africa |

**Ornithogalum**

| Species | Geo. Reg. | Ht. | Color | Bloom Time | Garden Uses | Moist. Req. | Sun Req. | Soil Req. | Native Habitat |
|---|---|---|---|---|---|---|---|---|---|
| *arabicum* | S, WC | M | white with black eye | spring | border, rock garden | medium, drier in summer | full sun | well drained | Mediterranean region |
| *dubium* | S, WC | M | orange, red, yellow | winter, spring | border, rock garden | medium, drier in summer | full sun | well drained | South Africa, Cape Province |
| *maculatum* | S, WC | M | yellow tipped brown | spring | border | medium, drier in summer | full sun | well drained | South Africa, S.W. Cape |
| *narbonense* | S, MA, BS, WC, PN | M | white | spring | border, rock garden | medium, drier in summer | full sun | well drained | Mediterranean, Caucasus |

| Species | Geo. Reg. | Ht. | Color | Bloom Time | Garden Uses | Moist. Req. | Sun Req. | Soil Req. | Native Habitat |
|---------|-----------|-----|-------|------------|-------------|-------------|----------|-----------|----------------|

**_Ornithogalum_**, continued

| Species | Geo. Reg. | Ht. | Color | Bloom Time | Garden Uses | Moist. Req. | Sun Req. | Soil Req. | Native Habitat |
|---------|-----------|-----|-------|------------|-------------|-------------|----------|-----------|----------------|
| _nutans_ | S, MA, BS, WC, PN | S to M | white striped pale green | spring | shade garden | medium to moist | part shade | adaptable | Europe, S.W. Asia |
| _saundersae_ | MA, BS, WC, PN | T | white | summer | border, cutting garden | medium | full sun | well drained | E. South Africa |
| _thyrsoides_ (Chincherin-chee) | S, W | M | white | winter, spring | border, cutting garden | moist in winter, dry in summer | full sun | well drained | South Africa, Cape Province |
| _umbellatum_ | S, MA, NE, BS, MW, RM, WC, PN | S | white | spring | shade garden, meadow, lawn | medium | sun to shade | adaptable | Israel |

## _Oxalis_ (Wood sorrel)

| Species | Geo. Reg. | Ht. | Color | Bloom Time | Garden Uses | Moist. Req. | Sun Req. | Soil Req. | Native Habitat |
|---------|-----------|-----|-------|------------|-------------|-------------|----------|-----------|----------------|
| _crassipes_ | S, WC | S | pink | winter, spring, summer | shade garden, edging | medium | sun to part shade | adaptable | S. Brazil |
| _deppei_ | S, WC | S | coral pink | winter, spring | edging, border | medium | sun to part shade | adaptable | Mexico |
| _purpurata_ var. _bowiei_ | S, WC | S | lavender pink | winter, spring | edging, border | medium | sun to part shade | adaptable | |
| _regnellii_ 'Triangularis' | S, WC | S | white, pale pink | winter, spring | edging, shade garden | medium | sun to part shade | adaptable | South America |
| _versicolor_ | S, WC | S | white with red | autumn, winter | rock garden, edging | medium | sun to part shade | well drained | South Africa, Cape Province |
| _violacea_ | S, MA, BS, MW, PN | S | lavender, pink | spring, summer | shade garden | medium to moist | part shade | humus-rich | U.S.: woodlands |

| Species | Geo. Reg. | Ht. | Color | Bloom Time | Garden Uses | Moist. Req. | Sun Req. | Soil Req. | Native Habitat |
|---|---|---|---|---|---|---|---|---|---|

## *Polygonatum* (Solomon's seal)

| Species | Geo. Reg. | Ht. | Color | Bloom Time | Garden Uses | Moist. Req. | Sun Req. | Soil Req. | Native Habitat |
|---|---|---|---|---|---|---|---|---|---|
| *biflorum* (syn. *commutatum*) | S, MA, NE, BS, MW, UM, RM, PN | M to T | white | spring | shade garden, border | moist to medium | part shade to shade | humus-rich | U.S.: eastern woodlands |
| *falcatum* | S, MA, BS, PN | M to T | white | spring | shade garden | moist to medium | part shade to shade | humus-rich | Japan, Korea: woodlands |
| *odoratum* | MA, NE, BS, MW, UM, RM, PN | M to T | white | spring | shade garden | moist | part shade to shade | humus-rich | Europe, Asia: widely distributed |

## *Puschkinia* (Striped squill)

| Species | Geo. Reg. | Ht. | Color | Bloom Time | Garden Uses | Moist. Req. | Sun Req. | Soil Req. | Native Habitat |
|---|---|---|---|---|---|---|---|---|---|
| *scilloides* (syn. *libanotica*) | MA, NE, BS, MW, RM, WC, PN | S | white and aqua | border, edging, shade garden | late winter, spring | medium, drier in summer | sun to part shade | well drained | Caucasus, Middle East: mountain meadow, stony hillside |

## *Ranunculus*

| Species | Geo. Reg. | Ht. | Color | Bloom Time | Garden Uses | Moist. Req. | Sun Req. | Soil Req. | Native Habitat |
|---|---|---|---|---|---|---|---|---|---|
| *asiaticus* | S, WC | M | various | winter, spring | border | moist in winter, dry in summer | sun to part shade | well drained | Middle East, long cultivated |
| *cortusifolius* | S, WC | M | golden yellow | summer | border, woodland | medium | sun to partial shade | adaptable | Canary Islands, Azores, Madeira |
| *ficaria* (lesser celandine, pilewort) | S, MA, BS, WC, PN | S | golden yellow | spring | shade and rock garden, border | medium to moist | partial shade | adaptable | S. European woodlands |

## *Rhodohypoxis* (Rose star)

| Species | Geo. Reg. | Ht. | Color | Bloom Time | Garden Uses | Moist. Req. | Sun Req. | Soil Req. | Native Habitat |
|---|---|---|---|---|---|---|---|---|---|
| *baurii* | S, WC | S | rose, pink, white | spring | rock garden, edging | medium | sun to part shade | well drained | South Africa, Drakensberg Mountains |

| Species | Geo. Reg. | Ht. | Color | Bloom Time | Garden Uses | Moist. Req. | Sun Req. | Soil Req. | Native Habitat |
|---|---|---|---|---|---|---|---|---|---|
| **_Rhodophiala_ (Ox-blood lily)** | | | | | | | | | |
| _bifida_ | S, WC | M | dark red | autumn | border, meadow, rock garden | medium | sun to part shade | adaptable | Uruguay, Argentina: meadows |
| **_Sanguinaria_ (Bloodroot)** | | | | | | | | | |
| _canadensis_ | MA, NE, BS, MW, UM, RM, PN | S to M | white | spring | shade garden | medium to moist | part shade to shade | humus–rich | U.S.: eastern woodlands |
| **_Sauromatum_ (Voodoo lily)** | | | | | | | | | |
| _guttatum_ var. _venosum_ | S, MA, BS, WC, PN | M to T | green and brown | spring | shade garden, streamside | moist to medium | sun to part shade | humus–rich | Asia subtropics |
| **_Schizostylus_ (Crimson flag)** | | | | | | | | | |
| _coccinea_ | MA, NE, BS, MW, RM, WC, PN | M | red, coral, white | late summer, autumn | border, streamside | medium to moist | sun to part shade | humus–rich | South Africa, Natal Province: along streams |
| **_Scilla_ (Squill)** | | | | | | | | | |
| _bifolia_ | MA, NE, BS, MW, UM, RM, WC, NW | S | blue, mauve, pink | late winter, early spring | lawn, border, edging | medium | sun to part shade | well drained | S. Europe, Turkey: slopes |
| _litardierei_ (_pratensis_) (Meadow squill) | S, MA, NE, BS, MW, UM, RM, WC, PN | S | amethyst purple | late winter, early spring | shade garden, meadow | medium | sun to part shade | adaptable | Bosnia: mountain meadows |
| _natalensis_ | S, WC | T | amethyst purple | spring | hillside, rock garden | medium | sun | well drained | South Africa, Natal Province |

| Species | Geo. Reg. | Ht. | Color | Bloom Time | Garden Uses | Moist. Req. | Sun Req. | Soil Req. | Native Habitat |
|---------|-----------|-----|-------|------------|-------------|-------------|----------|-----------|----------------|

*Scilla* (**Squill**), continued

| Species | Geo. Reg. | Ht. | Color | Bloom Time | Garden Uses | Moist. Req. | Sun Req. | Soil Req. | Native Habitat |
|---------|-----------|-----|-------|------------|-------------|-------------|----------|-----------|----------------|
| *peruviana* (Cuba lily) | S, WC | M | blue | spring | border, rock garden | medium | sun to part shade | well drained | Spain, Portugal |
| *siberica* | MA, NE, BS, MW, UM, RM, PN | S | blue, white | late winter, early spring | lawn, shade and rock garden | medium to moist | sun to part shade | adaptable | Russia, Caucasus, Iran |
| *mischtschenkoana* (syn. *tubergeniana*) (Milk squill) | MA, NE, BS, MW, RM, WC, PN | S | white | late winter, early spring | lawn, edging, rock and shade garden | medium to moist | sun to part shade | adaptable | Iran, Caucasus: stony hillsides |

*Smilacina* (**Solomon's plume**)

| Species | Geo. Reg. | Ht. | Color | Bloom Time | Garden Uses | Moist. Req. | Sun Req. | Soil Req. | Native Habitat |
|---------|-----------|-----|-------|------------|-------------|-------------|----------|-----------|----------------|
| *racemosa* | MA, NE, BS, MW, UM, RM, PN | M to T | white, red berries | spring | shade garden, streamside | moist to medium | part shade to shade | humus-rich | U.S.: northern and eastern woods |
| *stellata* | MA, NE, BS, MW, UM, RM, PN | M to T | cream, dark red berries | spring | shade garden, streamside | moist to medium | part shade to shade | humus-rich | U.S.: northwest woodlands |

*Sparaxis* (**Harlequin flower**)

| Species | Geo. Reg. | Ht. | Color | Bloom Time | Garden Uses | Moist. Req. | Sun Req. | Soil Req. | Native Habitat |
|---------|-----------|-----|-------|------------|-------------|-------------|----------|-----------|----------------|
| *elegans* | S, WC | M | peach | spring | hillside, border | medium, drier in summer | full sun | well drained | South Africa, Cape Province |
| *tricolor* | WC | M | cream, orange, purple | spring | slope, rock and cottage garden | medium, drier in summer | full sun | well drained | South Africa |

| Species | Geo. Reg. | Ht. | Color | Bloom Time | Garden Uses | Moist. Req. | Sun Req. | Soil Req. | Native Habitat |
|---|---|---|---|---|---|---|---|---|---|

## *Spiloxene*

| Species | Geo. Reg. | Ht. | Color | Bloom Time | Garden Uses | Moist. Req. | Sun Req. | Soil Req. | Native Habitat |
|---|---|---|---|---|---|---|---|---|---|
| *alba* (Little star) | S, WC | S | white | autumn, winter | streamside, meadow | moist | full sun to part shade | adaptable | South Africa, Cape Province: marshes |
| *canaliculata* | WC | S | yellow with maroon | autumn, winter | streamside, moist border | moist to medium | full sun to part shade | adaptable | South Africa, Cape Province |
| *capensis* | WC | S | white, yellow, pink | winter | hillside, rock garden | moist in winter, dry in summer | full sun | well drained | South Africa, Cape Province |
| *serrata* (Golden star) | WC | S | yellow | autumn, winter, spring | border, meadow | medium | full sun | well drained | South Africa, Cape Province |

## *Sprekelia* (Aztec lily)

| Species | Geo. Reg. | Ht. | Color | Bloom Time | Garden Uses | Moist. Req. | Sun Req. | Soil Req. | Native Habitat |
|---|---|---|---|---|---|---|---|---|---|
| *formosissima* | S, WC | M | crimson | spring | rock garden, border | medium | sun to part shade | adaptable | Mexico: rocky hills |

## *Sternbergia* (Golden chalice)

| Species | Geo. Reg. | Ht. | Color | Bloom Time | Garden Uses | Moist. Req. | Sun Req. | Soil Req. | Native Habitat |
|---|---|---|---|---|---|---|---|---|---|
| *candida* | S, MA, BS, WC, PN | S | white | winter, early spring | rock garden | medium | sun to part shade | well drained | Turkey: hillside |
| *clusiana* | S, MA, BS, WC, PN | S | yellow | autumn | meadow, lawn | medium | sun to part shade | adaptable, well drained | Middle East: slopes |
| *lutea* | S, MA, BS, WC, PN | S | yellow | autumn | woodland, hillside, lawn | moist to medium | sun to part shade | adaptable, well drained | S. Europe: hillsides, light woodlands |
| *sicula* | S, MA, BS, WC, PN | S | yellow | autumn | rock garden, border | medium | sun to part shade | well drained | Italy, Greece, Turkey |

| Species | Geo. Reg. | Ht. | Color | Bloom Time | Garden Uses | Moist. Req. | Sun Req. | Soil Req. | Native Habitat |
|---|---|---|---|---|---|---|---|---|---|

### *Tricyrtis* (Toad lily)

| Species | Geo. Reg. | Ht. | Color | Bloom Time | Garden Uses | Moist. Req. | Sun Req. | Soil Req. | Native Habitat |
|---|---|---|---|---|---|---|---|---|---|
| *flava* (Yellow toad lily) | S, MA, BS, WC, PN | M | yellow with purple | autumn | shade garden, border | moist to medium | part shade | humus–rich | Japan: light woodland |
| *formosana* (Purple toad lily) | S, MA, NE, BS, MW, WC, PN | T | rose purple | autumn | shade garden, border, streamside | moist to medium | part shade | humus–rich | Taiwan: light woodland |
| *hirta* (Hairy toad lily) | S, MA, NE, BS, MW, RM, WC, PN | M | white with purple | autumn | shade and rock garden | medium | part shade | humus–rich | Japan: shady rock outcrops |
| *macrantha* | S, MA, BS, WC, PN | M | yellow with brown | autumn | shade garden, border | medium | part shade | humus–rich | Japan: woodlands |
| *macropoda* (Spotted toad lily) | S, MA, NE, BS, MW, WC, PN | T | cream with purple | autumn | shade garden | moist | part shade | humus–rich | China: woodland |

### *Trillium* (Wake robin)

| Species | Geo. Reg. | Ht. | Color | Bloom Time | Garden Uses | Moist. Req. | Sun Req. | Soil Req. | Native Habitat |
|---|---|---|---|---|---|---|---|---|---|
| *grandiflorum* | MA, NE, BS, MW, UM, RM, PN | M | white | spring | shade garden | moist | part shade to shade | humus–rich | eastern U.S.: woodlands |
| *luteum* | S, MA, NE, BS, MW, RM, WC, PN | M | greenish yellow | spring | shade garden | moist | part shade to shade | humus–rich | Midwest and upper South: forests |
| *ovatum* | S, MA, NE, BS, RM, WC, PN | M | white | spring | shade garden | moist | part shade to shade | humus–rich | California and Pacific Northwest: redwood forests |
| *recurvatum* | S, MA, NE, BS, MW, WC, PN | M | purple | spring | shade garden | moist | part shade to shade | humus–rich | eastern U.S.: woodlands |

| Species | Geo. Reg. | Ht. | Color | Bloom Time | Garden Uses | Moist. Req. | Sun Req. | Soil Req. | Native Habitat |
|---|---|---|---|---|---|---|---|---|---|

### *Trillium* (**Wake robin**), continued

| Species | Geo. Reg. | Ht. | Color | Bloom Time | Garden Uses | Moist. Req. | Sun Req. | Soil Req. | Native Habitat |
|---|---|---|---|---|---|---|---|---|---|
| *sessile* | S, MA, NE, BS, MW, RM, WC, NW | M | maroon | spring | shade garden | moist | part shade to shade | humus–rich | eastern U.S.: woodlands |

### *Tritonia* (**Flame freesia**)

| Species | Geo. Reg. | Ht. | Color | Bloom Time | Garden Uses | Moist. Req. | Sun Req. | Soil Req. | Native Habitat |
|---|---|---|---|---|---|---|---|---|---|
| *crocata* | S, WC | M | peach, amber | late winter, spring | border, rock garden | moist to medium | sun to part shade | adaptable | South Africa, Cape Peninsula |

### *Tropaeolum*

| Species | Geo. Reg. | Ht. | Color | Bloom Time | Garden Uses | Moist. Req. | Sun Req. | Soil Req. | Native Habitat |
|---|---|---|---|---|---|---|---|---|---|
| *tricolorum* | WC, PN | T | orange with yellow and black | winter, spring | trellis, shrub support | medium | sun to part shade | adaptable | Chile, Bolivia |
| *tuberosum* (Scarlet flame nasturtium) | WC, PN | T | scarlet | spring | amid shrubs | moist to medium | sun to part shade | humus, peaty | Chile, Bolivia |

### *Tulbaghia* (**Society garlic**)

| Species | Geo. Reg. | Ht. | Color | Bloom Time | Garden Uses | Moist. Req. | Sun Req. | Soil Req. | Native Habitat |
|---|---|---|---|---|---|---|---|---|---|
| *simmleri* (syn. *fragrans*) | S, WC | M | mauve-pink | winter, spring | border, hillside | moist in winter | sun to part shade | adaptable | South Africa, E. Transvaal |
| *violacea* | S, WC | M | pink | winter, spring, summer | border, cottage garden | medium | sun to part shade | adaptable | South Africa, E. Cape Province: woodland |

### *Tulipa* (**Tulip**)

| Species | Geo. Reg. | Ht. | Color | Bloom Time | Garden Uses | Moist. Req. | Sun Req. | Soil Req. | Native Habitat |
|---|---|---|---|---|---|---|---|---|---|
| *acuminata* | S, MA, NE, BS, MW, RM, PN | S | yellow, white | spring | rock garden, hillside | medium | sun | adaptable | Middle East, known only in cultivation |
| *altaica* | MA, BS, MW, RM, PN | S | yellow with bronze, green | spring | border, rock garden | medium | sun | adaptable | Altai Mountains to Siberia |

| Species | Geo. Reg. | Ht. | Color | Bloom Time | Garden Uses | Moist. Req. | Sun Req. | Soil Req. | Native Habitat |
|---|---|---|---|---|---|---|---|---|---|

*Tulipa* (**Tulip**), continued

| Species | Geo. Reg. | Ht. | Color | Bloom Time | Garden Uses | Moist. Req. | Sun Req. | Soil Req. | Native Habitat |
|---|---|---|---|---|---|---|---|---|---|
| *batalinii* | MA, NE, BS, MW, RM, PN | S | yellow, bronze, red | spring | rock garden, lawn, border, cottage | medium to dry | sun to part shade | adaptable | central Asia: stony hillsides |
| *chrysantha* | S, MA, NE, BS, MW, RM, WC, PN | S | yellow and red | spring | rock, cottage garden | medium | sun to part shade | adaptable | Middle East to Himalayas |
| *clusiana* (Lady tulip) | S, MA, NE, BS, MW, UM, RM, WC, PN | S | red and white | spring | border, rock garden | medium | sun to part shade | adaptable | Middle East to Himalayas |
| *fosteriana* and hybrids | MA, NE, BS, MW, UM, RM, PN | S | red, white, pink, orange | late winter, spring | rock garden, border | medium | sun | adaptable | Bukhara: high meadows |
| *greigii* and hybrids | MA, NE, BS, MW, RM, PN | S | red, coral | late winter, spring | rock garden, border | medium | sun | adaptable | Turkestan |
| *humilis* | MA, NE, BS, MW, RM, PN | S | bright pink with yellow | spring | lawn, rock garden, dryland | medium to dry | sun | adaptable, well drained | Middle East to the Balkans |
| *kaufmanniana* and hybrids | MA, NE, BS, MW, UM, RM, PN | S | red, cream, yellow | late winter, early spring | rock and cottage garden, border | medium to dry | sun | adaptable | Turkestan: rocky slopes |
| *kolpakowskiana* | RM | S | yellow marked green | spring | lawn, rock garden, dryland | medium to dry | sun | adaptable | Afghanistan |
| *linifolia* | S, MA, NE, BS, MW, UM, RM, PN | S | scarlet | spring | lawn, rock garden, dryland | medium to dry | sun | adaptable | central Asia: high slopes |

| Species | Geo. Reg. | Ht. | Color | Bloom Time | Garden Uses | Moist. Req. | Sun Req. | Soil Req. | Native Habitat |
|---|---|---|---|---|---|---|---|---|---|

***Tulipa* (Tulip)**, continued

| Species | Geo. Reg. | Ht. | Color | Bloom Time | Garden Uses | Moist. Req. | Sun Req. | Soil Req. | Native Habitat |
|---|---|---|---|---|---|---|---|---|---|
| *pulchella* and selections | S, MA, NE, BS, MW, UM, RM, PN | S | wine red, magenta, white | late winter, spring | rock garden, border, dryland | medium to dry | sun | adaptable | Iran, Asia Minor: dry meadows, hills |
| *saxatilis* | S, MA, BS, RM, WC, PN | S | lavender-pink with yellow | spring | rock garden, border | medium | sun to part shade | adaptable | Crete |
| *sprengeri* | S, MA, NE, BS, MW, RM, PN | M | red | late spring, early summer | border, rock garden | medium | sun | adaptable | Turkey |
| *sylvestris* | S, MA, NE, BS, MW, RM, WC, PN | S | yellow | spring | shade and rock garden | medium | sun to part shade | adaptable | central Asia: Europe |
| *tarda* | MA, NE, BS, MW, RM, PN | S | yellow and white | spring | border, lawn, shade garden | medium | sun to part shade | adaptable, well drained | Turkestan |
| *urumiensis* | MA, NE, BS, MW, RM, PN | S | yellow | spring | rock garden, lawn | medium to dry | sun | adaptable | N.W. Iran |
| *vvedenskyi* | MA, NE, MW, RM | S | orange red | spring | border, rock garden | medium | sun | adaptable, well drained | central Asia: rocky scree |

**Uvularia (Merry bells)**

| Species | Geo. Reg. | Ht. | Color | Bloom Time | Garden Uses | Moist. Req. | Sun Req. | Soil Req. | Native Habitat |
|---|---|---|---|---|---|---|---|---|---|
| *grandiflora* | S, MA, NE, BS, MW, UM, RM, PN | M | yellow | spring, summer | shade garden, streamside | medium to moist | part shade to shade | humus-rich | southeast U.S.: woodland |
| *perfoliata* | S, MA, NE, BS, MW, UM, RM, NW | M | greenish yellow | spring, early summer | shade garden | medium to moist | part shade to shade | humus-rich | southeast U.S.: woodland |
| *sessilifolia* | S, MA, NE, BS, MW, UM, RM, PN | M | pale yellow | spring, early summer | shade and rock garden | medium to moist | part shade to shade | humus-rich | southeast U.S.: thickets |

| Species | Geo. Reg. | Ht. | Color | Bloom Time | Garden Uses | Moist. Req. | Sun Req. | Soil Req. | Native Habitat |
|---|---|---|---|---|---|---|---|---|---|

## *Veltheimia* (Winter red–hot poker)

| Species | Geo. Reg. | Ht. | Color | Bloom Time | Garden Uses | Moist. Req. | Sun Req. | Soil Req. | Native Habitat |
|---|---|---|---|---|---|---|---|---|---|
| *bracteata* (Forest lily) | WC | M to T | pink | winter, spring | border, shade garden | moist in winter, dry in summer | sun to part shade | well drained | South Africa: coastal woodlands |
| *capensis* | WC | M | pink | winter, spring | hillside, border | medium in winter, dry in summer | sun to part shade | well drained | South Africa, Cape to west: dry hillsides |

## *Watsonia* (Bugle lily)

| Species | Geo. Reg. | Ht. | Color | Bloom Time | Garden Uses | Moist. Req. | Sun Req. | Soil Req. | Native Habitat |
|---|---|---|---|---|---|---|---|---|---|
| *alectroides* | WC | M | pink | spring, summer | border, cottage garden | medium | full sun | well drained | South Africa |
| *borbonica* (syn. *pyramidata*) | S, WC | T | pink, coral, red | spring, summer | border, cottage garden | medium | full sun | adaptable | South Africa: fields |
| *humilis* | WC | M | white with pink | spring, summer | border, cottage garden | medium | full sun | well drained | South Africa |
| *laccata* (syn. *brevifolia*) | WC | M | lilac–rose | spring, summer | border, hillside | medium | full sun | well drained | South Africa |

## *Zantedeschia* (Calla lily)

| Species | Geo. Reg. | Ht. | Color | Bloom Time | Garden Uses | Moist. Req. | Sun Req. | Soil Req. | Native Habitat |
|---|---|---|---|---|---|---|---|---|---|
| *albo-maculata* | S, WC | M | white to yellow | summer | border, shade garden | medium to moist | sun to part shade | humus-rich, well drained | South Africa: meadows |
| *elliotiana* | S, WC | M | yellow | summer | cottage and rock garden | medium to moist | sun to part shade | humus-rich, well drained | South Africa, possibly a hybrid |

| Species | Geo. Reg. | Ht. | Color | Bloom Time | Garden Uses | Moist. Req. | Sun Req. | Soil Req. | Native Habitat |
|---------|-----------|-----|-------|-----------|-------------|-------------|----------|-----------|----------------|

**_Zantedeschia_ (Calla lily)**, continued

| Species | Geo. Reg. | Ht. | Color | Bloom Time | Garden Uses | Moist. Req. | Sun Req. | Soil Req. | Native Habitat |
|---------|-----------|-----|-------|-----------|-------------|-------------|----------|-----------|----------------|
| _aethiopica_ | S, WC | T | white | spring | streamside, border | moist to medium | sun to part shade | adaptable | South Africa: streams, bogs |
| _rehmanii_ | S, WC | M | plum, pink | summer | shade garden, streamside, border | medium to moist | sun to part shade | humus-rich | South Africa, Transvaal, Natal: moist grassland |

**_Zephyranthes,_ including _Cooperia_ (Rain lily)**

| Species | Geo. Reg. | Ht. | Color | Bloom Time | Garden Uses | Moist. Req. | Sun Req. | Soil Req. | Native Habitat |
|---------|-----------|-----|-------|-----------|-------------|-------------|----------|-----------|----------------|
| _atamasco_ (Atamasco lily) | S, MA, BS | S to M | white | spring | streamside, woodland | moist | part shade | humus-rich, acidic | southeastern U.S.: damp woodland clearings |
| _candida_ (White rain lily) | S, MA, BS | S | white | autumn | streamside, pond, moist border | moist | sun to part shade | adaptable | Argentina: along riverbanks |
| _citrina_ (_sulphurea_) | S | S | yellow | autumn | meadow, border, rock garden | moist to dry | sun to part shade | very adaptable | Mexico |
| _drummondii_ (_C. pedunculata_) | S | S | white with red | spring | border, meadow | medium | sun to part shade | adaptable | Texas, Mexico |
| _flavissima_ | S, MA, BS | S | gold | spring to autumn | streamside, moist border | moist | sun to part shade | adaptable | Argentina: damp low places |
| _grandiflora_ | S | M | pink | autumn | border, meadow | medium | sun to part shade | adaptable | Mexico |
| _insularum_ | S | S | white | autumn, winter | edging | medium | sun to part shade | adaptable | Caribbean islands |

| Species | Geo. Reg. | Ht. | Color | Bloom Time | Garden Uses | Moist. Req. | Sun Req. | Soil Req. | Native Habitat |
|---------|-----------|-----|-------|------------|-------------|-------------|----------|-----------|----------------|

***Zephyranthes,* including *Cooperia* (Rain lily)**, continued

| Species | Geo. Reg. | Ht. | Color | Bloom Time | Garden Uses | Moist. Req. | Sun Req. | Soil Req. | Native Habitat |
|---------|-----------|-----|-------|------------|-------------|-------------|----------|-----------|----------------|
| *pulchella* | S | S | gold | autumn | border, meadow | medium to moist | sun to part shade | adaptable | Texas, Gulf coast |
| *rosea* | S | S | rose pink | autumn, winter | path and border edging | medium | sun to part shade | adaptable | Cuba |

# SOURCES FOR BULBS

## DOMESTIC

Ambergate Gardens
8015 Krey Avenue
Waconia, MN 55387-9616
*Some choice woodland and border bulbs,*
*including martagon lilies, Scilla numidica*

Autumn Glade Botanicals
46857 W. Ann Arbor Trail
Plymouth, MI 48170
*Unusual South African and woodland*
*bulbs*

B&D Lilies
3030 P Street
Port Townsend, WA 98368
*Catalogue $1*

Bakker of Holland
Louisiana, MO 63353
*Spring bulbs*

Bear Mountain Alpines
P.O. Box 2407
Evergreen, CO 80439-2407
*ck garden and border bulbs*

Bundles of Bulbs
112 Green Springs Valley Road
Owings Mills, MD 21117
*Wide selection*

Crutchers Colors
18900 South Pear Rd.
Oregon City, OR 97045
*Catalogue $1; Lily specialists*

The Daffodil Mart
Rt. 3, Box 794
Gloucester, VA 23061
*Catalogue $1; wide selection of Narcissus,*
*Crocus, and Tulips as well as hard-to-find*
*Allium, Brodiaea, Camassia, Fritillaria,*
*Iris, Ixia, Lachenalia*

P. de Jager & Sons
P.O. Box 2010
South Hamilton, MA 01982
*Wide selection*

Dutch Gardens
P.O. Box 200
Adelphia, NJ 07710
*Wide selection*

Fairyland Begonia/Lily Garden
1100 Griffith
McKinleyville, CA 95521
*Catalogue $1*

Joy Creek Nursery
20300 N.W. Watson Road
Scappoose, OR 97056
*Some choice border and woodland bulbs*

Logee's Greenhouses
141 North Street
Danielson, CT 06239
*Catalogue $3; exotic houseplants,*
*including some bulbs*

Long's Gardens
P.O. Box 19
Boulder, CO 80306
*Iris specialists*

McClure & Zimmerman
108 W. Winnebago
P.O. Box 368
Friesland, WI 53935
*Wide selection including hard-to-find*
*species tulips, Anemone, Freesia,*
*Fritillaria, Galanthus, Ipheion, Iris, Ixia,*
*Lachenalia, Leucojum, Scilla, Sparaxis,*
*Veltheimia, Watsonia*

Messelaar Bulb Co.
P.O. Box 269
Ipswich, MA 01938
*Wide selection*

Mitsch Daffodils
P.O. Box 218
Hubbard, OR 97032
*Catalogue $3*

Mt. Hood Lilies
15361 SE Bluff Road
P.O. Box 1314
Sandy, OR 97055

Old House Gardens
536 Third Street
Ann Arbor, MI 48103
*Antique and species bulbs*

Park Seed Co.
Cokesburry Road
Greenwood, SC 29674-0001
*Wide selection including Babiana,
Bletilla, Canna*

Plant Delights Nursery, Inc.
9241 Sauls Road
Raleigh, NC 27603
*Mainly perennials but unusual bulbs in-
cluding Achimenes, Agapanthus, Alocasia,
Arisaema, Canna, Colocasia,
Hedychium, Iris, Kniphofia, Polygonatum,
Sauromatum, Smilacina, Tricyrtis,
Uvularia, Zephyranthes*

Pleasant Valley Glads
P.O. Box 494
Agawam, MA 01001

John Scheepers, Inc.
P.O. Box 700
Bantam, CT 06750
*Wide selection of spring bulbs*

Spaulding Bulb Farm
1811 Howey Road
Sebring, FL 33870
*Caladium*

Alex Summerville
R.D. 1, Box 449
Glassboro, NJ 08028
*Gladiolus*

Ty Ty Plantation
Box 159
Ty Ty, GA 31795
*Catalogue $1; exotics including Canna,
Colocasia, Crinum, Hedychium*

K. Van Bourgondien & Sons, Inc.
P.O. Box 1000
245 Farmingdale Road, Rt. 109
Babylon, NY 11702-0598
*Spring and summer bulbs*

Van Engelen, Inc.
307 Maple Street
Litchfield, CT 06759
*Wide selection of spring bloomers*

White Flower Farm
Litchfield, CT 06759-0050
*Spring bulbs and Clivia, Convallaria,
Cyclamen, Freesia, Lilium, Zantedeschia*

## INTERNATIONAL

Avon Bulbs
Burnt House Farm
Mid Lambrook, South Petherton
Somerset, England TA13 5HE
*Choice border and rock garden bulbs*

Broadleigh Gardens
Dept AGS 1 Bishop's Hull,
Taunton, Somerset
England TA4 1AE
*Dwarf bulbs*

CKS
Box 74
708 00 Ostrava
Poruba, Czech Republic

Potterton and Martin
Cottage Nursery, Moortown
 Road
Nettleton, Caistor, Lincolnshire
England LN7 6HX
*Dwarf bulbs and alpines*

Tile Barn Nursery
Standen Street
Iden Green, Benenden, Kent
England TN17 4LB
*Cyclamen*

# BIBLIOGRAPHY

Bryan, John E. *Bulbs,* Vol. I, II (Portland, Ore.: Timber Press, 1989).

Davies, Dilys. *Alliums, The Ornamental Onions* (Portland, Ore.: Timber Press, 1992).

Doutt, Richard L. *Cape Bulbs* (Portland, Ore.: Timber Press, 1994).

Glattstein, Judy. *The American Gardener's World of Bulbs* (Boston: Little, Brown and Company, 1994).

Griffiths, Mark, ed. *The New Royal Horticultural Society Dictionary Manual of Bulbs* (Portland, Ore.: Timber Press, 1995).

Heath, Brent, and Becky Heath. *Daffodils for American Gardens* (Washington, D.C.: Elliot & Clark Publishing, 1995).

Hobbs, Jack, and Terry Hatch. *Best Bulbs for Temperate Climates* (Portland, Ore.: Timber Press, 1994).

Kohlein, Fritz. *Iris* (Portland, Ore.: Timber Press, 1995).

Lawrence, Elizabeth. *The Little Bulbs* (Durham, N.C.: Duke University Press, 1986).

Mathew, Brian. *The Smaller Bulbs* (London: B.T. Batsford Ltd, 1987).

Ogden, Scott. *Garden Bulbs for the South* (Dallas: Taylor Publishing Company, 1994).

Snyder, Sandy. "Bulbs in a Buffalo Grass Lawn," *The Brooklyn Botanic Garden Record,* 1991, pp. 32–36.

# INDEX